NATIONAL UNIVERSITY
LIBRARY    SAN DIEGO

# Forbes®
# Great
# Success
# Stories

# Forbes

# Great Success Stories

## Twelve Tales
## of Victory
## Wrested
## from Defeat

### Alan Farnham

John Wiley & Sons, Inc.

New York • Chichester • Weinheim • Brisbane • Singapore • Toronto

This book is printed on acid-free paper. ⊗

Copyright © 2000 by Forbes Inc.

FORBES is a registered trademark. Its use is pursuant to a license agreement with Forbes Inc.

Published by John Wiley & Sons, Inc.
Published simultaneously in Canada.

No part of this publication may be reproduced, stored in a retrieval system or transmitted in any form or by any means, electronic, mechanical, photocopying, recording, scanning or otherwise, except as permitted under Sections 107 or 108 of the 1976 United States Copyright Act, without either the prior written permission of the Publisher, or authorization through payment of the appropriate per-copy fee to the Copyright Clearance Center, 222 Rosewood Drive, Danvers, MA 01923, (978) 750-8400, fax (978) 750-4744. Requests to the Publisher for permission should be addressed to the Permissions Department, John Wiley & Sons, Inc., 605 Third Avenue, New York, NY 10158-0012, (212) 850-6011, fax (212) 850-6008, E-Mail: PERMREQ@WILEY.COM.

This publication is designed to provide accurate and authoritative information in regard to the subject matter covered. It is sold with the understanding that the publisher is not engaged in rendering legal, accounting, or other professional services. If legal advice or other expert assistance is required, the services of a competent professional person should be sought.

PHOTO CREDITS: Aaron Feuerstein, © Malden Mills; Tom Monaghan, © Tom Monaghan; Larry Ellison, © Oracle Corporation; Ruth Handler, © Mattell, Inc.; Ron Popeil, © Ron Popeil; Emma Chappell, © United Bank of Philadelphia; Donald Trump, © Donald J. Trump; Don King, © Don King Productions, Inc.; Bruton Smith, © Charlotte Motor Speedway for Bruton Smith; Earl Stafford, © Howard M. Kaye; Jim Stovall, © Narrative Television Network; Kevin Maxwell, AP/Wide World Photos.

ISBN 0-471-38359-7

Printed in the United States of America.

10 9 8 7 6 5 4 3 2 1

# CONTENTS

# FOREWORD

THE THEME OF THESE STORIES—success, setback, comeback—is perpetually appealing. We all know from our own experiences that life rarely runs in a straight line but is a series of zigzags and ups and downs.

What makes these tales so collectively intriguing is that they're about flesh-and-blood people grappling with real-life crises—troubles arising from "irrational exuberance," the sheer skepticism of capital providers (usually lenders), intensified competition, changed conditions in the marketplace, playing too close to the edge of the law, a stroke of bad luck, or even physical impairment (Jim Stovall's becoming blind at age 29).

When faced with a setback, many people lose their verve and nerve, like some defeated, middle-aged character in a John O'Hara novel. But our subjects fought back. What makes their stories worth reading is that their comebacks were never easy and usually involved considerable heartbreak and disappointment along the way. Moreover, several of these business titans could crash yet again.

In business, success is transient, never permanent. As my father liked to say, "When you think you have arrived, you're ready to be shown the door." Entrepreneurs, often starting with nothing but ambition, will always strive in a free society to create new products, services, and ways of doing things. This inventive, innovative spirit is the font of progress— but it also brings constant turmoil, with constant thrusts against the status quo. "Creative destruction" is what famed economist Joseph Schumpeter termed the process of economic progress.

Such progress is not orderly. Most new businesses never make it. And most existing, dominant corporations eventually succumb, ending up merged, submerged, or in the corporate graveyard. Of the 500 largest companies dominating the economy at the time of *Forbes* magazine's seventieth anniversary in 1987, less than half remain in the top 500 today.

Eighteen years ago *Forbes'* first list of the 400 richest Americans was dominated by those whose wealth came from oil and real estate. Today—who knows about tomorrow—high-tech-related wealth dominates.

My siblings and I were taught at an early age that business is similar to a bakery—you can't sell yesterday's bread tomorrow; you have to earn your way in the market each day. We were suckled on stories of *Forbes* magazine's roller-coaster history. Started in 1917 (the same year as the Russian Revolution) by our once-penniless, immigrant grandfather, B. C. Forbes, the magazine achieved enormous success during the Roaring Twenties. In 1928 the powerful press lord William Randolph Hearst offered grandfather today's equivalent of tens of millions of dollars to buy *Forbes*. Immensely flattered and gratified, independent-minded B. C. Forbes proudly turned down the offer. Then came the stock market crash and the Great Depression. By 1932, *Forbes* was bankrupt in all but name, surviving only by the heroic efforts of its founder and his colleagues. For years, B. C. Forbes couldn't cash his own paychecks because there wasn't enough money in the bank to cover them.

Some people still believe that business and economics are dry as dust, just a lot of mind-numbing numbers. But properly portrayed, business is gripping drama. As any observer or participant knows, numbers are simply a form of shorthand, and balance sheets are just snapshots of a rapidly moving, ever-changing picture. My grandfather used to say that you'd learn more about a business by sizing up the "headknocker" (his word for CEO) than you would from the company's balance sheet.

Given human nature and the oft-messy process of creativity, it is no wonder business is rarely the smooth progression beloved by analysts and economists.

Jim Stovall puts it as well as anyone: "You and I only have one right in this world and that is the right to choose. We can't always choose what happens to us, but we can always choose what we are going to do about it."

So read and see what these people "did about it"—and be inspired.

Steve Forbes

# INTRODUCTION

O UR SUBJECT, HERE, is not "simple" success, but success captured on the rebound—victories wrested from defeat.

Prepare to meet 12 men and women of steel, who took the worst fate had to hit them with, and yet survived. What's more, they prospered. Superman has nothing on our 12. And yet our victors, as you'll soon discover, are anything but superhuman. All were changed and humbled by their experiences, and most still bear their scars today. That's part of what makes their stories so affecting—their willingness to tell the truth about the price they paid for their success—not just to win it, but, once lost, to win it back.

Such reversals of fortune, as Aristotle was the first to note, are the mainspring of great drama. Long before the dawn of capitalism (let alone dot-com-ism), the best and most engaging plots have been those that turned upon some near-fatal upset. They still are today.

No one cares about a person whose life is easy, whose worst on-the-job injury is a paper cut. Suffering, though, *real* suffering—especially when coupled with brave struggle—always holds our rapt attention. The kid who travels frictionlessly from Groton to Harvard to the chairmanship of Morgan Stanley, before decorously retiring from the presidency of the World Bank, causes not a yawn. But the kid who gets thrown *out* of Groton, who manages somehow to get into Harvard nonetheless, who almost loses the family fortune along the way to doubling it, and who, in his or her dotage, invents a machine for curing cancer, only to have the blueprints blow out the window while driving to the patent office—*that* kid keeps us glued to the edge of our collective seat. Why? Because unimpeded progress is simply not part of the human experience. The second kid's story rings truer of the two; we recognize ourselves in that kid.

In selecting the tales that follow, our criteria were few. We wanted stories of individuals, not of faceless institutions. The world's shelves were full enough, we figured, of dull casebooks recounting how a bunch of bureaucrats at XYZ Corporation turned things around. Thus, the only corporate turnarounds you'll find in here are those, such as Larry Ellison's at Oracle or Aaron Feuerstein's at Malden Mills, where the hero and his or her company are one and the same.

It didn't matter to us if our protagonists were rich or not-so, white or black, famous or obscure, young or old, male or female. For that reason, you'll find this to be a heterogeneous group. There's a banker, a blind person, a boxing promoter, and a pizza maker, among others. There's Donald Trump—he seemed inescapable—but you'll also find people you've probably never heard of, until now.

We didn't stipulate the types of setbacks, either, so long as they were doozies. Hurdles surmounted include fire, jail, cancer, racial prejudice, bankruptcy (including the biggest financial *pfffft* in history), and—maybe most difficult of all—the consequences of success itself, including hubris and complacency.

While it would have been nice if, like Dante, each of our 12 had come back from the Grey Line Tour of Hell with a set of lessons poetically expressed, we didn't insist on that, either. Where necessary, we inferred the lessons.

So, what *did* matter to us? Just two things, really: the intrinsic drama of the stories; and that all of our protagonists be people currently alive, so that we could meet them, shake their hands, and, wherever possible, get their stories from them in their own words. With one exception—Larry Ellison—this proved possible to do. (You wouldn't want a book on setbacks to be perfect, would you?)

A final word: It lately has become the fashion among business pundits to dismiss setbacks and defeats as matters of small consequence. Like the chicken pox, they are seen as precursors to maturity. Employers now *seek out* candidates who've driven businesses into the ground. Failures, it is argued, are just so many speed bumps on the road of one's career.

Is this really true? Our survivors offer a less glib perspective. It hurts to go to jail, to suffer blindness, to lose a breast, to see your family's business burned to ashes. One has but to talk with people who've suffered lesser disappointments to know the truth of this.

"I hear," a well-intentioned visitor once said to William Randolph Hearst, "that there's money to be made in movies."

"Yes," wistfully replied Hearst, who'd lost a bundle in the film business, "mine."

In these pages, failure is no abstraction. It's not something that happens only to other people. It's immediate and real—and its bite is feared. Yet it can be beaten back, and therein lies the message and the promise of this book.

The oft-quoted remark by F. Scott Fitzgerald—that there are "no second acts" in Americans' lives—is refuted here on every page. No *second* acts? Scottie must have been hanging out with the wrong crowd. Our 12 stalwarts didn't just have second acts; they went on, in some cases, to enjoy a third or fourth. They thus proved themselves star survivors. And one suspects they'll keep taking curtain calls until the Great Stage Manager yells, "Get the hook!" When your ego and your wallet and your name are all in jeopardy at once—as entrepreneurs' so often are—you fight like hell to hold the stage.

# Forbes®
# Great
# Success
# Stories

Aaron Feuerstein

# Aaron Feuerstein

## CEO and Owner of Malden Mills

### *"Did you ever read the book of Job?"*

T HE NIGHT OF DECEMBER 11, 1995, began happily enough for Aaron Feuerstein, chief executive officer (CEO) and owner of Malden Mills—one of Massachusetts's largest, oldest, and most innovative textile makers. The occasion was a surprise party for his seventieth birthday. The place: Café Budapest, one of his favorite restaurants (and one of Boston's best). Family, friends, and coworkers had gathered there to fete Feuerstein amid toasts and laughter, for there was much to celebrate.

The company had flourished for better than a decade, thanks largely to a single product—Polartec (originally, Polarfleece)—a soft, fuzzy, fleecelike synthetic fabric patented by Malden engineers in the late 1970s and first sold to customers in 1981. For Feuerstein, this fleece literally had been golden.

Its attributes—warmth, light weight, moisture-absorbency—made it ideal for outdoor garments worn by everyone from professional athletes and mountain climbers to joggers and weekend gardeners. Tens of pages of every L.L. Bean and Lands' End catalog (to name but two of Malden's customers) were devoted regularly to touting Polartec-based coats and jackets, gloves, hats, vests, booties—even bathrobes and pajamas. Not only was the fabric warm and snuggly—it also was politically correct. Made mainly from recycled plastic soda bottles (80 percent), it could be worn with pride by environmentalists. Here was the quintessential feel-good product. By promoting it aggressively, Malden Mills had created a $3-billion retail market. Sales hit $400 million the year Feuerstein hit 70.

The company's situation was unique within the textile industry, its hold on life growing stronger at the time other mills were losing theirs.

Traditional mills, not having a proprietary product comparable to Polartec, had been forced to compete principally on price. And on that basis, New England's mills, since the 1950s, had been losing out to mills with lower operating costs—ones situated in southern states, Mexico or Asia. More than a few of Malden's peers had declared bankruptcy, closed, or pulled up stakes and moved. Result: There were no "Café Budapests" in Lawrence, Massachusetts, Malden Mills' home town. The section of Lawrence where Feuerstein's century-old redbrick mill buildings were located was considered by locals to be among the city's toughest—a wasteland of shuttered shops and broken windows. Malden's Victorian-looking complex ran through three blocks of it, along the Lawrence–Methuen border.

Life for working men and women in Lawrence had never been exactly easy (the city was the scene for 1912's "Bread and Roses" strike by 25,000 workers), but at least the city had once bustled with commercial activity. Now, it ranked twenty-fourth among the poorest cities in the United States, no longer famous for manufacturing but for being a crack-cocaine capital and a magnet for newly arrived immigrants. Though only 30 miles north of Boston, it might as well have been in the third world. Malden Mills' workforce comprised 52 different nationalities—among the most diverse in the textile industry.

Yet Feuerstein had steadfastly refused to move, in part because he didn't have to (Malden's margins, thanks to Polartec, were so robust he didn't need to shop for cheaper labor); in part because he felt a civic obligation, as Lawrence's largest employer, to remain; and in part because he was—well—at the age of 70, a stubborn old man.

Not that he looked or acted old. Snapshots from the night of his party show him spry and straight-backed, vigorous, his blue eyes alive with humor. Since childhood, he had been physically unable to sit still. The weight he carried on his 5-foot, 11-inch frame (150 pounds) was 2 pounds *less* than what he'd weighed in college. He exercised daily, and was something of a health nut.

Though Feuerstein recently had appointed a chief operating officer at Malden Mills—the first such delegation of power in the company's history—he himself professed no interest in taking life any easier, let alone retiring. If he had, however, who among that night's celebrants

could have begrudged him a bit more leisure? After four decades at
Malden's helm, he had more than earned the right to spend more time
with his wife, Louise; more time reading the literature he loved—
Shakespeare, Shelley, the romantic poets generally, the Talmud, and the
Psalms.

What Feuerstein did not know, as he prepared to blow out the lone
candle on his cake, was that a tragedy was unfolding at that same
moment. Whatever his private vision of the future might have been, as
he made his birthday wish, it was about to be eclipsed—incinerated, in
fact, by that night's subsequent events. He blew the candle out.

When the Feuersteins finally arrived home around 11 P.M. to their
suburban Brookline condo, the phone was ringing. It had been ringing,
they later learned, for hours. Aaron raised the receiver. A voice told him
there had been a fire—that Malden Mills was blazing, dying.

## A Business Gone Up in Smoke

As the Feuersteins' car sped north in the dark up Highway 93, Aaron
and Louise could guess the fire's size long before they got near
Lawrence. Ahead of them, the winter horizon glowed red. A drive that
should have taken 30 minutes was stretched out to an hour as they
encountered first smoke, then snarled traffic, then general confusion.

When at last they arrived at the sprawling, 29-acre complex, the hour
was midnight.

"By the time I got there, it was a veritable holocaust—the buildings
all burning—everyone standing dazed and crying—helpless," Feuerstein remembers. He says he managed to keep his own feelings in check
only by reciting to himself, privately, words he had memorized once
from *King Lear:* he would not weep, he vowed, though his heart "break
into a hundred thousand flaws."

Nor was he alone in such despair.

From a hillside cemetery looking down upon the factory, some
5,000 townspeople and workers shivered in the freezing cold, watching spellbound as the blaze reached its zenith. Flames whipped by 45-
mile-per-hour winds leapt 50 feet into the air. Embers "the size of
basketballs" (as Louise remembers) spread fire from one building to
the next. To her it looked like Rome burning. To Aaron, Dresden. In
slow succession, seven brick and wood-frame structures—comprising

some 600,000 square feet of manufacturing space—caught fire, tottered, and collapsed.

What was burning was more than just a set of buildings. To Feuerstein, it represented a family heritage spanning three generations. At the end of the nineteenth century, his grandfather Henry Feuerstein, a Hungarian Jew, had immigrated to New York City, making his living by selling rags from a pushcart. In 1906, Henry founded Malden Knitting in Malden, Massachusetts, first producing wool bathing suits and sweaters, and later—during World War II—military clothing. The company expanded, and, in 1956, with Aaron at its head, it moved to Lawrence. Aaron had never worked anywhere else. He had gone to work at Malden directly out of college. The factory wasn't a "second home" to him—it was more like his first: Along with all the many tons of machinery being burned and melted were his own private keepsakes—his baseball trophies, won in grammar school; his two oil paintings of his parents.

To Feuerstein's workers—3,100 men and women—the mill represented the only dependable, high-wage employment in an otherwise bleak landscape. Malden Mills was a union shop in an otherwise nonunion town. Even rarer, it was a union shop with cordial and cooperative management–labor relations. As Paul Coorey, president of Local 311 of the Union of Needletrades, Industrial and Textile Employees (UNITE), watched the mill collapsing, his son (who also worked at Malden) turned to him and said simply, "Dad, we just lost our jobs."

Malden's wages were better by $2 an hour than any others to be found in town. While pay nationwide for textile workers hovered around $9.50, at Malden it was $12.50. That meant an income of $26,000 a year in a city where the average income was barely $15,000. The majority of Malden's workers—first- and second-generation Dominicans and Puerto Ricans—lived paycheck to paycheck. They had no cushion, and for them the fire could not possibly have come at a worse time—two weeks before Christmas. Without December's paycheck there would be no rent, no heat, no food, no presents.

Feuerstein admits he briefly gave in to an emotion alien to him—self-pity. " '*How could such a tragedy befall me?*' Yes, I can't deny I felt some of that," he says. "But to me, this was not a tragedy of money. It was that everything I wanted to accomplish in business was burning down in front of my eyes. It was dying, there, in front of me."

Then his thoughts turned in a more characteristic direction: "I thought, What can I do to better the situation?" He took quick stock of the situation: What *hadn't* burned?

"I had my offices, my books, my inventory." (All that had been in separate buildings that were still standing.) He still had some knitting capacity, thanks to a satellite facility up in Maine. The one thing he absolutely could not do without, he realized, was the company's capacity to "finish" Polartec—to give the fibers their characteristic nap and feel.

"In our business," he explains, "we knit a fabric which ultimately, after dyeing or printing, is made into a fleece. And the fleece-making, which we call 'finishing,' is a highly specialized technique, in which we are superior to others in the business. Without the finishing, I'm out of business. If I could just save this small finishing plant, I thought I might be able to make it. That little building was the 'genius' of the company." This was a structure known as Fin2, which, Feuerstein now could see through the smoke, was starting in to smolder. But, like the celebrated bush of the Old Testament, it was burning but not consumed—at least not yet.

Feuerstein said to his director of engineering that he thought there was a chance they could save Fin2. The time was now approaching 1 A.M., and Malden Mills was growing into a 51-alarm fire—meaning fire companies from 51 different municipalities had converged to fight it.

"He looked at me in bewilderment," remembers Feuerstein. " 'Aaron,' he said, 'You've always been a dreamer. That building will be down to the ground with all the others by seven o'clock tomorrow morning. It's *over*, Aaron.' "

Feuerstein didn't listen. Instead, he went and spoke to his director of security, to whom he made the same suggestion: "You know, that building hasn't burned down yet. But it will burn down. Maybe there's some way of saving it." What, exactly, was Feuerstein proposing to do, the director asked. "Well, we'll take our best people . . . and we put them into that building—which is a danger, of course; there's always a risk. We put them in there and see if we can prevent that fire from spreading—see if we can save it." The director pointed out that the fire department would not permit this; that they had forbidden anyone to get that near to the fire. Said Feuerstein, "Don't listen to them. Let's see if we can do it." Louise, fearing the old man might try to fight the fire himself, along with the other men, insisted he come home with her and get some rest.

Next morning, no one's heart beat any easier. Daylight only revealed the full scope of the devastation. Officially, the fire ranked as having been the worst in Massachusetts in the twentieth century, and among the top-10 worst industrial fires ever in the United States. Three enormous block-long buildings had been leveled. All that remained of them was a five-story brick tower, entwined by blackened girders. Ice entombed the ruins.

## Surveying the Wreckage

Feuerstein reappeared at 7 A.M., still wearing the same brown tweed suit he'd worn at the birthday party—only now it reeked of smoke. He took in the devastation like a general surveying the remnants of his defeated army, taking damage reports from his lieutenants.

There were three pieces of good news. First, no one had been killed. Of the 500 people working in the mill that night, only 33 had been injured. Of those, the nine hurt worst had been air-lifted to burn units of Boston's hospitals. Second, the company had been carrying just a little over $300 million worth of insurance. And third, among the buildings that remained was Fin2.

By now, employees were starting to show up for work. With no work to go to, they wandered around aimlessly in the cold. Feuerstein ordered them taken into one of the surviving buildings. And it was there, *en famille,* that he did what some considered an impulsive thing: He announced that he would rebuild the mill.

That was on December 12.

On December 14, Malden Mills' employees, summoned by a notice placed by the company in the local newspaper, assembled in a high school gymnasium to hear what Feuerstein had to say about their future.

No one knew for certain what he'd say, of course, but most had made an educated guess. Throughout the United States at that time, layoffs were in the air. AT&T alone had cut legions of workers. "Chainsaw Al" Dunlap was winning points with shareholders by sloughing off employees like so much dead skin.

Malden, being privately held, had no shareholders to answer to. But workers knew what was in the wind in boardrooms. They had reason to suspect that Feuerstein's morning-after vow was one his board might possibly have talked him out of.

Union president Coorey, for one, was ready to hear that it was all over—that Feuerstein would say he had decided, on reconsideration (and with great regret, of course) to close down the mill. He would pocket his $300 million in insurance and retire. Or maybe, if he wasn't ready to retire, he'd set up a new mill elsewhere—in the South, maybe, or Mexico—some place where costs (read: *labor* costs) were cheaper.

Feuerstein entered the gym, paused to shake snowflakes off his coat, and then walked the length of the long aisle to the front of the room, where there was a stage. Every eye followed him. By the time he reached the podium, the room had fallen silent.

## "We're Going to Continue to Operate"

Feuerstein's words, when they came, were brief. "I will get right to my announcement," he began. "For the next 30 days, our employees will be paid their full salaries." The traditional Christmas bonus of $275 also would be paid, just as in prior years. Healthcare coverage would continue, too, for 90 days—as would other benefits. "But over and above the money," he concluded, "the most important thing Malden Mills can do is to get you back to work." By January 2, he said, operations would resume. In 90 days the mill would be fully operational again. Then, addressing himself to the reporters present, he said: "We're going to continue to operate in Lawrence. We had the opportunity to run South many years ago. We didn't do it then, and we're not going to do it now."

The room exploded with pent-up feeling.

Men cried. Women cried. Television news crews, sent to cover the event, cried. People hugged and kissed whoever was sitting next to them. It was like V-E Day, New Year's, and the Fourth of July all rolled up into one. From 52 nationalities represented in Malden's polyglot workforce, hosannas rang in Quebecois French and Spanish, in Portuguese and German, in Italian, Irish, Hebrew, and English. Paul Coorey told reporters, "Thank God we've got Aaron."

And that was only the beginning—the first spontaneous outburst of affection from the local Malden family. Nationally, in the days that followed his announcement, praise for Feuerstein grew. He was lionized and lauded by every interest group except the Brotherhood of Pyromaniacs.

Unions coast to coast applauded him. Labor Secretary Robert Reich said Feuerstein had displayed the kind of leadership that *every* CEO should emulate.

Reporters vied for superlatives to wrap around his 70-year-old brow. ABC's Peter Jennings made him the network's "person of the week." NBC's Tom Brokaw, not to be outdone, called Feuerstein first "the best boss in America," then later "a saint for the nineties." The banner headline of *Backpacker* magazine declared: "From Ashes to Fleece: In the Wake of Tragedy, a Shining Example of Compassion Emerges."[1] *Reader's Digest* called him "one boss in a million."[2]

For weeks the media buffed his halo to such high luster that it seemed all but impossible to pick up a magazine that didn't have his picture on it or in it. *Parade, People,* and *Reader's Digest* profiled him. He was swamped with speech invitations and interview requests.

Meanwhile, donations and offers of help for Malden Mills were pouring in from every quarter—from banks, customers, and suppliers. The apparel company Dakota sent $30,000. Patagonia sent $64,000. UNITE sent $100,000. The Bank of Boston sent $50,000. The Merrimack Valley Chamber of Commerce sent $150,000. Feuerstein, overwhelmed, declared: "The money is not for Malden Mills. It is for the Malden Mills employees. It makes me feel wonderful. I have hundreds of letters at home from ordinary people, beautiful letters with dollar bills, ten-dollar bills." Not a few newspaper commentators borrowed the imagery of Frank Capra's holiday movie *It's a Wonderful Life:* Lawrence suddenly was Bedford Falls, and Feuerstein a Jewish Jimmy Stewart.

Colleges awarded him honorary degrees (12 doctorates in all). Even the commander in chief weighed in. The president phoned with personal congratulations, and Feuerstein found himself invited to breakfast at the White House and to a State of the Union Address as the first lady's guest.

Nor were the high and mighty the only ones who honored him. A woman in Colorado Springs, sitting under her hair dryer in her beauty salon, was so impressed by what she read about Feuerstein in *Reader's Digest* that she got up, went to the phone, called Malden Mills, and asked if she could drop by and congratulate him in person. "Sure," said Feuerstein's secretary. So she boarded an airplane, flew to Boston, and did.

Nationwide, there was a brief upswing in the number of parents naming newborns Aaron.

But the acknowledgment Feuerstein found personally most touching was a patchwork quilt made for him out of strips of Polartec by the children of a Hebrew day school. Inlaid on it were the words "Who is honored? One who honors others."

All of this was pretty heady stuff for a guy who, until the age of 70, had never been interviewed by a reporter or asked to speak anywhere outside his own company. Through it all, though, he held up nobly, managing to keep not just his modesty and sense of proportion, but his focus on the job at hand—getting Malden Mills back on its feet, and its employees back to work.

He worked incessantly. For two weeks straight, he insisted on wearing the same brown tweed suit he'd been wearing on the night of the fire. Maybe it smelled of smoke, but he said wearing it somehow made him feel better.

People unfamiliar with him marveled at his stamina and self-discipline, his dedication, his physical and mental strength. Yet to anyone who knew the Feuersteins' history (or Aaron's in particular), it all seemed perfectly in character. In him, tragedy had found an extremely well-prepared foe. Feuerstein's rabbi put it best: "When crunch time came, he was standing upright."

Who *was* this guy?

## Developing His Purpose in Life

The single most impressive thing about Feuerstein (and the fact that makes him somewhat daunting, for anybody aspiring to emulate him) is that he was *born* upright: He was, and is, a congenitally moral man, long set in his ways. "Early in life—I was two, maybe three," he remembers, "I developed what I would call a 'sensitivity to the good'—with a capital G—what man should be doing in this life. That was my purpose in life, I discovered: being good." Referring to the fire, he laughs, "I was preparing for that *before* day one—when I was in the womb!" He means it.

He was born in Brookline in 1925, a few blocks from where he lives now, the fourth of five children born to Henry and Mitzi Feuerstein. From them he acquired a love of literature and religion. After attending the prestigious Boston Latin school, where he first became familiar with Milton, Keats, and Shakespeare, he graduated in 1947 from New York City's Yeshiva University, majoring in English and philosophy. He entered the family business, working first in quality control, then moving on to a supervisor's job in yarn making.

His father shaped him, in civics and religion. Henry Feuerstein, an Orthodox Jew, was one of the original founders of the Young Israel synagogue in Brookline—now New England's largest—which began in the Feuerstein's suburban living room in 1926. Much later, Aaron and his brother helped rebuild its temple after a fire with a $2 million pledge in 1994. Today, when faced with tough decisions, he often says, "I know what my father would have wanted." From Henry he also learned a 2000-year-old aphorism written by the philosopher Hillel, which, he says, has come in handy to him more than once: "When all is moral chaos around you, do your best to be a man."

As kids, Aaron and his brother wished that their father could have joined them when they played on Saturday mornings. But Saturdays were when Henry met with emissaries from the charities that he supported. Aaron inherited that responsibility. Before the fire, his own habit for a decade had been to make year-end visits to local charities—donating, for example, $100,000 to charities in Lawrence. Even after the fire he made the rounds. In late December, he gave reporters the slip, delivering personal checks for $80,000 to shelters and to soup kitchens.

Feuerstein practices strict self-discipline in both mind and body. He rises daily at 5:30 and either runs five miles or performs an hour of strenuous calisthenics. His daughter, Joyce, says he needles family members whom he deems overweight: "He bullies anyone who gains a pound." He monitors his pulse constantly, eats sparingly, and says that he intends to live to be 120—Moses's age. When his daily habit of eating a dozen oranges was described in profiles of him following the fire, fruit sent by the Florida Orange Growers Association and by private individuals began piling up in his office. His vices? Few. He likes chocolate, and every now and then drinks a little Scotch.

He subjects his mind to equal care: On even-numbered days, while exercising, he recites from memory an hour's worth of Shakespeare, Milton or the other English poets; on odd days, he recites in Hebrew from the psalms and prophets, or from the Talmudic dictates on ethics. When he speaks in public, he does so without notes.

What his audiences see is a lean, sagelike figure: blue-eyed, white-haired, slightly reminiscent of 1950s television's Mr. Wizard. In dress, he describes himself as being "from the old school"—meaning he prefers to wear a three-piece suit for virtually all occasions—even napping. After logging 10 or 12 hours at the mill, he typically comes home to Brookline and lies down. Joyce says he naps "all dressed up—like a corpse."

In the office, he cuts a formal, even a fastidious figure—except for footwear. He often wears sneakers with his suit. The combination is less fashion statement than practical necessity. Constantly in motion, walking the mill floor to see what's doing, he has over many years build up a great equity of good will with workers. He's no prima donna. As Joyce told *People* magazine, "I remember as a child that in summer, when it was 110 or 115 degrees in the factory, he would sweat it out for two or three hours right in there with the bottom of the line workers, making sure things happened right."[3] He practices a true open-door policy—on those rare occasions when he's in his office, sitting still. Workers, who refer to him as Mr. A.F., know they can take any grievance to him. Says one, "I'd take a bullet for Mr. A.F." The mayor of Lawrence has called him "the kind of guy everybody wants to support."

It's good they do, because Feuerstein, in his willingness to take risks, has gotten Malden into tight spots. In the early 1980s, a Feuerstein-led foray into fake fur fizzled, putting the company into Chapter 11. Louise ascribes her husband's bulletproof self-confidence to his having grown up in prosperous and secure surroundings. She herself, she says, is no optimist, and serves (in her words) as the family's "designated worrier." The two met onboard an airplane in 1984, shortly after Feuerstein's first wife, Merika, died. He was returning home to Boston from a Salt Lake City business trip. She, head of the rug department at a Boston auction house, was returning from a friend's wedding. They chatted and exchanged cards. He mentioned that he had a houseful of old rugs, and she asked if he would like to make an appointment with her. (She had in mind an appraisal.) No, he said, he'd like to take her out to dinner. Despite the fact that she was 11 years his junior—and had been raised a Mormon—they married 3 years later, after she had converted to Judaism. Artistic by temperament and training, she assumed responsibility for architectural and design questions when construction of the new mill began.

## Rebuilding the Mill—and the Business

The physical rebirth of Malden Mills had started almost as soon as December's embers cooled. Polartec's season—the peak time for delivering new shipments of the fabric—kicked off in February, so there was precious little time. If Feuerstein could not meet those deliveries, his buyers would go elsewhere. The whole ball game, he told his executives, would be lost.

As workers removed debris, they found several tractor trailers full of still-usable manufacturing equipment, which had been ordered as part of a planned expansion. Though the trailers themselves were dented and buried under rubble, the contents were in serviceable condition. Other new equipment, intended for a facility Malden had begun in Germany, was ordered shipped to Massachusetts. Dyeing and printing operations—a total loss—could be subcontracted out to other mills.

And the company still had Fin2.

On the tenth day following the fire, Feuerstein got a call from the men who had been working nonstop to get the Polartec finishing process restarted. They asked him to come over to see something.

"It was quite a moment," he remembers. "All my workers were standing on the production line with smiles of accomplishment and tears of emotion, and they were standing there while the fabric was coming off the equipment—finished, first-class fabric." His feelings overwhelmed his reserve. "I, too, couldn't hold back tears then. I went and shook hands with each and every one of them, and I said thank you to each person." One worker vowed to him, "We'll pay you back tenfold, Aaron." Together they would surmount all obstacles.

While this accomplishment gave everyone a tremendous lift, production was still just a trickle compared to what it had been before the fire. The men told Feuerstein they thought getting operations back "for real" would take two to three months. That wasn't good enough:

" 'We've got a *little* time,' I told them. 'But not that much. Let's see what you can do.' "

By late December, production had improved enough that 300 workers—about 10 percent of the workforce—were back on their jobs.

In early January, Feuerstein authorized a team of architects to begin designing a new, state-of-the-art mill, to be built directly on the burned and blackened footprint of the old one. The goal: To have it finished in 13 months. By mid-January, 65 percent of the workers had come back. Feuerstein told those still out that he would continue paying benefits and wages for another 30 days.

He extended that offer once more in February—by which time 70 percent were back, and only 800 remained out. It was around this time that a few business writers, self-styled realists, began to question what they characterized as Feuerstein's profligate generosity. It was all very well for him to behave responsibly, but wasn't he carrying things a bit too far? Wasn't he, in fact, jeopardizing Malden's ability to come back by spending money from which he was getting no practical return? In the press at large, theirs remained a minority view.

As March 1 approached, Malden Mills had plenty to be proud of: Not only were most employees back at work, but the plant was turning out more than 200,000 yards of Polartec a week (though that was just a quarter of the prefire peak). Customers for the most part had stayed loyal, believing Feuerstein's promise that Malden would honor its commitments. If deliveries could not be made from new production, he told them, the company still had a backlog of inventory stored in its warehouses. Feuerstein proved a tireless salesman, traveling around the country—and the world—reassuring worried customers.

With spring, 80 percent of employees were back at work, and erection of a new $130 million mill was underway. As it took shape, the roads along the Lawrence–Methuen border became choked with trucks carrying pallets of construction materials and machinery. Deliveries of steel, stone, and concrete rumbled down the highways. What was rising on the ruins of the old mill was something to see. Feuerstein, with Louise's help, was rebuilding in what the *New York Times* termed "the grand style,"[4] restoring not only substance but the old mill's costly architectural details. On June 2, Malden's customers who had remained loyal and patient were given a tour of the fast-rising plant.

Feuerstein seemed revitalized by the challenges he faced, adhering to a schedule that would have taxed a 25-year-old. He not only met the exigencies and crises of construction, but maintained all his habits—his morning runs and his recitations of poetry and psalms.

On September 14, 1997—just 21 months after the fire—the new mill was dedicated in a ceremony rich with fanfare and heartfelt feeling. "I thank you, God," said Feuerstein, as television cameras hummed and a crowd of 15,000 townspeople, employees, politicians, and labor leaders watched. "I thank you, majestic God of the universe, for restoring to Malden Mills and its employees, our life and soul." Former U.S. Labor Secretary Robert Reich led the crowd in a cheer, "Let's hear it for America's number-one mensch!" (Yiddish for a supremely stand-up guy).

The 610,000-square-foot factory was absolutely current in technology yet Victorian in appearance, faced in copper and red brick. It had 30-foot ceilings and was flooded with natural light, which streamed in through translucent panels. It was so rich in re-created period detail that the National Trust for Historic Preservation gave it its 1996 Honor Award.

Now all but 70 of Feuerstein's employees were back at work, and Polartec sales had risen 25 percent since before the fire. What was more, the promise given Feuerstein by the men of Fin2—that they would pay him back tenfold—was beginning to fruit: productivity was up 25 percent and climbing.

## Struggling with Unprofitable Operations

It was at this point that the world tuned out on Malden Mills. The television crews packed up and went away. The spotlights dimmed. Collectively, a million readers yawned, turned the pages of their newspapers, and moved on to the next story. Why shouldn't they? The story of Aaron Feuerstein and his mill was over, wasn't it? People naturally assumed that everything was hunky-dory now; that the Malden family was reunited, its business reestablished; and that everyone would live happily ever after.

This wasn't entirely the case. Not only was the story far from over, but the version spun on television was so sweet, so simple, it amounted almost to a fairy tale: *Things looked awfully bad for Malden Mills; now they looked good. A kindly, white-haired wizard had slain the fire-breathing dragon, armed only with decency and kindness.*

This version omitted a few important facts: Polartec was indeed flourishing, but Polartec was not the whole of Malden Mills' business. The company had two other divisions as well—flock (cheap synthetic upholstery, used primarily in automobiles) and high-end wovens. These were unprofitable, dragging the business down. Total sales might be up, but the company still wasn't making any money. Yet Feuerstein had pledged to put *all* employees back to work, even those who worked in those unprofitable operations. His struggle to do this—and the price he paid—amounted to what Paul Harvey likes to call "the rest of the story."

*That* story was less simple and less sunny. It involved missed deadlines, lost business, financial strains, and tense partings of the ways between Feuerstein and two of his top three lieutenants. Even the weather, at one point, seemed to conspire against the company's struggle to recover. The real comeback story was no smooth and muscular ascent, but a lurching, herky-jerky climb—one step backward for each two forward. It was not scripted by Frank Capra but by an infinitely higher, less glib, more unfathomable authority—one that would force Feuerstein, before all was over, to resort to expedients he found both painful and distasteful.

"Did you ever read the book of Job?" The time is November 1999, and Feuerstein has posed this question during a visit *Forbes* had paid the patriarch in his private office, furnished in Stickley furniture, exposed brick, and Malden Mills' own jacquard fabrics and upholsteries (both now discontinued). On the wall behind his desk hangs a lithograph showing the mills as they looked at the turn of the last century, before the night when fire destroyed so much. Since that night, four years have passed; but Feuerstein looks hardly any older. Dressed in a gray chalk-stripe three-piece suit (smelling not at all of smoke), he is in an expansive, retrospective mood, seeking to put the whole story of his company's struggles into a larger context.

"Did you ever read the book of Job?" he asks again, this time with rhetorical flourish. "Well, go back and read it." And without missing a beat, he launches into his own precis: "Satan goes to God and says, 'You know, this guy, Job—he's very successful; he's the prince in his area. He's a big business success, honored by his community. He's very righteous. He does good; he helps people. He observes all Your commandments and objectives. He's just a fabulous guy.' "

Feuerstein, still acting out the Devil's part, continues: " 'You know *why* he's so good? He's good because it came easy to him. He never went without food, so it was easy for him to give charity to the hungry. He never had to suffer in business, so it was easy for him to do the right thing. But strip him of his conveniences and honors, and you'll see he's *just like everybody else.'*

"God demurs: 'No . . . my Job . . . he's terrific.' And the Devil says, 'Okay, so let me *test* him.' And the deal is made. The book of Job describes this testing, this *stripping* of him—all the hurdles that are put into his way. That's Job's story: Very few guys keep going when you raise the hurdles."

He ought to know.

Behind the scenes at Malden Mills—beyond the view of television—Feuerstein, in the days following the fire, found himself confronting hurdle after hurdle—some political, some financial, all personal.

## Dealing with Conflict over How to Rebuild

Feuerstein and one of his three top executives came into conflict over the direction the new Malden Mills should take. Patty Fitzpatrick, director of manufacturing, saw rebuilding as a chance to further automate Malden's operations. Though Feuerstein was not opposed to this in principle, he disagreed with her about the degree of automation that was possible or appropriate. In his view, parts of the Polartec process required such skill and attention that they were better left to people. The two reached an impasse, and Fitzpatrick—a 10-year veteran of the company—abruptly left in May 1996, escorted off the property in tears by Malden Mills security guards. This drama took place at about the same time Feuerstein was being photographed having breakfast at the White House, an event that got far more publicity.

Tensions had been building between Feuerstein and others of his top advisors. In his absolute determination to do the right thing, he was proceeding partly on facts, partly on faith. The faith part bothered pessimists. Feuerstein assumed, for instance, that Malden's insurance would more than cover the rebuilding costs. And he assumed, also, that if production could be restarted quickly enough, something close to 1995's level of sales ($400 million) could be maintained.

Toward these goals (and in service to his moral imperative), he had originally planned to keep all idled workers on full wages and benefits indefinitely. Not only was this the right thing to do, it made, to him, good business sense: It guaranteed that Malden's highly skilled workforce, essential to the company's high-tech, high-margin operations, would not disperse. They could, when needed, be called back on short notice.

The more cautious among Feuerstein's directors, however, were concerned that Malden Mills was proposing to spend what it didn't have—at least not yet. They urged him to be a bit less specific about how *long* Malden would continue paying wages to those furloughed. Such payments, they estimated, could cost the company between $10 and $14 million at a time of pinched revenues and zero profit. Feuerstein put their advice to one side, and soldiered on.

One hurdle proved especially daunting, and unexpectedly so. "There were many problems we encountered," he now recalls. "But the insurance problem—that was a hell of hells that would have broken anybody."

The company's lead insurer, Commerce and Industry Insurance (CII) held up payment on the company's policy at the very moment Malden Mills most needed money. Not only was the company hemorrhaging $1.5 million a week in pay and benefits, but it had started spending heavily on materials for the new mill. CII was demanding more and more documentation as to the fire's cause, which investigators were having trouble establishing. (No definite cause ever was established, beyond a chance combustion of synthetic fiber particles. The fire marshal's report did, however, absolve Malden Mills of any negligence.)

Seven months after the fire, Malden had received only $78 million on its $302 million policy. To meet bills and payroll, Feuerstein had to borrow. The amount owed to banks quickly climbed to more than $100 million—a substantial sum for a company whose prefire sales had been $400 million. (1997's sales would be just $240 million.)

Through the summer of 1996, these financial pressures mounted. Sales were coming back, but the company still wasn't making any money. The contracting out of dyeing and printing operations further eroded margins. Feuerstein had to cancel a party organized to mark groundbreaking for the new mill. The company could ill afford the party's cost, either in money or in downtime.

Getting Polartec production back to where it had been was only one of Feuerstein's imperatives. He was simultaneously trying to rehabilitate Malden Mills other two divisions, flock and wovens. Though these divisions made a significant contribution to sales, neither had been profitable before the fire.

Efforts to restart flock hit several snags. Delays eventually cost it its 1997 buying season, and Feuerstein's chief financial officer (CFO) warned that continuing to push forward on rebuilding flock—spending $45 million for new machinery and $60 million to house it—was more than the company overall could afford. A second of Feuerstein's top lieutenants took personal responsibility for the delays, and resigned.

## The Most Painful Decision: Letting People Go and Shutting Down Divisions

Finally came a black day: July 11, when Feuerstein was forced to tell the 400 flock workers still unemployed that he could no longer guarantee them jobs. Emotionally, he told them that he had committed "a profound mistake" by trying to restore everything at once. Though some of these workers eventually were hired back in new capacities, others never returned.

In October 1997—the same month that the trade journal *Textile World* named Feuerstein Leader of the Year and pronounced Malden Mills "stronger than ever"[5]—sales still languished below the prefire $400 million. Exceptionally mild winters in 1997 and 1998 only made matters worse, because they cut demand for Polartec.

Then, on February 25, 1998, came a second black day: Feuerstein had to announce the shutdown of the company's unprofitable wovens division, with a loss of nearly 400 more jobs. The company's total sales for 1998 dropped to $228 million, and Malden recorded a second loss.

On it went, each advance coming in lockstep with new setbacks. Workers were rehired, only to be laid off again. A showpiece of a new mill was up and running, but other operations, which Feuerstein had fought hard to save, had shut their doors.

As a hurdler, then, he had turned in a mixed performance: He'd stayed the course; he'd been brave; he'd done the best he could—but he hadn't cleared them all.

## "Be Strong and Be Courageous"

Feuerstein here offers his own hard-won perspective:

> One person, he gets a hurdle, he loses confidence in himself, he drops. Very few can keep going. Raise the bar higher, and pretty soon you eliminate almost everybody. Except there are a few guys who are so . . . so . . . *convinced* that their way is just, and so self-confident of their ability to do good, that you can't break them. And that's the story of Job. Exactly the story of Job.

As his own case illustrates, it's possible to miss a hurdle here and there and still acquit yourself honorably. What you take away, he says, is justifiable pride that when you were in the troughs, "You didn't let any of this stuff get you down and you didn't lose your vision and you didn't lose your hope and you didn't degrade yourself into living *like an animal.*"

If someone suffering a setback (or perhaps anticipating one) were to telephone him tonight, what advice would he give him?

> I think the best thing I could say to him is that he should develop or strengthen his will to overcome his difficulty—to have a determination that is strong enough to move walls. And he should couple that with some very creative entrepreneurial kinds of thinking. [For example, the kind of thinking Feuerstein displayed when the mill was going up in flames around him: What *hadn't* yet been burned? What could still be saved?]
>
> Why some people have determination and some don't is a tough, tough question. Why does the American bicyclist [Lance Armstrong] who had cancer—who's told he's through—have a determination over and above the cancer, over and above everything else—to win? Why does he have a determination to go into a race—a three-day marathon

that will test everybody down to their last strength, when he himself has had his strength weakened by the chemotherapy? Yet he was determined to win it, and he did.

Is it possible to strengthen one's determination, we asked. Yes, thinks Feuerstein—through a rigorous reexamination of one's own deepest-held beliefs:

> Think out carefully your purpose and your vision, so that you know clearly why the effort is . . . if it's worth this terrible effort and price. You have to be satisfied in your own mind that what you're doing is good and important and worthwhile on this earth. And then you have to couple that with self-confidence. How you develop self-confidence, I don't know. But I can tell you this: At the end of Deuteronomy, Moses gives advice to Joshua, the younger leader who's going to succeed him: "Be strong and be courageous." That's all that's told to Joshua. God doesn't prescribe a certain course of action. He doesn't tell him, "I want you to have this kind of rifle instead of that kind," or "I think you should go north instead of south." God doesn't tell him anything except to be strong and be courageous. And as Joshua took it seriously, he was successful. This guy who's going to call me on the telephone—if he has the ability to be strong and courageous in impossible situations—then he probably will be able to see it through.

Self-confidence, he notes, usually arises naturally, as a by-product of the exercise he recommends: reexamining and revalidating one's beliefs. That exercise can be performed anytime, at any age. Like memorization, it gets easier with practice. Feuerstein thinks his own strength, which he drew on in his time of testing, was large because he started young: "I was prepared from a very early age, because there was a conviction within me that—over and above—I would overcome."

By exercising that muscle proactively, you can help ensure that you—like Feuerstein—are standing upright when crunch time comes.

The crucial moment in Malden Mills' comeback may have been when Feuerstein and the men of Fin2 looked each other in the eye and vowed jointly to overcome all obstacles: "From that moment on, all I was just a cheerleader," he says. Then he adds, on reconsideration:

No, I was more than that. I created the spark, the hope, the will to overcome and salvage a situation that had seemed impossible. I was able to
influence others to participate in that dream. Not just by the few words
I said that evening. It had to do with a history together of treating
human beings as God's creatures—my confidence that they all had a
spark in them, and that they could all do it. My confidence that they all
had the divine spark.

Tom Monaghan

---

## CHAPTER 2

# Tom Monaghan

## Founder of Domino's Pizza

*"I feel that all these setbacks were tools for me to learn from."*

T HE LIVES OF MANY successful entrepreneurs in the United States are frequently compared to the rags-to-riches stories penned by nineteenth-century American novelist Horatio Alger. Alger's heartwarming tales promised that any American boy—through grit, hard work, pluck, and perseverance—could rise from the most humble of beginnings to climb the ladder of success and attain great wealth. The boys in the stories were usually of society's lowest rank—foundlings, shoeshine kids, newspaper or delivery boys—and the books always reflected their lowly early stages of life in titles like *Ragged Dick* or *Tattered Tom.*

The life of Tom Monaghan is the perfect Alger story: orphanage at 4, multimillionaire at 33. But in looking back on a life spectacularly well lived, one sees other literary stories, such as *Oliver Twist* and young Oliver's constant request for "more." Or another, more modern-day work also comes to mind—the movie *The Graduate,* in which young Benjamin, the recent college graduate, was offered the key to business success in one word: "Plastics." Tom Monaghan would also follow a one-word suggestion to develop the Midas touch. And that word was *pizza.* The name of the pizza that Tom Monaghan made famous was Domino's.

## The Keys to His Success

In his autobiography, *Pizza Tiger,*[1] Monaghan wrote about the importance of having boyhood dreams: "I have a lot of dreams, and I don't think I'll ever achieve them all. I hope not. I don't like having to think about the day when I might stop having new ones." The dream would eventually multiply a small, local, three-pizzeria business into a giant one with over 5,000 locations internationally.

Idealism also provided the springboard for Monaghan's success. But it was idealism mixed with the power of one person making the decisions. At the start-up stage, when the business was small, his hands-on decision making proved essential to the success of the entity. Later, critics—especially executives, who seemed to come and go in a revolving-door scenario—would say that he lacked the skills to delegate, and this cost the chain millions of dollars as competitors cut significantly into Domino's dominant—and, at one time, almost monopolistic—market share of the delivery segment of the multi-billion-dollar pizza business.

He perceived that success was a mix of idealism, dreams, and self-determination:

> To me, the real substance of life and work is in a constant battle to excel. I am determined to win, to outstrip the competition. But to my mind, winning in business is nothing unless you do it strictly according to the rules. Ideals are what saved the company. They kept hope alive, Eventually, they provided the fuel that propelled our corporate growth.[2]

Monaghan's brilliance at the outset of his career, when he owned only three pizzerias, was focused on streamlining the time to make and deliver a quality, fresh-baked pizza. Those first three pizzerias would later play a symbolic role in the company's brand logo signature.

From this humble three-store beginning, Monaghan would begin the swift ascent to riches beyond his or anyone's imagination. He would realize every childhood dream and fantasy and spend money with the profligate extravagance of an Indian rajah. Along the way, his journey would sometimes resemble the ancient Greek myth of the trials of Sisyphus, a person doomed to repeatedly push a huge stone to the top of a mountain only to have the stone tumble him to the bottom. Yet after each of the many setbacks, Monaghan would dust himself off and continue to climb back up the hill.

For some founders of businesses, losing control of the company one time marks the ultimate trauma, but Monaghan almost lost Domino's four times. "Along the way to success," he said, "I might have had eight or nine setbacks, two or three of them serious, and the last one was the most severe. The others were just bumps on the road that I had to handle compared to the last one. But I never lost hope that things would work out in my favor. Never." He would remain an eternal optimist and a man possessed of great faith.

One key to his success was that Monaghan loved working. It never bothered him to put in 100 hours a week or, years after the success, to roll up his sleeves and make dough if it was required: "I think people are at their best when they combine love and their work. Life is too precious to be wasted in doing work you don't love." His enthusiasm for jumping in when the moment called for it rubbed off on others, as well. "There isn't one executive in Domino's who will stand by and look on if a crew is working short-handed," he said. "A spot of pizza sauce on your suit during inspections isn't a sign of bad grooming; it's a badge of honor."[3]

Eventually, his meteoric climb to the pinnacle of fast-food pizzadom would make him a billionaire, ranked by *Forbes* as one of the nation's most wealthy individuals. And after 40 years of unparalleled business success, owning enormous wealth, he would make plans to give almost all of his millions away to worthy and newly formed Catholic charities and institutions.

## An Orphan Boy's Childhood Values

When Monaghan was 4 years old, his father died on Christmas Eve. His mother, Anna, tried to keep the family together but was unable to support her two sons. She turned the children over to a Catholic orphanage, the St. Joseph Home for Boys in Jackson, Michigan, where Tom and his younger brother Jim were to be raised by priests and nuns. Monaghan recalled the sad story of his father's death: "My life would have been completely different if my father had lived. I remember stepping up to his casket and trying to reach in and shake him."

Monaghan began imagining a life after the orphanage, often day-dreaming while polishing the oak floors of St. Joseph's. He took unusual pride in his work, usually rubbing the floors with wax-coated paper bread wrappers and then following by buffing with a blanket. The home emphasized the Catholic value of a strong work ethic, a model which Monaghan would adopt for the rest of his life.

In St. Joe's, he also discovered a love of handcrafted objects, especially the ornately carved Victorian staircase. He hoped to turn his appreciation into a career as an architect. In the home, where daily chores often cut into playtime, he could not play baseball frequently, yet always fantasized that one day he would be the shortstop of his beloved Detroit Tigers. He also kept a scrapbook of cars, which represented another boyish passion. From an early age, Monaghan kept his dream machine going.

## False Steps on the Career Ladder

Becoming a priest was one early career dream that went astray when a pillow fight in the seminary ended Monaghan's quest. He enlisted in the Marines and was discharged in 1959 with $2,000 in savings. An oil promoter conned him into a get-rich-quick investment and the savings vanished. Penniless and homeless, Monaghan headed back to Michigan, where he worked at a newsstand to raise tuition money to attend Ferris State College in Big Rapids, Michigan.

Soon afterward he enrolled at the University of Michigan, but became ill and dropped out. He worked for a while and reenrolled, but had to abandon the course work because it was too difficult. Instead, he attended high school courses at night in Ann Arbor. His dream was still to become an architect.

Then his younger brother Jim suggested that they buy a pizza place from an Ann Arbor restaurateur named Dominick DiVarti. The parlor was located in Ypsilanti, at the campus of Eastern Michigan University, and the selling price was $500 plus assumption of a few thousand dollars of debt. The brothers decided to take a stab at running a pizza parlor although neither had ever been in the food business. They decided to keep the Dominick's name because Monaghan Brothers Pizza didn't sound either Italian or authentic. They took over the store in December 1960.

But eight months later, the 23-year-old Tom Monaghan watched his brother Jim drive off in the Volkswagen Beetle that they had purchased together. Jim had traded Tom his 50 percent equity in the pizza parlor for full ownership of the car. It had been Jim's ability to borrow $900 from his post-office credit union that had financed the 1959 VW—Tom had no cash and no credit. The plain fact was that Jim had lost hope of enjoying any financial success in running the small pizzeria. Jim preferred the steady work—and steady paycheck—at the post office.

## "If It Is to Be, It Is up to Me"

For Tom, Jim's departure would represent the first of a lifetime of business obstacles that would temporarily halt—but never deter—his inner spirit and his desire to succeed. He became inured to both the small and large stumbling blocks that impeded his path. He wrote of his brother's departure: "It was a setback, but I took it in stride and was optimistic. I thought of all the dreams I'd had of being wealthy and successful and I told myself, 'If it is to be, it is up to me.' "[4]

Even when other business defeats increased in magnitude over time as Monaghan's business flourished—even when he lost control of his company to the bank and stayed on as a measly $200-a-week employee—he would not despair. Nor would he rail against God as Job had wailed in the Bible. In fact, Monaghan's faith—his strong, rock-hard Catholic belief—would be one of the many sources of his strength and, years later, his admitted spiritual salvation.

In truth, Monaghan could not fault his brother's decision. The pizza parlor had done a fair to middling seasonal business while students attended classes from September to June. But in the summer months, the restaurant's income had dropped a drastic 75 percent, echoing the famous line about the retail trade: "No traffic, no revenues."

With his brother and only coworker gone, Tom had to perform all the many labor-intensive tasks himself. The pizza-making business required hours of preparation to ensure that the hand-rolled dough, freshly diced toppings, and original sauces were lined up and ready for the customers' arrival. Often, Tom worked 18 hours a day, starting at 10 A.M. and ending work at 4 A.M. by cleaning the kitchen and swabbing the floors. What bothered him that summer was the thought that he would be too busy operating the pizza parlor to continue at college and fulfill his life's ambition of becoming an architect like his boyhood idol, Frank Lloyd Wright.

## Expanding and Improving the Fledgling Pizza Business

Because necessity is often the mother of invention, Tom searched for and found a new partner: a fast-talking local cook, who had pizzeria experience and knowledge of a special tomato sauce, and who had also been a pioneer in the trade by offering free home delivery—an idea no one else had tried up to that time. The man wanted a 50-50 equity split and offered $500 as a buy-in. Monaghan agreed, leaving the business in his own name because the new partner had previously gone bankrupt. He put the degree in architecture on the back burner. Pizza was calling.

Once the delivery method was set in place, Monaghan struggled with different ideas to improve the entire pizza-making system in order to make certain that the pizza arrived undamaged. Initially, he conceived of two pizza-business innovations: the square, multisized corrugated box (strong and easily stackable) and the "hot box," or insulated pouch, to keep the pizza hot during delivery. He is also credited with designing the conveyer oven, pizza trays, and a vertical cutter—all

implements that streamlined the laborious and time-consuming process
of making a fresh pie.

Monaghan opened two additional college-based pizzerias in Ypsilanti
under the name Pizza King, and his new partner operated two restaurants under different names. Monaghan doggedly put in 100 hours per
week to keep up with demands of the three pizza locations. In whatever
spare time he could manage, he would think of ways to make the operation more efficient without lessening the quality of the pizza. Above all,
he searched for ways to trim down the time needed to produce and
deliver a fresh-baked pie.

Monaghan now had the time to reflect on the nature of the operations. He realized that college towns would provide the optimum profitable locations for his pizzerias, particularly if the pizzas were delivered.
Students—most without cars—could stay in the dorms and order pies to
share with friends. For college students, pizza was an inexpensive meal,
a respite from the drab and predictable college fare, and the ideal hot
finger food to eat with beer.

Monaghan had not counted on the college practical-joke mentality.
Students would conspire to call for delivery at the same time of the
evening, knowing that the pizzeria couldn't make so many pies in a short
time frame. Worse, when Monaghan showed up to deliver one pie,
pranksters would steal the other pizzas from his car. He waited in the
car with a baseball bat to deter the thieves.

The one upside of delivering pizza to college dorms was meeting his
wife, Margie, a student at Central Michigan University in Mount Pleas-
ant. Ironically, he never would have met her had he not conceived of the
pizzeria's college expansion. How did he court her? On their second
date, he presented her with a heart-shaped pizza for Valentine's Day.

## Staving Off Bankruptcy and Starting Over

Unfortunately, while Monaghan was busy growing his three-store pizza
business, his unsupervised partner was skimming cash from the two
restaurants. The cook went on a spending spree, purchasing automobiles
and property and making expensive home improvements. Although
friends pointed out the partner's obvious fiddling with the receipts, Monaghan, naive and trustworthy, paid no notice to their warnings. He said:
"I believed I wouldn't get hurt if I played fairly. I was naive and trusted

him. He was older than I and a real sweet talker so maybe I was somewhat frightened of his age and experience."

In 1964, Monaghan finally dissolved the partnership, taking the pizzerias and leaving the cook the restaurants. A year later, the cook declared bankruptcy—but Monaghan took the financial hit, because all the stores were still in his name. He was left with a bill for $75,000 in back taxes, which he had to pay off or lose his good name. He said: "I worked so hard to build this business, to make it grow. I couldn't imagine losing it." To the lawyer who suggested that the easiest way out was for him to declare bankruptcy, Monaghan said emphatically: "I hate the word bankruptcy. So forget that. I want to work my way out of this thing. I know I can do it."[5]

Monaghan vowed to repay all creditors, and he also decided to rid himself of the negative association with the bad-luck Dominick's name. At first, he considered Pinocchio's, which had an Italian flavor and was easily remembered. But Pinocchio's was rejected. His workers were invited to come up with new names; finally, a manager suggested the name Domino's. Monaghan thought it was perfect because it wouldn't confuse the existing clientele with a brand-new name. He also cleverly reasoned that the change would still leave the "D-O-M-I-N" beginning of the name intact and in the same alphabetical place in the phone book.

Buoyed by this new start, a business rebirth, and the second occasion of bidding farewell to a less-than-productive partner, Monaghan buckled down, cut costs, and turned a $50,000 profit in 1965. He also talked to an ad agency for the first time: It recommended an eponymous logo of a domino with three dots, one pip for each store. The idea was that as Monaghan opened other stores, additional dots would reflect the growth. No one knew then that if the company followed this ingenious idea, the logo today would contain thousands of domino spots.

Monaghan also realized that the extra expense of premium ingredients and his crew's hard work would go for naught if pizzas were delivered tepid or cold. To maintain an objective for the stores to strive for, he suggested the goal of delivering each order to the customer in less than 30 minutes. At first, this 30-minute idea was just a time target to shoot for; later, it would become the signature hallmark of the Domino's franchise and would change a local pizzeria chain into a recognizable American brand.

Two of the three aspects of Domino's future pizza domination were set in place: a familiar and easy to recognize domino logo and name, and a promise of a hot pizza delivered in 30 minutes. The one variable missing to generate greater profits was additional stores. This would represent the next business phase. But first, Monaghan would experience another catastrophe and roll down the hill again.

In 1967, a fire destroyed the anchor store, resulting in a $150,000 loss only partly covered by a paltry $13,000 in insurance. The financial beating was only part of the calamity; Tom and Marge lived in the house connected to the pizzeria. Monaghan ordered the remaining stores to organize along a single-ingredient assembly line plan—one store made the dough, another shredded the cheese, and the third made sauces. This allowed all the stores to stay open without receiving supplies from the anchor location.

## Expanding through Franchising Causes Huge Cash-Flow Problems

By 1968, Monaghan believed he had found the magic combination to pizza success and was determined to expand as quickly as possible. He perceived that franchising—all the rage back in the mid-1960s when newspapers were full of franchising opportunities—was the business model to spread the Domino's story. He tried to pattern the franchise system after Kentucky Fried Chicken and McDonald's. In those go-go days of proliferating fast-food chains sprouting up on every highway street corner, it seemed all a company had to do was open a store and wait for the traffic. This was not the case with Domino's.

Monaghan also basked in his celebrity status, having garnered the reputation of being the boy wonder of Ypsilanti's business community. Everyone in town had heard of the Domino's expansion, and Monaghan became the example of the hard-working hometown boy who had made good. He reveled in the new adulation.

In the first 10 months of 1969, Domino's opened 32 new stores, bringing the total to 40 pizzerias. All the new locations underperformed drastically and the more established company-owned Domino's stores had to forgo profits to keep the newer entries afloat. Part of the problem was that Domino's was an unknown chain in areas outside of the Michigan heartland. In Ohio or Indiana, it was perceived as just a new mom-and-pop pizzeria, not as part of any celebrated chain.

The cash-flow problems escalated from the too-rapid expansion. Monaghan couldn't pay the insurance premiums, and the company was falling behind on its sales tax payments. The bottom finally blew open when the company's checks started to bounce. To exacerbate the dilemma, an errant decimal-point error resulted in a withholding tax payment to the IRS of $4,000 instead of $40,000. Monaghan, the optimist, wrote: "I thought that solving our IRS problems would put us in pretty good shape. But we had so many stores losing money, it was like being in quicksand."[6]

When Monaghan finally assessed the financial bleeding, he was astonished to discover that the company's debt totaled $1.5 million. The creditor bank was not interested in the Pollyannaish hopes of the company's founder and main stockholder. One autobiographical sentence summed up Monaghan's position: "I lost control of Domino's on May 1, 1970."[7] The bank and the creditors allowed Monaghan to remain as the supervisor for 12 stores. In one year, as he said, "The boy wonder of Ypsilanti had become the village idiot."[8]

What Monaghan did not then know was that there was still no beacon of real light shining at the end of his tunnel of despair. As humiliating as the end of his dream of a whole world of Domino's franchises was, more serious drawbacks still awaited. His confidence in himself and his pizza franchisees would be severely tested.

## Recovering from $1.5 Million in Debt

The first step for Monaghan was to agree to a bank-approved plan whereby another person would assume ownership for two years while his stock was placed in trust. The arrangement staved off bankruptcy and reduced some of the demands from the hordes of infuriated creditors, many of them Domino's suppliers. Everyone who had done business with Domino's cursed its name and railed against its founder, who had, in their opinion, allowed his own unrealistic sugar-plum dreams of fame and fortune to blind him from perceiving his lack of sound business judgment.

Within a year, Monaghan had negotiated to have his entire stock returned, and the new owner took charge of a well-paying pizzeria and the property that went with it. Most of the creditors became unnerved at the move, apprehensive that Monaghan would declare bankruptcy with his financial overseer out of the picture. Monaghan had the entire company back but he did not have the confidence of his storeowners or creditors. He remembered these dire times in his autobiography: "I planned to pay everybody back a hundred cents on the dollar. But there was no way I could pay anybody back yet."[9] Some creditors agreed to go along with his plan, but, surprisingly, the once-loyal franchise owners pressed an antitrust lawsuit against the corporation. This represented the lowest point of Monaghan's business life. He said, "When I was served notice that they'd filed against me, I sat at my desk and cried."[10]

Somehow Monaghan found the inner courage to confront the rebellious and litigious owners. He visited each operation, persuading anyone who would listen that suing him was futile: if he—Domino's—went under, they—the franchisees—would lose everything, because there was neither cash nor assets to pay off the judgment. His speech was part begging, part business, but over the next three years every franchisee lawsuit was dropped. Some owners sold their stores back to Monaghan at a premium price, but in the long run, gathering stores back into the corporate fold would reap dividends for Domino's for years to come. The first big bump in the road was crossed.

By the end of 1972, Monaghan had compiled a final list of the mistakes that had almost caused him to lose the business. He said: "We had overexpanded and added new stores to territories before the first stores were firmly established. We also made the mistake of sending in untrained managers with no experience to run the new stores and [we] overstaffed our home office. A final and, in my mind, potentially fatal mistake was the lack of good financial statements available on a timely basis."[11]

In overexpanding without a sound plan, the franchising move appeared to be another in a series of near-fatal errors. Monaghan seemed to be caught in a repeating pattern of flying too high and then crashing in flames. Over time, he would learn to make sounder business decisions. Yet, lurking somewhere up ahead, were still other serious errors of judgment, as well as one trademark lawsuit that would cost the company millions.

The one recurring note throughout the painful restructuring was Monaghan's optimism and self-confidence. He was proud to toot his own horn, the cheerleader encouraging the team to win: "I could see that Domino's had barely scratched the surface of its potential, I knew we already had the best-run pizzerias in the country—any of our competitors would have to admit that. We weren't too well thought of in financial circles, but that would change." And he was right.

## Getting National Attention and Turning the Business Around

In 1971, the East Lansing store experienced a fantastic one-day pizza output when it promoted a $1 pizza on Super Bowl Sunday. This annual professional football championship was not then a rite of American television viewing, a ritual pastime like watching the Academy Awards or the Miss America pageant. But for males eager to see the game with their pals, what could be tastier than ordering delivery of a pizza or two or three? The one-shot promo resulted in an amazing 3,500-pizza day.

A year later, in 1972, Monaghan and some of his owners assembled in the East Lansing store to help with the expected demand from the second Super Bowl Sunday promotion. This store featured Big Red, the largest oven in the United States at that time. The company hired an unheard-of 37 drivers to handle the deliveries. Monaghan invited one of the executives of the North American Pizza Association to watch the ordering frenzy. The event produced 5,000 pizzas in five hours, an output of Guinness' record-book proportions. The pizza executive wrote a press release that was picked up by the Associated Press and United Press International, and soon everyone in America learned of the avalanche of pizzas that had descended on East Lansing. More important to Monaghan, all America read the name Domino's Pizza for the first time.

That day's Super Bowl event, coming after those terrible soul-searching years of lawsuits and creditor bills, was the proverbial shot in the arm for Monaghan's tired soul. He wrote glowingly of the camaraderie: "Get a bunch of people with sauce in their veins working together in a situation like that, and you have a pizza man's dream of heaven."[12] It was a joy for him, finally, to be surrounded by positive and nurturing Domino's employees.

Monaghan hired the pizza association executive as a part-time consultant, and the new hire's first step was to recommend the first all-company meeting. It was held in the modest surroundings of Howard Johnson's in Ypsilanti. Years later, Monaghan would recount with irony of the choice of the once-famous ice cream chain: "When I was a boy, Howard Johnson's was the only place along the road to stop for food east of the Mississippi. Today they've all but disappeared. At one time,

Domino's was the only pizza delivery chain in America and twice we almost came close to disappearing."

At that first company meeting, Monaghan gave the keynote address with one vital message to pass on to the managers and the franchise owners: Deliver in 30 minutes. He emphasized the target time by telling them: "Whenever your franchisees think about me in the future, I want you to remember me by my initials, TSM (Thomas Steven Monaghan), but in *this* order, TMS which stands for thirty-minute service."[13] He recalled the laughter that ensued, but he was very serious about the delivery time and put many stores on notice that he meant business. It was at this first company powwow that everyone realized Monaghan was back in form and running the show.

By 1973, Domino's had 76 stores in 13 states and showed a small profit. Monaghan realized he had one business nut left to crack for the chain to explode nationwide: a successful franchising system to replace the failed one from years before. By chance, he met an executive from the Kirby Vacuum Cleaner Company who described his company's successful program for launching new distributorships: a sponsorship program in which higher-ranking managers recommended lower-ranking employees as being worthy to run a franchise. For Monaghan, this was the key solution: "I'd create our own sponsorship programs whereby franchisees would encourage their best managers to open their own new Domino's stores. It contained a double benefit for franchisees because it not only gave them added income, it also provided them with a powerful new tool in their recruiting efforts."[14]

Inherent within this promotion system was Monaghan's savvy method of rewarding good workers who might never generate the capital for down payment on a franchise and who might otherwise have accepted managerial offers from competitors. It also kept loyalists within the Domino's family. A loyalist, a true believer, was a Domino's employee whose mantra was "TMS—thirty-minute service."

Monaghan believed that "dependable delivery" was the most important variable in customers' minds when they decided to order pizza: "Sure quality, taste, and value were important to the consumer. But if it you couldn't deliver that pizza in less than thirty minutes, it didn't matter how good the pizza tasted or what price was paid. I'm convinced that Domino's success came from the guarantee that a pizza could reach a home in less than thirty minutes."

## Fighting to Maintain the Company Name— and Keep the Franchisees

The year was 1972 when Domino's filed to amend its articles of incorporation by adding the appellation "Pizza" to the company name. It would now and forever be called Domino's Pizza, Inc. Monaghan recorded that moment by stating: "Never again would I apologize for being what I am, a pizza man. I'm proud of my calling and I'm proud that Domino's is a *pizza* company."

Two years later in 1974, when the U.S. Patent Office's *Official Gazette* published its new listings to the public, the Amstar Corporation, makers of Domino Sugar, filed a trademark infringement lawsuit. The battle over the company name with another corporate powerhouse would constitute the second big bump in the road for Monaghan, and it would drag on for five years. Just when he could see the profits ahead on the horizon, he had to spend valuable time and money to fight what seemed on the surface a ludicrous suit—who would ever mistake a retail pizza chain for boxes of sugar on a store's shelf? Visually, there was not a smidgen of similarity between the familiar yellow box of sugar and the red and blue pizza carton. However, Amstar believed that it had built up such positive equity in the Domino name from years of advertising ($54 million from 1947 to the time of the lawsuit) and sales (around $300 million per year) that any trademark similarity—even in such a disparate product as pizza—represented a dilution of the established brand name.

Monaghan perceived that Amstar thought he would settle the suit quickly. For a while, he toyed with changing the name to Red Domino. But the expense to alter every sign, every napkin, and every telephone-book listing seemed prohibitive. Monaghan puzzled over what action to take, because he had two sets of lawyers voicing different opinions. Finally, he said, "We would not switch to Red Domino. We would fight to register Domino's Pizza, and if we lost and Amstar sued us, we would battle them for all we were worth."[15]

By 1976, in the midst of the Amstar dispute, Monaghan fired his executive vice president, who had tried to convince Monaghan to sell out and leave the company. The VP had excellent organizational skills, but did not believe that franchise stores would maximize corporate profits: He wanted all Domino's outlets to be company-owned stores. Naturally, when the franchise owners learned of this proposed attempt to drop them, they turned their anger toward Monaghan. Once again, he was faced with franchisee mutiny, and again the venom was expressed in a lawsuit. The owners claimed they were paying royalties on a Domino's name that the company no longer could use because of the Amstar trademark suit.

For Monaghan, the franchise fight was another huge obstacle to face at a time when he had not yet settled the trademark problem. But the franchise problem represented another possible loss of the company. So Monaghan got into his car and visited all the dissidents, telling them that the old way of operations had returned. Six months later, Domino's was again one happy family, albeit one unsure of what it could legally call itself.

In November 1978, Domino's opened its 200th store, and the chain added 28 additional stores that year. But the guillotine fell in 1979, when the judge in the case announced that Amstar had prevailed: Domino was permanently prohibited from using the Domino name. Monaghan calculated that the name changes would cost Domino's $2 million.

As the appeal went forward, the company was caught in a curious limbo: It could keep the Domino's name in the states where it was already doing business, but stores opened in new states had to go under a new name, Pizza Dispatch. A year latter, the appellate court overruled the judge and reversed the decision. Domino's Pizza could keep its name. Monaghan was overjoyed and said, "I got a big smile on my face and then I burst into tears. I grabbed Margie and for twenty minutes I cried. I was a complete basket case."[16] Monaghan had weathered two huge obstacles, and it was time for him to enjoy the fruits of his labor.

## Spending Lavishly on Himself and the Corporation

As the 1980s began, Monaghan had not formulated any plans for what he would buy for himself and his wife now that all his legal and franchise problems had ended. But once he first took out his wallet and began to procure objects that he wanted or had dreamed about, there was no end to his flagrant—and, occasionally, ostentatious—material acquisitions. The man with the Midas touch in pizza wanted all the wealth of King Midas, and more.

Remember that Monaghan had held onto 97 percent of the company, so when the cash started flowing into headquarters during the 1980s, millions upon millions ended up in his bank account. He said, "I couldn't believe the cash flow of that decade. I had never had so much money coming in from all the outlets. I felt it was time to spend some of my hard-earned money."

Spend it he did. He bought a rare Bugatti sports car for $22 million. He bought a collection of Frank Lloyd Wright memorabilia valued at $40 million, including Snowflake, a house Wright had designed, in Plymouth, Michigan; stained-glass windows; and a dining room set from the Husser House in Chicago. He also purchased a 173-foot-tall ship, which he named the *Domino Effect*. And then, in the final statement of "Look, world, I've got it made!" he bought what every kid dreams of—a baseball team. In 1983, he purchased his beloved Detroit Tigers from legendary owner John Fetzer for $53 million. The orphan boy had amassed every dream of his youth and, in an ending not even Hollywood would write, the Detroit Tigers won the World Series in 1984, one year after Monaghan had purchased the team.

Monaghan's love and veneration for Frank Lloyd Wright resulted in his building the company headquarters in Ann Arbor, Michigan, in the style of the great architect who had died in 1959. Originally, Monaghan had hoped to construct the headquarters in a larger version of an unfinished Wright house designed for Edith Rockefeller McCormick in 1900. But Gunnar Birkitts, the architect on the project, pointed out that the house was never intended as a large corporate building.

The finished building was a compromise, a Wright-Birkitts collaboration, sleeker than most of Wright's houses, and more reserved than Birkitts's previous buildings. Monaghan tipped the memory in Wright's favor by naming the structure Prairie House. Monaghan's own duplex suite in the building cost a reputed $2.5 million, containing walls of African mahogany, leather floor tiles, and a vaulted gold-leaf ceiling. The complex also featured a working farm, museums, and a mime center directed by Marcel Marceau. The total bill for company headquarters topped out at more than $150 million.

Monaghan continued to spend lavishly on himself and the corporation. Eventually, he would amass more than 150 classic cars worth more than $150 million. There would be a Domino Lodge in northern Michigan, where Monaghan and his wife would occasionally treat guests to a $1 million, three-day bash, presenting Tiffany trinkets to the invitees. One building project conceived in the 1980s never was realized. It was another Monaghan idea called the Leaning Tower of Pizza, a 35-story conference center that would tilt 15 degrees eastward.

When asked about all his fanciful indulgences, Monaghan replied: "I'm allowed to have hobbies. So are my franchisees. I think I've done a pretty good job of having my hobbies complement Domino's."

Monaghan's obsession for Frank Lloyd Wright cannot be simply a case of youthful dreams unrealized. Monaghan's feelings for the master were more visceral. He said, "What I like about the Wright architecture is hard to say. It just makes you feel good. At times it almost brings you to tears." For many years afterward, Monaghan had plans to complete unfinished Wright designs, but these were never accomplished.

## Dealing with Despair—A Decision to Sell the Company

During the 1980s, the millions of dollars of purchases put Monaghan into the public limelight, with two different consequences: The media depicted him as a show-off kid who had run wild in a candy shop, but the public reaction to the new millionaire, who displayed so much passion and appreciation for the realization of his dreams, was positive. Everyone anticipated that as Monaghan's fortune grew, his acquisitions would also increase.

No one anticipated what happened next. Monaghan read a book, and it transformed his life. The year was 1989 and the tome was *Mere Christianity* by C. S. Lewis, the British author. The chapter on pride, "the great sin" was a "rude awakening" to Monaghan. He felt suddenly trapped by the enormity of his possessions, reflecting, "I lay awake virtually all night and realized I had more pride than any person I know. I took a millionaire's vow of poverty."

Motivated by a newly found and sincere devotion to God, Monaghan decided to sell his 97 percent share of Domino's. If there was one terrible decision that ranks as the worst, this one, in 1989, wins the gold medal in a lifetime of poor decisions. The main reason for the error was that as Monaghan was trying to get out of the pizza business, Pizza Hut was trying to get into the delivery segment, in direct competition with Domino's. This crisis would be the ultimate test of Monaghan's ability to rise from the ashes of defeat; this crisis was more than just a bump in the road.

Monaghan was confident he could sell out his shares and take the monies to invest in Catholic charities. He used two of Wall Street's most savvy merger and acquisition firms, Goldman Sachs and J. P. Morgan, as agents. As he said, "I thought they would find me a buyer in less than two months. In that time, I did not anticipate any short-term harm to the Domino's business."

The next two and a half years would be a calamity of horrible proportions: The sale never materialized, and as it dragged on, the once-profitable business started to nosedive. He said, "The biggest reason why the sale did not go through was bad timing. It was two years after the Crash of 1987 and there just weren't the leveraged buyouts going on at that time."

The important numbers to remember are that in 1989, Domino's market share of the delivery pizza segment was 54 percent, and three years later, it had dropped drastically to 16 percent, losing share to Pizza Hut and also being undercut by Little Caesar's clever marketing strategy of offering two pizzas for the price of one.

While Monaghan waited confidently for the sale to go through, he devoted his time to philanthropic work for Catholic charities and let a management team operate the company. But in his absence, Domino's floundered. Financial analysts agreed that part of the reason why no offer ever came in was that Monaghan's finances and assets were so commingled with the company's, no accountant's rendering could really come up with a true statistic on what the company was worth. The Wright headquarters also turned out to be a millstone, because rents would not cover the mortgage.

Marketing experts also cited the fact that the captain had left the helm of the ship and no one knew in which direction the ship was headed. The corporate team was unwilling to spend millions of dollars for promotion and advertising without knowing whom the new buyer would be. Monaghan said: "Everything was put on hold. A lot of things that should have been done, were not, like building for the future and upgrading. Everything pretty much stopped and there was no expansion program. Worse, our people in the field were losing confidence in Domino's."

## Confronting Disaster: Closing Stores and Selling Assets

For the next two and a half years, Domino's floundered on the choppy seas of indecision and absentee ownership. It would seem that at this juncture in his life, with the big crises threatening his wealth and his reputation, that Monaghan might have caved in and bailed out. But he relied on his renewed faith to confront this disaster.

Without a sale forthcoming, Monaghan had no choice but to take over the helm and return to the CEO position. By 1992, the company faced a technical default of nearly $200 million in debt. For the second time in Domino's history, the banks sent up red flares of doubt that the company could survive. Assets sales were cutting costs, but large bank fees from the default were impeding the company's ability to stay afloat.

"The thing that kept me going every day was a belief that sooner or later it would all turn out all right," Monaghan said. "I had to deal with a new executive team and franchisees on the warpath. They didn't believe in the system or in me. Sales were down and the banks wouldn't let me make any moves. I couldn't take money and move it from one account to another."

His only comfort in these times of trouble was to work endlessly on scratch pads, making cash-flow predictions for the future until he could envision the company returning to profitable years down the road. This daily exercise proved part of his salvation: "I would write down different scenarios of all the key indicators—average sales per store, profit per store, debt—in the present time. Then I would project three months, six months, a year, two years, or five years down the road until I found a profit. In this method, I was able to live with the present situation knowing that one day the company would be out of the red. And over time it happened, my projections came true."

The goal for the reluctant and returned CEO was twofold: to restructure the company and to bid farewell to all of his personal assets. Painfully, all the toys and all the possessions went on the market for a fraction of their original price. Monaghan installed a new computer software system that provided better data on profitability. The new data resulted in the closing of many company stores that were not making target sales.

In the midst of this crisis, Domino's was hit by a lawsuit from a St. Louis woman who had been injured by a Domino's delivery driver. The jury found that in the rush to deliver a pizza in less than 30 minutes, the driver had been negligent. The award totaled $78 million, and, more serious, Domino's had to give up its established signature benefit, guaranteed delivery in less than 30 minutes.

During the restructuring, Monaghan changed his life forever by renouncing most of the many and wondrous material assets he had accumulated. Much to America's surprise, the now-billionaire divested himself of the huge fortune he had amassed. Out went the Sikorsky S-76 helicopter, the corporate jet, the classic and expensive automobiles, the tall ship, the Detroit Tigers, and, so, finally, did his beloved Frank Lloyd Wright collection. Never one to do anything in half measures, Monaghan wore his hair shirt and announced to the world: "Everything about me was pride, going way back to my childhood. I was always the most competitive in sports. Why? Because I wanted to impress people. I didn't to it because God wants me to do it. I came to the conclusion that I should be impressing God and not other people."

After five years of cost cutting and realigning the company, Domino's achieved steady sales growth. Monaghan had worked another miracle, saving his company from the jaws of defeat.

## "You Just Can't Quit"

In 1998, Monaghan successfully sold the company for $1 billion to Bain Capital, a Boston-based equity company, leaving him with a personal fortune of $900 million. In the big capital rush of the 1990s economic boom, the company had found a buyer, and Monaghan could finally exit with pride and profit.

With the large sum of money, he started a number of new Catholic organizations over the years, including Legatus, an organization for Catholic corporate leaders; the Thomas More Center for Law and Justice; *Credo*, a weekly magazine for Catholic households; the Ave Maria School of Law; and missions to Honduras to improve the life of the people in that country. He has never been busier or more content.

Asked what advice he would give to those businesspeople who experience the occasional downturn in their careers, he replied: "You just can't quit. Keep going. Make projections over and over again. Escape into fantasy if that's helpful. Then after you make the projections, you try to achieve the results."

Tom Monaghan now devotes all his time to the many Catholic institutions that he started. He stands in line at airports like any other coach-class passenger and tries to live a life of service and without pride. But the company that he created took great pride in raising $100,000 to endow a prize given annually to a new Domino's franchisee. It's called the Thomas S. Monaghan Entrepreneurial Award.

Larry Ellison

# CHAPTER 3

### Larry Ellison

*Founder and CEO of Oracle*

*"When we hit the wall, we hit it very, very hard."*

IN 1991, LARRY ELLISON, cofounder and chief executive of the hugely successful California-based computer software company Oracle, and one of the richest people in the world, decided to spend the winter holidays in Hawaii. It had been a grinding year for him. Against all the odds, Oracle had established itself as a hot company in the hottest American industry, but staying on top in Silicon Valley is almost as tough as getting to the top. For the past couple of years, Ellison had been busy putting out fires and otherwise dealing with problems arising from too-rapid growth and lax controls. For a respite from killer competition and internal problems, Ellison was looking forward to some sun, sand, and diversion with his then-girlfriend, Kathleen O'Rourke.

On Christmas Day, 1991, on the Big Island of Hawaii, Ellison went body surfing. He should have paid attention to the signs indicating that the beach was closed, or to the red flags posted to indicate the threat of 12- to 15-foot waves. But Ellison had not gotten where he was in life by paying attention to rules or by timidity in potentially perilous situations. He favored fast cars and flew his own jets, and his 6-foot, 1-inch frame was in remarkably good physical condition considering that he was 47 years old.

The only people braving the conditions that day were three Hawaiian teenagers. But Ellison figured what the hell, he'd go for it. This had always been his attitude, whether in business or in his personal life. So he jumped on his surfboard and headed into the sea. For a brief moment, it was exhilarating. A 13-foot wave caught him and his board and shot him forward like a bullet. "For the first half second I thought:

This is amazing. I couldn't believe the acceleration of this wave," Ellison later recalled.

The exhilaration suddenly faded. The huge water formation propelling Ellison began pushing faster, harder, sending him pitching forward, utterly out of control. "Holy smokes. I knew I had to bail out of this wave before I got onshore or I was going to be maybe killed. So I duck. I go into a tuck and try to get out from underneath the wave. The wave took me down. It was taking my head right for the sand and would have snapped my neck like a twig, but I finally just rolled and got back onto my right shoulder."[1]

That reflexive effort saved his life, but at tremendous cost. "Within a couple of seconds I started hearing a sound in my ears that sounded like someone with a handful of shredded wheat, just crushing all this shredded wheat." What he heard was his own body being rent asunder. "I heard three bones fracturing in my shoulders. It was a very surreal experience. My board exploded into three pieces—one piece jammed into my neck and broke my neck—broke my sixteenth vertebra," he says. "Then I heard my ribs snapping one after another, and finally one of them went into a lung and punctured and collapsed my lung. When the wave finally subsided, my right shoulder was down where my waist was supposed to be."[2]

Ellison did not even realize his neck had been broken until four days after the surfing accident. He was taken to the hospital, where his broken collarbone was set. The doctors could do little about his broken ribs. Luckily for the software tycoon, his neck was broken with a stable fracture that did not pose a threat to his neuromotor functioning.

Ellison was back at the office a short time later, but still was unable to resist pushing things to extremes. While bike riding as part of a physical therapy regimen for the damage his body sustained during the body-surfing mishap, Ellison refused to slow down when he hit some railroad tracks. He hit the rails, and his bike upended. Ellison went airborne. When he slammed into the ground he did so squarely on his left elbow, shattering most of the bones in the elbow and arm. Once again, he was taken to the hospital, this time to the University of California at Davis. "The doctor who finally fixed it said it looked like a war wound, like I'd been shot with a high-powered rifle," Ellison has said.

Again, luck—and medical competency—were on Ellison's side. The physicians carefully reconstructed the shattered mass of skeleton in his left arm. The operation was a complete success, and Ellison regained full use of his arm. He was so happy with what the Davis surgeons had done, in fact, that he pledged $5 million to the school for the establishment of a new musculoskeletal institute.

In both these incidents, Ellison was acting true to character. He gloried in pushing the envelope, whether in business or in physical activity. At about the same time that he was being buffeted by waves and slammed into the ground, the Oracle Corporation, the source of his vast wealth and the company he ruled over like a medieval warlord, was suffering the worst setbacks of its existence. Many of its troubles were traceable to his penchant for pushing things to extremes. Oracle had doubled its sales in 11 of the first 12 years of its existence (it was founded in 1977 and shipped its first product in 1979) and had doubled both sales and operating profits every fiscal year from 1983 to 1990. Ellison became so rich in good part because he has always been reluctant to finance growth by selling additional shares, which amounts, in effect, to taking in new partners. But he wasn't about to slow growth just because he lacked the money to fund it adequately. He kept pushing his people to take chances.

They took a few too many. In the early 1990s, the big wave hit—and the company's bones began cracking like shredded wheat. In the first fiscal quarter of 1991 (ended August 31, 1990) the company recorded its first-ever loss, amounting to some $36 million. That was not the end of the bad news. For the entire fiscal year 1991, Oracle posted its first ever annual loss—some $12.4 million. As on that beach in Hawaii, Ellison had pushed too far.

Shareholders sued; critics called for Ellison's ouster; and the SEC would became involved in an investigation of the company. To make matters worse, Ellison would shortly be sued by an Oracle employee with whom he had had a sexual relationship for "wrongful termination, failure to prevent discrimination, and negligent mental distress."[3]

It had happened often enough in high tech in the 1990s. Many brilliant founders of successful companies had soared to the heights within a few years, only to crash into oblivion. There was Edson deCastro at Data General and Ken Olson at Digital Equipment. Ellison's close friend Steve Jobs, another entrepreneurial CEO, had been kicked out of the company he had cofounded, Apple Computer. (Jobs has, of course, since made a dramatic comeback at the same company).

Investors were quick to punish Oracle for its slide. The company's market capitalization plummeted from close to $4 billion to around $700 million; its shares—of which Ellison owned 24 percent—dropped from the $25 range to around $5. In the words of the publication *Which Computer?*, "the bubble burst" at Oracle.[4] The industry publication *Tech Street Journal* compared Oracle to Donald Trump, another business celebrity who nearly went bust around the same time.[5] Of Ellison, *Forbes* later wrote, "It seemed that another Silicon Valley legend had flamed out."[6]

At the time that Oracle began to topple, Stephen Imbler, the company's vice president of corporate finance, visited Oracle's lavish indoor gym, which was fitted out with stationary bicycles, basketball courts, and other things you might expect to find in a world-class gymnasium. Looking around himself at the impressive exercise furnishings, though, Imbler felt only a cold sense of dread. "I had this fin de siècle feeling. It was like being at an Austrian ball in Vienna just before the war broke out," he recalled. Ellison's damn-the-obstacles personality wouldn't let him slow his bicycle for those railroad tracks or stay on dry land when the surf was billowing dangerously. Why expect he would run his business any differently?

Risk-taking had gotten Ellison to where he was. He wasn't about to stop taking risks. When you take risks you sometimes lose. What made Ellison different from most was that he didn't let those setbacks floor him. After all, much of his life had been about battling against discouragement.

## "You'll Never Amount to Anything"

Lawrence Joseph Ellison was born on August 17, 1944, to an unwed mother, Florence Spellman, on the Lower East Side of Manhattan. Though today the Lower East Side is home to many trendy bars and boutiques, in the 1940s it was largely the preserve of working-class immigrants, mainly Jewish, who had come to America seeking a better life for themselves and their progeny. It was not a good place to raise a fatherless child in those days—Ellison's father was nowhere to be found—and Spellman almost lost her infant son to a bout of pneumonia.

So Spellman made a decision that is never easy for a mother. She decided to give him up. But rather than subject her child to the vagaries of an orphanage or an adoption agency, Spellman sent her baby boy to be raised by her aunt, Lillian Ellison, and Lillian's husband Louis, on the South Shore of Chicago.

The Ellisons were not wealthy people. Louis was a Russian Jew who had fled his native country in the back of a hay cart in 1905. His Russian name had been Anglicized to "Ellison" upon his arrival at—as you might have guessed—Ellis Island, the point of arrival for millions of immigrants in New York harbor at the turn of the century.

Larry Ellison did not learn that he was adopted until he was 12 years old; nor did he learn that his adoptive parents were blood relatives until he was an adult. Naturally obsessed with his origins, Ellison hired a private investigator to locate his birth mother in 1991. (Florence Spellman turned out to be living in New Haven, Connecticut; Ellison bought her a home in California and put his half-sister through college. He never found out what had happened to his biological father.)

Louis Ellison was not a kindly guardian. A small-time real estate operator, he eventually lost his business and went to work for a public housing agency as an auditor. He managed to provide his family with a decent home in a respectable, if modest, Chicago neighborhood, but he was a bitter man—and he took out much of his bitterness on young Larry. The family occupied a two-bedroom, one-bath flat at Clyde Street and Eighty-second.

Later, Ellison grew fond of telling reporters that he grew up in a tough neighborhood on Chicago's South Side. "The truth," according to Ellison biographer Mike Wilson, "was that Ellison did not grow up in a tenement, his family was not poor, and his neighborhood was not rough—at least not while he was there. South Shore, along the shore of Lake Michigan, was once one of the South Side's most desirable neighborhoods."[7] A boyhood friend of Ellison recalled, "It was a pretty nice way to grow up."

Ellison has fictionalized his childhood to make his rise sound more dramatic, but in one important sense he did have a rough upbringing: Perhaps soured by his own lack of success in life, Louis Ellison would often needle Larry and attempt to make him feel insignificant. One time, during a basketball game—Ellison has been a lifelong devotee of the sport, continuing to play it when his schedule permits and remaining a die-hard Chicago Bulls fan—Ellison accidentally scored a hoop for the opposing team. A local newspaper took note and recorded this fact. Ellison says his father cut the story out of the paper and held onto it so he could embarrass him with it. Build the child's self-esteem? Louis Ellison wasn't big on that. His standard greeting to Larry was "You'll never amount to anything." This continual humiliation and searing debasement seems to have played a large part in shaping the man that Ellison was to become. Far from crushing him, it made him determined to prove himself as worthy, over and over, in the surf or in business. When you constantly and habitually test yourself, you are bound to fail sometimes. That constant drive to excel—in everything—is as responsible for Ellison's victories as for his defeats. Notes Mike Wilson, "From the beginning he felt he had something to prove."[8]

And he would do it on his own and on his own terms. Though the Ellison family was Jewish, Ellison refused to be bar mitzvahed at the age of 13. Ellison apparently felt that he didn't need the sanction of religion to prove himself a man. (Though he identifies himself as Jewish and is interested in Jewish history, especially the Holocaust, he does not attend synagogue. And though he is a lover of Japanese culture, he seems to never have fallen under the sway of Buddhism or other Eastern beliefs.) Whereas others need causes and religions, Ellison essentially believes in himself.

Ellison graduated from South Shore High School in Chicago in 1962 and enrolled at the University of Illinois's main campus at Urbana-Champaign. He showed up on a three-wheeled Harley-Davidson motorcycle that he had acquired at a bargain price at a police auction. Other than the Harley, though, Ellison's tastes and aims seemed conservative; he was planning on going premed and becoming a doctor. However, it was probably inevitable that Ellison would never follow so settled a path. He never did earn a degree from the University of Illinois. The reasons remain murky. It has been said that Ellison was asked to leave for failing to maintain a C average—which, given his dislike of rules and the strictures of others, is entirely possible. However, Ellison maintains that he left because his adoptive mother, Louise, died during finals week. The loss, he says, was so overpowering that he simply could not carry on with his studies.

Certainly, the loss of his adoptive mother, who must at least have played the role of buffer between young Ellison and her carping husband during his youth, must have hit him hard. But it is not at all clear that this is what drove Ellison out of the university. In fact, one is left with the distinct feeling that Ellison rearranged the chronology of his mother's demise to supply his biography with a good reason for leaving college. This is classic Ellison: Reinvent your own story—and, if necessary, reinvent the facts to make that story salable. As a person who has essentially invented himself, Ellison apparently sees nothing wrong with throwing in bits of drama to make the invention more interesting.

After leaving the University of Illinois, Ellison enrolled at the University of Chicago. Again, he failed to graduate. His failure to graduate may or may not have been due to a refusal to take a required French proficiency test. Even if the truth is somewhat different, such a refusal seems vintage Ellison. At any rate, rather than continuing to try his hand at academics, the future CEO of Oracle made other plans: "In 1966," writes Mike Wilson, "he headed to California where he attempted to prove his father wrong."[9]

## Getting Started in a Career: Computer Programming

Once on the West Coast, Ellison drifted a bit. He motored about in an aqua blue Ford Thunderbird and was drawn, like many of his generation, to the San Francisco Bay Area, which was a hothouse of cultural ferment. But rather than getting caught up in the countercultural scene that Berkeley and its environs offered, Ellison was drawn to a different aspect of Bay Area life that would have a more positive impact on America than the liberal rebellion of the 1960s: Ellison enrolled in the cyber-revolution.

Taking what strengths he had in the sciences, Ellison began teaching himself the art of computer programming. In late 1966, he went to an employment agency seeking a job in computer programming. The demand for computer programmers wasn't what it is today, but the agency offered him a job as a career counselor.

Ellison took the job but remained there only about long enough to meet a young woman named Adda Quinn. She had recently graduated from San Jose State University with a degree in Chinese history, and was working at the agency to make ends meet. She caught Ellison's eye—or, rather, each caught the other's. By January 1967, just as young America's rebellion was nearing its peak, Larry Ellison and Adda Quinn had married. "I agreed to marry him because he was the most fascinating man I'd ever met in my life," Quinn has said. Though the couple remained together for only seven years and had no children, they have remained friends over the years.

With marriage, Ellison began to be successful. He finally got into computer programming, working in the 1960s for several banks and major companies such as Wellsco Data Systems and Fireman's Fund Insurance. Mostly, he was programming the big IBM mainframe computers that then were the information backbone of many large companies. He did everything from hanging the tapes that backed up data to overall systems upkeep and maintenance. By the late 1960s, Ellison was living well: He owned his own home, as well as an expensive sports car and a sailboat. "He had champagne tastes on a beer budget," recalls Adda Quinn. The marriage was beginning to come apart.

"If you stay with me, I will become a millionaire," Ellison promised Quinn during a session with a therapist who was helping them work on their ailing marriage. In the end, she didn't stay with him, but he did go on to keep his share of the bargain. Even when Oracle's troubles were at their worst, in the early 1990s, he was a centimillionaire.

Like most computer types in the early 1970s, Ellison moved from one job to another, eventually landing at a Silicon Valley technology company called Ampex, based in Sunnyvale, some 30 miles southeast of San Francisco. Although he did not last long at Ampex, he met two men who would play a mammoth role in his future life: Bob Miner and Edward Oates. Miner and Oats were computer techies; Ellison would eventually found Oracle with them.

Miner in particular was the key player. For much of Oracle's history, Miner proved an essential balance to Ellison. If Ellison was into swagger, and into pushing the envelope, Miner was a hard-headed engineer with simple tastes and a down-to-earth mentality. Whereas Ellison pushed and drove those under him, Miner typically encouraged his underlings to lead balanced lives. "If Larry Ellison was to be the brains behind Oracle Corporation, Bob Miner was surely the company's heart," says Mike Wilson.[10]

## Code Name: "Oracle"—Creating a New Business

At Ampex, Ellison found his true calling: sales and marketing. One of Ampex's customers, the Central Intelligence Agency, needed Ampex's help with a project code-named "Oracle." Ellison, Miner, and Oates got the job of writing software that would make the Ampex system work for the CIA. The CIA not only unwittingly gave Ellison the name of his future company (and its main product), it would also prove to be Oracle's first customer, in 1977.

Ellison was clearly on the rise now, his youthful drifting behind him. He left Ampex and went to work for Precision Instrument, a company that specialized in products used for the storage and retrieval of information. At Precision Instrument, Ellison was given a raise and was made vice president of systems development. At the time that Ellison joined, Precision Instrument was trying to market a device called the PI 180, which would store data visually and do so more effectively than a microfilm or microfiche device. The problem was that the PI 180 needed software to function properly, but nobody at Precision knew how to create that software.

This was a major turning point for Ellison. He called Ed Oates and Bob Miner, his former Ampex colleagues, and suggested that they form a company and make a bid. They did so, and their fledgling outfit, called Software Development Laboratories, Inc. (SDL), won out. SDL, which would shortly be renamed Relational Software, Inc., and eventually would become Oracle, had its first official day of business on August 1, 1977, and Ellison soon left Precision Instrument. SDL issued 100,000 shares of stock upon its creation; Ellison bought 60 percent of the shares for 2 cents apiece, or $1,200 total. That $1,200 was the seed capital for a company whose revenues in 2000 were nearly $10 billion and whose market capitalization exceeded $200 billion. But at the founding of SDL, those heights must have seemed unattainable even to the cocky Ellison.

In June 1970, a researcher at IBM named Edgar H. "Ted" Codd had published an article on databases in a technical journal. The contents of this article eventually propelled Ellison into the big time. Codd basically proposed that information could be stored in large data tables and that such tables could be linked together, thus relating the information in one table to the information in another. The advantage to such a system was that it held the possibility of transforming raw data into usable information. You could ask it all kinds of specific questions, and it would provide the answers quickly and reliably. This "relational" model of databases may not seem impressive given the capacities of computers today; however, it was a marked improvement—in theory, anyway—over the hierarchical and network species of database that existed at the time. Faster computers would have to be developed to make relational databases a reality, but that is exactly what happened.

By the mid-1970s, IBM was interested enough in Codd's theory that it assigned a group of engineers and programmers to come up with a working relational database. In order to do so, the IBM group had to come up with a language that would allow users to communicate with the computer. Eventually, they came up with a new, simple language that used plain English characters. They called this new computer language Structured Query Language (SQL). With SQL, users could ask the computer housing a relational database fairly straightforward questions and—voila!—the computer would spit out the information requested. A relational database stores information in several related tables, rather than one large table. This makes the information easier to use.

SQL was the magic formula that would turn Ellison into a billionaire. Ellison and his colleagues did not invent SQL, nor the idea of relational databases. Rather, they took a good idea and ran with it, heedless of the obstacles and the brashness of competing with companies like IBM. Though such borrowing of ideas contradicts the popular myth of the Great Inventor toiling in solitude in the laboratory, it has in fact been quite common in the development of computer technology. Bill Gates and his partners did not invent the Disk Operating System (DOS) that was the source of Microsoft's initial success; they bought it from someone else. Nor did Apple invent the mouse or the cute graphical interface that millions of computer users associate with the Macintosh and its progeny; those innovations came from Xerox. What Ellison and Miner brought to the party was an early understanding of the power of the idea plus a refusal to worry much about the risks. They began marketing a relational database product three full years ahead of IBM. It was a nervy move, but of such bold gambles are great successes built.

Ellison and Miner's first client was the CIA, which paid $50,000 for a database product. The Air Force was another early customer. But Ellison knew that the big market for relational databases would be the private sector. He and his team knew that corporations would be attracted to a properly functioning and easy-to-use database product like tornadoes zeroing in on a trailer park. So, using SQL, they came up with a product called Oracle. Oracle would permit companies to retrieve data based on whatever parameters they wished. If, say, executives at a company wanted to find out which widget salesmen in a particular region had sold more than $1 million worth of widgetry during a particular quarter, they could now do so.

Ellison and his colleagues also made another decision in developing Oracle that would prove amazingly farsighted and contribute greatly to their future success. Although Oracle was initially created to run on the Virtual Address Extension (VAX) computer invented by Digital Equipment Corporation, Ellison saw to it that the program was extended to run on a variety of platforms. Smart move: Digital Equipment, once second only to IBM in the computer industry, went into a prolonged tailspin, and VAX never really caught on. Ellison had Oracle software designed to run on all computer platforms, a rarity among database programs. That way Oracle 2 was not dependent on the success of any single computing platform. The same software package could travel from one type of computer to another and work just as well (in theory, anyway). Today, when Digital Equipment is just a footnote in the computer history books, Oracle software works on IBM mainframes; Unix servers made by Sun Microsystems, IBM, and Hewlett-Packard; and PC servers from myriad computer makers that use the Microsoft Windows NT software package.

Ellison also made sure that his company's product was highly connectable, meaning users could seamlessly synchronize Oracle databases running on several different machines. This, too, proved a brilliant decision. In a sense, people could now access data stored in various far-flung points on a computer network as though it were stored on a single server—even if that data was coming from a different kind of computer than the computer being used to pull it up. Oracle was created to be fully compatible with IBM's relational database software. This was especially important at the time of Oracle's founding, because IBM ruled the world of mainframes and companies wishing to compete in that market had to make their devices IBM compatible.

So, with its portable, connectable, and compatible database software, Oracle was off to a promising start. Ellison shipped his first product in 1979, and recorded sales of $2 million in 1982 (the year IBM shipped its *first* relational database product). Over the next few years, Oracle was a runaway success. It racked up sales of $55 million by 1985, and $1 billion by the early 1990s. More and more big companies turned to Oracle to solve their information-processing needs. Ford Motor, Boeing, General Electric, Texaco, Shell Oil, Sara Lee, American Airlines, Pacific Bell, and others all became Oracle users in due time. As if to illustrate the product's popularity in diverse milieus, both the Joint Chiefs of Staff and the Peace Corps began using Oracle software. By 1999, Oracle boasted 120,000 customers in 145 countries around the world. Those customers were able to use Oracle to store and retrieve information about all their vital functions, from customer lists and account information to financial records and employee data.

## First Problems: Sloppy Accounting and Overly Aggressive Salespeople

Oracle's breathtaking growth did not come without cost. A more prudent manager might have slowed growth in order to build a deeper organization and to accumulate more capital. Prudence is not Ellison's style—not in surfboarding, not in business. But decisions made to help the company rack up bigger and bigger returns ended up having a near-fatal effect on the organization. In emphasizing growth at all costs, Ellison paid little attention to such fundamentals as accounting controls, sales procedures, and cash-flow needs. "I knew eventually this would hit us—at some time we would invest for very rapid growth and we would get nailed. And when we hit the wall, we hit it very, very hard," he said.[11]

Take the matter of receivables. Ellison pushed his salespeople to meet higher and higher quotas each quarter. In order to meet their minimums, the Oracle sales force often gave customers extremely lax terms. This did not bother the salespeople. They had to meet quotas, but they didn't have to meet payrolls. After all, they were allowed to book the future revenues from a sale instantly even if it would take months—or even years—to collect those revenues. "Oracle's highflying accounting practices . . . inflated quarterly revenue statements with receivables that proved difficult or impossible to collect," wrote *Management Review* in 1992.[12] And the trade publication *Information Week* noted that Oracle's "salespeople pushed products that didn't yet exist—a not uncommon practice in the software trade."[13] In many cases, customers were permitted 150 to 200 days to pay for Oracle's expensive software (the industry average was about 60 days).

All this created huge cash-flow problems. Put simply, though the business was booming, cash was flowing out faster than it was flowing in—and you can't meet payrolls with uncollected cash. But Ellison didn't care. His idealist's eye was forever focused on the future, on growth, on the ever-expanding fortunes of his electronic empire. To him, such things as accounts payable and receivables were for bean counters, people who did not share his Alexandrian vision.

In 1989, Oracle hit the beach with a crash. In that year, Oracle tallied revenues of $584 million and yet was yoked with receivables amounting to $262 million. The following year, revenues grew to $971 million, but receivables swelled to $468 million. Oracle was even recording revenues—and paying commissions—on the sale of software products that were still in the early stages of research and development. Again, such practices were common in this explosively growing industry, but they are dangerous. But when did danger ever deter Ellison?

Ellison gives a number of reasons for the lack of stricter financial controls and the snowballing problem of accounts receivable. "We were an adolescent company," he says. "Our goal was growth, much like an adolescent's. Every year we were older and twice as large." Not everyone was willing to forgive Ellison for spreading an "adolescent" attitude at Oracle. *Software Magazine* argued that the company showed a distinct "lack of an adult mentality in the financial area."[14]

To make matters worse, Ellison had put Jeff Walker, a software guy, rather than someone with formal accounting training, in charge of finance at Oracle. For a time, Ellison even restructured the company so that the sales department was in charge of reviewing and approving terms and contracts, instead of having an objective, non-commission-oriented department in charge. Stephen Imbler, the company's vice president for corporate finance, later said that this was tantamount to "putting the fox in charge of the chicken coop."[15]

By the late 1980s, "In its exhilarating push for growth above all else—the marching orders of founder Lawrence J. Ellison—Oracle paid little attention to such things as management controls. So nobody was prepared when things started going wrong," wrote *BusinessWeek*.[16] Similarly, *Fortune* said, "As chief executive, he ran Oracle the same way he drives his Acura NSX: pedal to the metal."[17] *Forbes* said simply that Ellison had used "smoke and mirrors" to pump up his company.[18] Fair enough, but smoke and mirrors are common equipment in fledgling new-economy companies.

## More Problems: Quality Control, Measly Profits, and a Plummeting Stock Price

Ellison was not, of course, responsible for every mistake committed by his aggressive sales force. But there is no question that he had imparted his own cowboy personality to the company. As long as the sales staff met its quotas, Ellison paid little attention to its methods. At least one Oracle package, called Oracle Financials, was released before all the bugs were fixed. A humorous e-mail made its way around the high-tech world: Consider what it would be like if certain computer industry companies made toasters rather than software or hardware. If Oracle made toasters, "They would claim that their toaster was compatible with all brands and styles of bread, but when you got it home, you would discover the Bagel Engine was still in development, the Croissant Extension was three years away, and indeed the whole appliance was just blowing smoke."[19]

As it often does, humor had caught the spirit of the situation. Vaporware—products announced but not yet perfected—is a feature of life in Silicon Valley, and Ellison and Oracle produced plenty of it. Scott McNealy, founder and chairman of Sun Microsystems, said of Ellison, "There's a bit of P. T. Barnum in him."[20] It takes one to know one: A consummate showman himself, McNealy is well practiced at the art of using publicity to advance his corporate goals. Nevertheless, there is no question but that Ellison pushed his luck too far.

On March 27, 1990, Oracle released its financial results for the third quarter of the 1990 fiscal year. The upshot: While revenues increased 54 percent to a record $236.4 million, profits increased by a staggeringly measly 1 percent. This was remarkable for a company that had boasted record profits for just about every quarter of its existence. Afraid of what was to come—and of what Wall Street's reaction might be—Ellison began speaking of "conventional growth" and employing other terms of modesty that were wholly uncharacteristic of him. The day after the disappointing earnings were announced, the investing community dealt Oracle a blow worthy of a World Wrestling Federation Smackdown. The company's stock plummeted nearly $8.00, to $17.50. In one day, Ellison's personal fortune atrophied by $366 million.

There was more bad news to come: During the first quarter of fiscal 1991, the Oracle Corporation announced its first-ever loss, amounting to some $36 million. For the fiscal year as a whole, Ellison's company came up negative in the earnings department to the tune of $12.4 million. It also had to restate its financial results for several of its 1990 quarters because it became clear that Oracle would be unable to recover millions in receivables. Shareholders sued. The stock sank even lower (down to under $5, less than a fifth of its high of about $25). For a time, it seemed as if everything Ellison had built was hovering on the brink of extinction—just as Ellison's life hung on a thread on that Hawaiian beach. Yet in both instances, Ellison snapped back and went on to even bigger things. He reconceived and restructured the Oracle Corporation in a way that mirrored the skill of the doctors who knitted his body back together after the surfing and biking accidents. The task wasn't easy. It did not help that the U.S. economy was in recession, that money was tight, and that the market for Oracle's software had become glutted. Oracle's latter-day CFO Jeff Henley even admitted that the company was "facing default" if things kept going they way they had been.

## The Road to Financial Recovery: Facing Problems Head-on

It must have been tough for him to admit it, but the first thing Ellison did was to concede that there were some problems in the way his company did business. Rather than ignore matters such as receivables and financial controls, or banish them to his accountants, he started to see them as things he'd have to deal with, as problems to be solved, just as he once viewed the creation of database software or the need to take sales out of his competitors' coffers. He also began to concede that there were quality problems with Oracle software. All in all, the change of attitude served Oracle well, because by 1992, the company was described as having "performed one of the most remarkable mea culpa atonement and transformation acts in IT [information technology] industry has ever seen."[21]

Ellison announced layoffs—some 400 people, or 10 percent of the U.S. workforce—which constituted the first large-scale staff cuts growth-oriented Oracle had ever made. But even while he was reducing Oracle's numbers, Ellison had the good sense and surprising humility to admit that he needed help managing the company. Ellison's aplomb at making such a decision ought not to be dismissed. One of the hardest things for entrepreneurs to do is to ask outsiders into the houses they themselves have built for advice on how to keep them standing. Ellison hired Jeff Henley, who had been CFO at Pacific Holdings, to become Oracle's chief of finance and to tighten the company's books. This turned out to be a wise and much-lauded decision.

Ellison also hired Air Force General James Abrahamson, who had been head of NASA's shuttle program, to take over as chairman, replacing his own exalted self (Ellison held onto the title of CEO and has since reclaimed the title of chairman). And he lured Ray Lane, who had been a senior vice president at the consulting firm Booz Allen & Hamilton, to become president with the promise of 300,000 stock options. These three came to be regarded as the saviors of Oracle. All in all, Ellison replaced 6 of Oracle's top 12 officers. He had realized that the people who had helped Oracle to grow in the first place were not the best people to manage and run a huge, maturing company. "The people who were in charge," said senior vice president of marketing Terence Garnett, "had come up through the ranks. One day they were managing a group of 10 people, the next year they were managing 50 people, and the year after 200. In a lot of cases, they didn't have the experience."[22] Wall Street analysts even began issuing higher ratings on Oracle stock, based in good measure on the addition of Ray Lane and the other new professionals to the company's staff. Ellison's senior appointments were seen by the industry as both impressive and far-sighted. In fact, the chief of information systems at nearby Argonaut Insurance later said, "If Oracle goes back to being a Larry Ellison-driven company, they can go fly a kite."[23]

Ellison, who had also prided himself on never having taken a dime of venture capital—remarkable for a Silicon Valley company—did something else even more remarkable: He went outside Oracle for cash. First, he arranged (or rather, Corporate Finance Vice President Stephen Imbler and Treasurer Bruce Lange arranged) a $250-million credit line from a syndicate of banks to stanch the shortfall. Then, after some negotiating, he took $80 million from the Japanese company Nippon Steel in return for an option to purchase 25 percent of Oracle's Japanese subsidiary. Finally, Ellison made a concerted effort to improve the quality of Oracle products.

Quality had long been a thorn in Ellison's side. By the middle of 1992, Oracle had effected a quality assurance program whereby products at each stage of the development cycle had to chalk up zero defects before being allowed to advance to the next phase. Software that once was pushed out the door was being tested extensively.[24] The company began awarding bonuses to its developers based on how few defects their work contained rather than how well it sold. All told, Oracle's Version 7, released in 1992, was subjected to 10 times the quality testing that Version 6 had undergone.

Ellison's makeover of the company and his new willingness to admit his mistakes were perhaps made more difficult in that they coincided with his recovery from two serious physical accidents. Perhaps they were even related. Perhaps the accidents—to his body and to his business—made him, if not prudent, at least more willing to take the counsel of others. Like his recovery from his surfing and bicycle mishaps, Ellison's business setbacks forced him to deal with the entirety of himself and the things he had produced in a new way. His body may have been badly broken, but it was not beyond repair, and Ellison took a quick and active role in its recuperation. He did very much the same thing for the broken Oracle Corporation.

In addition to releasing higher-quality products, Oracle began to book revenues from those products more conservatively, usually over the life of a contract rather than entirely up front, prior to full payment from a customer. Terms were tightened as well; the time it took customers to pay began to shrink closer to industry averages. Ellison was especially pleased with the cadre of seasoned executives who now comprised his cabinet. As if to contrast them with his top execs back in Oracle's "adolescent" days, he began calling Henley, Lane, and their peers "the adults."

By the summer of 1992, the *San Francisco Chronicle* was reporting that "the biggest changes are philosophical, not technical. . . . Oracle now claims to be a kinder, gentler company with a new religion—product quality, customer service, and conservative accounting."[25] Oracle Corporation emerged triumphantly from its crisis. In mid-2000, the well-respected Silicon Valley publication *Red Herring* called Oracle the Comeback Company of the Year.[26] Ellison's $1,200 investment had become a $10-billion-revenue company with a market value of over $200 billion—and the size of Ellison's personal fortune, worth $27.5 billion in mid-2000, was challenging the Microsoft nestegg of his old rival, Bill Gates. Oracle had over 43,000 employees (many of whom were Oracle stock millionaires) in the United States and 55 other countries. *Red Herring* marvelled: "[Oracle's] databases, enterprise, and e-business applications . . . are once more taking the new economy by storm."[27]

Best of all, Oracle's products are central to the fast-developing business-to-business applications that promise to revolutionize the world economy via the Internet: Oracle has signed such high-profile customers as Wal-Mart, Sears, and Ford Motor. In May 2000, a *BusinessWeek* cover that dwelled heavily on Oracle's Internet strengths proclaimed: "Oracle is cool again." Ellison told *BusinessWeek:* "We have a chance to pass Microsoft and become the No. 1 software company. If I had said that two years ago, I would have been sedated and locked up. But now we're the Internet and they are not."[28] That is clearly an overstatement, but hype—and even exchanges of insults—are routine in the combative air of Silicon Valley. The point remains that Microsoft doesn't own the Internet the way it owns the desktop and probably never will.

Ellison's yacht, *Sayonara*, was the winner in its class in the Sydney-to-Hobart race in February 1998, but by all reports Ellison is spending less time with his toys these days and more time running his business. "Ellison may have matured, but he has not been humbled," observed *Information Week*.[29] "The difference between God and Larry Ellison," Mike Wilson once wrote, "is that God doesn't think he's Larry Ellison."[30] But that was years ago. Today, it is safe to say, Ellison knows he is not God.

Ruth Handler

C H A P T E R  4

## Ruth Handler
### Cofounder of Mattel Toys

*"I've been proving myself my whole life; I still am."*

COUNT A SECOND IN TIME: You remember how it goes, "one, one thousand." Well, in that second, two Barbie dolls were sold somewhere on the planet. Multiply those seconds by purchases, and the math indicates that Barbie has become a billion-dollar dolly. Specifically, more than 1½ million Barbies are sold each week, every week, making the doll the most popular toy in the world. But she's more than a toy, more than a never-ending, money-pumping cash cow for the toy giant, the Mattel Corporation—Barbie has become an icon for generations of girls past and for generations yet to come.

In one of the more poignant ironies of twentieth-century American business, a federal grand jury would wrench the mother of Barbie away from her creation to suffer the shame and embarrassment of a venomous stockholder suit and indictment. From the moment the wheels of justice started to turn, mother and "child" would be separated commercially forever. Like a sudsy ending to a Joan Crawford tear-jerker, the beautiful daughter would continue to enjoy a life of fame and fabulous riches, while the "badly behaved" mother would retreat into the dark shadows of obscurity. But she didn't disappear into the darkness forever; instead, she went on to found a second business completely unrelated to Mattel but financially successful nevertheless and a source of great personal pride.

### Inventing Barbie—and Mattel

Ruth Handler was the marketing and retail mastermind who created and marketed Barbie in 1959. She birthed it, nurtured it, and—most important—she accessorized it. It all began in 1944, when she founded a small toy-making company with Harold "Matt" Matson. To create a name, she used *Matt* and her husband *El*liot's name to create Mattel. Matson would exit in 1947; he did not have the stomach to roll the new-product dice every year in the volatile and risky toy business. His departure left the Handlers to run the fledgling company themselves.

To be more exact, it was the gutsy, energetic and retail-savvy Ruth who handled the sales and marketing decisions. The shy Harold, a creative artist and industrial design genius, preferred the artisan's life of the studio. Ruth always said that their relationship was a match made in heaven. The marriage has lasted for over 60 years. The business collaboration is one of mutual admiration. Ruth said: "From the first day I met Elliot I admired his immense artistic and creative talents. Elliot, in turn, respected my talents: self-confidence . . . and above all, my willingness to attack the impossible."[1]

Sales the first year, in 1944, totaled $100,000; 20 years later, this Mom and Pop business—originally operating out of a garage—grossed $200 million. During the next two decades, in the 1950s and 1960s, the toy industry in America was dominated by the name Mattel. In 1955, the company was the first to advertise on network television, a stroke of Ruth Handler's marketing brilliance that forever changed the dynamics between toy manufacturers, retailers, and the consumer. It is impossible today to imagine that toys were *not* advertised on children's television programs.

The petite and attractive Ruth Handler basked in the glow of Mattel's commercial success. Possessed of a gravely smoker's voice and a direct manner (which some people found off-putting), she was regarded as the creative spark, the energetic dynamo of the company, especially in introducing and then expanding the Barbie line. Toy buyers and toy retailers waited expectantly every year for what Ruth and Elliot Handler would think of next.

## Success and Recognition

Few women in American corporate business of the prefeminist 1960s were as highly praised or as highly regarded as Ruth Handler. But her femininity would also represent the main obstacle that she had to over-come: "In those days back when I started in the business, there were no other women running a company. The biggest hurdle for me was to be accepted as a boss, and as a leader. In retrospect, the fact that I was a woman was sort of an advantage because men didn't know how to react or read me."

In 1973, *Fortune* included her on its list of the 10 highest-ranking women in business, along with Dorothy Chandler of the Times Mirror Company in Los Angeles, Katharine Graham of the Washington Post Corporation, and Bernice Lavin of Alberto-Culver. And of the 10 women on the list, Handler was one of only three who been cofounders of their businesses.

In truth, Ruth Handler became as successful as the doll she created. And the honors poured in: first female vice-president of the Toy Manu-facturers Association; outstanding Business Woman of 1961, awarded by the National Association of Accountants; named 1968's Woman of the Year in Business by the *Los Angeles Times;* named the first female member of the Federal Reserve Board; appointed by President Nixon to the Business Advisory Council in 1970. Everything was coming up roses for Ruth Handler.

## Confronting Cancer

Then, in 1970, Handler had a mastectomy, and this painful loss started the tragic downward spiral of a brilliant career. This painful event represented the major crisis in her life. She said: "Breast cancer destroyed my self-confidence. The image of myself was shattered. I wanted to retain my femininity in a world of men. People had wanted me to be a real rough gal but for years I exercised and kept my figure so I would retain that soft femininity. But to me, losing a breast was such a terrible blow to my self-esteem."[2] So she returned to Mattel "and found that because I believed my femininity and attractive-ness were gone, my self confidence was gone, too,"[3] More frequently, with her self-confidence ebbing, she turned decisions over to other executives.

Even though she held onto the title of Mattel's president's after her return from the hospital, she retreated in mind and spirit from an effective leadership position. This would prove to be the wrong choice, the slip of the will that would open the door to disaster. In 1974, only four years after the mastectomy and one year after making the *Fortune* list, Ruth Handler would stand in a courthouse in Los Angeles to be photographed, fingerprinted, and almost incarcerated in a jail cell filled with prostitutes and pickpockets. Her redemption would be years away. She would have to endure public humiliation, inflexible court-supervised probation, and menial work. The irony would be that her salvation and later triumph would itself be inspired by her mastectomy.

## An Early Work Ethic: "I Simply Preferred Working over Playing with Other Kids"

To look back on the tapestry of Ruth Handler's life—to try to understand how a woman of modest beginnings rose meteorically to the presidency of the largest toy company in the world—requires some understanding of second-generation European immigrants and the American businesses that were open to them.

Handler was born Ruth Mosko in 1916 in Denver, Colorado, the tenth and last child of Polish-Jewish parents. As her father Jacob (né Moskowicz) told the story, he had deserted from the Russian army, but other relatives would remember him as a gambler who had been forced to flee creditors. What's important is that upon arriving at Ellis Island in 1907, when asked his vocation, he replied, "Blacksmith." Mr. Jacob Mosco (the "wicz" didn't make it past customs) was placed on a train west, with Denver and horseshoeing the last stop.

By 1908, the entire family had left Warsaw and joined Papa Jacob in Denver. When Ruth was born eight years later (her mother was then 40), the Mosco children numbered 10, ranging in age from 20 (sister Sarah) to baby Ruth. The fragile Mrs. Mosco suffered a gall-bladder attack and the dutiful Sarah, newly married, brought the infant Ruth into her household and assumed the maternal role. Ruth would never live with her parents again. Although she loved them dearly, she often said that owing to their age they seemed more like grandparents.

For some children, being separated from their birth parents can be a horrible trauma that causes feelings of abandonment and loss. But

Ruth was blessed with a nurturing sister who not only showered her with love but also served as a role model for a working woman. Sarah and her husband opened a pharmacy–cum–soda fountain. Sarah was the driving force behind the business and assumed different marketing, sales, and accounting positions. It was in this retail establishment that 10-year-old Ruth worked every day after school as cashier, waitress, and soda jerk. Ruth recalled her sister fondly: "My older sister was a leader in the business world. She helped me believe that I, also, could do that."[4]

Handler loved working: "I simply preferred working over playing with other kids. I never formed the kind of intense friendships that most kids build their childhoods around." One can speculate that work represented a younger sibling's grateful emulation of a beloved older sister. Whatever the reason, from an early age Handler was comfortable dealing with and selling to customers, the prerequisite to being successful in any business. More important, she was comfortable dealing with and talking to men.

As a teen-ager in Denver she met Elliot Handler, a student at the Denver Art Institute, also a second-generation Jewish immigrant. They married in 1938 and settled in Los Angeles, where Ruth had been working as a secretary at Paramount Pictures. Elliot had abandoned hopes of pursuing a career as an artist and had begun hand-making giftware items like bookends, candleholders, and trays in a room above a Chinese laundry. Ruth would sell his beautifully crafted wares. This unpretentious commercial beginning would signal the Handlers' successful method of business—Elliot would design and make the products, and Ruth would sell them. It was a marriage and a partnership.

## Getting Started in the Toy Business: "I Shall Have a Career!"

Before World War II, the toy industry in the United States was a straightforward business, mainly, but not exclusively, consisting of single products. Some of the more well known classic American toys were 1902's teddy bear; Erector sets, made by the A. C. Gilbert Company, first shown in 1913; Raggedy Ann and Andy dolls, created by artist John

Gruelle in 1915; Lincoln Logs, invented by John Lloyd Wright (son of the famous architect Frank) in 1916; the yo-yo, discovered by Donald Duncan in 1931 on a street corner in Los Angeles; Lionel trains, introduced in 1933; American Flyer trains, first exhibited by the A. C. Gilbert Company in the mid-1930s; and a large offering of baby dolls from many manufacturers.

In the postwar period, some of the new single-product toy stars introduced were Slinky, in 1945; and Lego, Silly Putty, and Mr. Potato Head, in 1958. The emergence of plastic as the basic material used in toys and the process of injection molding would revolutionize the industry and would transform forever the single-product, small-company market into one dominated by huge toy conglomerates. With the flexible plastic material and the new process, hand-making toys became a relic of the past. The key to success—and Lego's plastic interlocking bricks in many colors illustrate this perfectly—was to stamp out one shape after another after another.

By 1944, Elliot began to craft a few toys, including a wooden dollhouse furniture line, which first appeared in a chain of women's clothing stores. Ruth was smart enough to realize that dollhouses needed to be sold in toy departments, not clothing stores. That year she set out on a cross-country train pilgrimage to the Mecca of toy retailing, the famous Toy Building on lower Fifth Avenue in New York City.

This voyage by Ruth Handler, wife and mother of a 3-year-old daughter, would eventually catapult a small company into mega-million-dollar balance sheets and, many years afterward, would offer generations of women a true champion of their gender: a woman who thrived in a male-dominated business environment. Although the trip did not have the historic revolutionary impact of Lenin's crossing to the Finland Station, it was a bold, groundbreaking, and radical statement. In a voice probably heard only in her own psyche, Handler trumpeted, "I am breaking the mold. I shall have a career!"

Probably no other woman in America in 1944 assumed that her role in life was to be a senior executive in a burgeoning commercial business. Even with two children (a son was born later that same year), Handler never believed that a woman's place was in the home. As she related later, "I'm a little lost at home, I'm just not efficient." But more succinctly she stated: "One option was to wait until the children were grown before I returned to work, but that prospect filled me with dismay. What if by then, I'd lost my spark, my ambition, my powers of persuasion?"[5]

Handler was cut of a different cloth from her female peers of her generation. She might have been one of the first American prototypes of the "superwoman," that whirling dervish of mother, wife, and career-person in perpetual motion. The emotional tug on the heartstrings between children and career would damage her relationship with her daughter. Handler would title one chapter of her own story "Good Mother/Bad Mother."

In the late 1940s, Handler quickly learned the basics of the toy business, as it existed in those first years after World War II. She and Elliot recognized that servicemen were coming home in droves to marry and start families. The toy business—not yet dominated by large corporations—offered entrepreneurs (and Jews) a chance to make money if they could find unique products for the marketplace. The Handlers possessed the creative and artistic genius of Elliot, who always seemed to be at the avant-garde of toy design. What Elliot could make, Ruth could sell.

In 1947, Mattel introduced the Uke-A-Doodle musical instrument to seize the momentum created by television host's Arthur Godfrey's playing of the ukulele. A few years later, the company sold a small toy piano with black and white keys and real scales. These two instruments and other toys represented a series of Mattel musical products that would total 20 million sales by 1952. The Handlers, conscious that the toy business needed new concepts to spark buyer and consumer interest each year, recycled the music-making toy idea through an entire line of products, like the Chuck Wagon that played "Oh, Susannah," the Lullaby Crib that played "Rock-A-Bye Baby," and a jack-in-the-box that cranked out "Pop Goes the Weasel."

During the 1950s, the Handlers were rolling merrily along. Sales were up and profits were high. Mattel ranked as the third-largest toy company in the world. The family had moved to the fashionable west side of Los Angeles in a beautiful home and had live-in help to do the household chores (which Ruth detested doing).

In the summer of 1956, the Handlers took a six-week business and vacation trip to Europe. They also brought along their children. The kids' names—in case you didn't know or never guessed—were Barbie and Ken.

## Discovering Barbie

In a small shop in Lucerne, Switzerland, Ruth Handler discovered a row of Lilli dolls, 11-inches high, German-made, adult looking, and dressed in different ski outfits. Lilli featured natural-looking hair and sported an anatomically perfect body. The doll was based on a popular European comic strip of the same name, and some said that the lithe shape was patterned after sex kitten Brigitte Bardot. One fact was certain, though: Lilli the doll was no cherubic-faced, big-tummied, flat-chested, squatty-thighed image of a chubby baby that little girls could use to play-act being a mommy.

Who knows how many thousands of American women had gazed on Lilli or how many had brought the doll back to the States? It would take Ruth Handler's experienced toy-savvy eyes to realize that Lilli had enormous sales potential. But that's only one part of the story. You see, Handler had been waiting expectantly for Lilli for seven years. As she wrote, "Here were the breasts, the small waist, the long, tapered legs I had enthusiastically described all those years ago."[6]

Back in 1950, daughter Barbara, then age 9, started to play make-believe with cutout paper dolls. Handler was surprised that her daughter preferred one-dimensional cutouts to real, roly-poly baby dolls. The child's play time also incorporated a behavioral curiosity (at least to her mother)—Barbara fantasized about the lives and careers of the female and male paper cutouts. She imagined adult futures for these paper creations: stewardesses, secretaries, or college coeds. For Handler, her daughter's play activities signaled a new product opportunity for Mattel: "I realized if we could three-dimensionalize the adult paper dolls, we'd a meet a very basic play need."

In the early 1950s, when Handler had presented the idea of a three-dimensional adult doll, Mattel's team of all-male designers reacted with flat-out rejection. They insisted that little American girls only wanted to emulate their mommies and play with baby dollies. This was during the Eisenhower years, and who listened then to the few women in business? Even Elliot, usually warm and supportive, was preoccupied with creating a talking doll called Chatty Cathy.

In Lucerne, Handler purchased three Lilli dolls, each dressed in a different ski outfit. The male designers back in Los Angeles would have to confront a real model of her adult doll idea. They would now risk rejecting a model in hand, carried by their powerful boss.

Handler intuitively realized that Lilli would have to undergo some American transformation to be sold in the States. First, she realized that Lilli's body was too sexy for the conservative-minded American market. But although she fattened the curves slightly and reduced the doll's breast size, she insisted that for all intent and purposes, the new doll resemble a young teen-age girl's shape.

From the very outset in the research and development stage, the project called out for a name. For Handler, the creator, there was only once choice: Barbie, her daughter's nickname. After all, it had been 9-year-old Barbara who had played with those paper cutouts and had inspired the project in the first place.

Many of those early decisions about making Barbie arose from the available material and not from a conscious desire to create a perfectly chiseled beauty. In fact, Handler fretted about how a too-attractive Barbie might affect young girls: "I was worried that if Barbie was too glamorous, little girls wouldn't be able to identify with her." This considerate apprehension would prove false: Little girls loved the shape and look of the doll.

Handler's instincts also proved invaluable in the look and attire of the first Barbie. She hired a hairdresser to experiment with hairstyles, and the result was the now-famous blonde ponytail. She hired a dress designer to design a complete wardrobe of clothes, and the result was quality clothing never before seen on any manufactured toy doll. Barbie's outfits came with sewn hems, zippers, bust darts, buttons, and buttonholes.

In 1959, after three years of experimentation, the green light was given to the Kokusai Boeki Company, a Japanese toy manufacturer, to start making the first Barbies. The initial small shipment sent to Mattel was perfect in every detail: The blonde ponytail looked real because the hair was rooted into the head, and the beautifully made black-and-white bathing suit seemed ready for a walk down a Paris runway. One small detail was wide of the mark—the dolls had Oriental eyes!

## First Setback: Market Resistance from Toy Buyers

With Barbie's eye problem corrected, the Handlers geared up to present the doll to the 1959 Toy Show in New York, which attracted 1,600 manufacturers and more than 15,000 buyers. Each annual Toy Show was like the opening night of a new Broadway production. If the buyers liked what they saw and gave a rave review, the orders poured in. But if the buyers didn't like a new toy and gave it a thumbs down, this spelled disaster, because the manufacturers created huge factory inventories based on preshow forecasts to meet the hoped-for high demand.

As they entered the Toy Show, the Handlers brimmed with enthusiasm, especially Ruth, because Barbie had been her idea. She had also insisted that the toy not be named simply "Barbie," but rather "Barbie, the Teen-Age Fashion Model." There were two reasons for Handler's naming decision. The first was a practical one: Barbie would come with an extensive wardrobe of clothes (sold separately) to generate additional revenues (recall Mattel's musical toy extensions). And second, Barbie would enjoy a career. Handler wanted to give girls a doll that would encourage fantasizing about being grown up.

Handler had been so confident of the doll's success that she gave orders to the Japanese factory to increase production, anticipating that initial orders taken at the show would result in 1 million dolls and 2 million pieces of clothing sold the first year. But Handler met a stone wall of male buyer resistance. Almost to a man, each said, in so many words, "Ruth, you've made a major mistake with this doll. Little girls want cutesy, cuddly baby dolls. They all want to pretend to be mommies."

The response from Handler—a mother and a career woman—contradicted this narrow-minded male impression. She replied, "No, little girls want to pretend to be bigger girls." But she could not convince enough men to buy into this radical toy doll idea. There was also the problem of Barbie's postpubescent sexuality, which further exacerbated male buyer apprehension: What decent American mother would buy her daughter a doll with *breasts?*

On that first night of the show, Handler remembered, "I went to my hotel room and burst into tears of grief. My *baby* had been rejected."[7] Handler's tears did not last long. In the first year, Barbie, the Teen-Age Fashion Model walked—make that galloped—off the store shelves.

Stores could not keep up enough product in stock. It would take Mattel three years to catch up with burgeoning consumer demand.

## First Success: Skyrocketing Sales

In 1964, five years after the 1959 Toy Show, Mattel's net sales totaled $96 million, compared to 1957's pre-Barbie $9 million. Four years after the company went public in 1960, the Handlers were worth $44 million on paper. But Ruth Handler could point to another statistic that told a more powerful story: From 1957 to 1963, Mattel's sales had multiplied 20 times while total toy industry sales had only doubled. Barbie was a gold mine, producing blonde gold with no bottoming out in sight.

Handler's retailing genius became clearer with the "family" extensions of each new Barbie-line product introduced. Barbie would not only have a finite but unbounded wardrobe, she would also have siblings, cousins, friends, and pets, each with their own names and identities. First came boyfriend Ken in 1961, with the now-famous groin-area bump. Then Midge, Barbie's best friend, appeared in 1963. How could Barbie and Ken go on a double date with Midge? Enter Allan, Midge's beau, in 1964. Dancer, Barbie's pony, arrived in 1971, followed by the other ponies, Dallas and Dixie and their baby, Midnight.

The toy industry had never witnessed such a proliferation of products and costumes emanating from one toy. Barbie was the central hub of a mammoth retail rail system, radiating spokes of siblings, friends, cousins, and pets, and many of these toys were sending off sidetracks of their own friends and animals. Eventually, American girls between the ages of 3 and 10 would own an average of eight Barbie toys.

But importantly to Handler, Barbie herself evolved to have career after career. The next three Barbies introduced by 1961 were a ballerina, a registered nurse, and an American Airlines stewardess. In the 1960s, as women started the slow process of moving into executive business and other professional positions, Barbie would be an astronaut, a fashion editor, and a teacher. By 1973, surgeon Barbie would become the first female doll made in America with an MD degree.

No one can estimate the degree of confidence building that young girls experienced through playing at careers with the Barbie of their choice. No doll delivered that adult world but Barbie. Handler, a dedicated careerist herself, said, "My whole philosophy was that through the doll, a little girl could be anything she wanted to be." The exact motto of Ruth Handler.

## The Beginning of the Downfall:
## Loss of Management Control

The heyday decade of the 1960s saw skyrocketing revenues at Mattel. Sales totaled $100 million by 1966 and $200 million by 1969. The company's market share was 12 percent of the $2 billion toy market, most of it powered by Barbie's exponential growth. The Handlers hired MBAs, CPAs, and industrial designers to harness the company's growth potential.

The balance sheet was increasing, and the cash reserves were overflowing. In 1967, the company hired a well-known acquisition specialist as vice president of finance, and this one appointment signaled to Wall Street the good news that Mattel was ready to become a big player via diversification. The company's stock price rose dramatically on this one piece of news. But this event marked the moment that foreshadowed the downfall of the Handlers' hegemony at Mattel and, later, Ruth's decent into judicial torment. Henceforth and forever, executives crunching numbers with an eye toward maximizing shareholder equity would run Mattel. It would no longer be a mom-and-pop—an Elliot and Ruth Handler–run toy business.

The drive to acquire other companies in youth-related businesses had begun in earnest. Within a few years, Mattel had bought Metaframe (pet supplies), Turco (playground equipment), and Audio Magnetics (audiotapes and cassettes). With each new purchase, the leadership of the Handlers receded further into the background—they could not keep their hands on so many pieces of pie, many of them in businesses outside of Mattel's core toy center.

If only to remind themselves of the fun that the toy business engendered, the Handlers decided to have Mattel acquire Ringling Brothers Barnum and Bailey Circus. Ruth Handler was overjoyed at the merger and stated: "Ringling Brothers fit into our plans for Mattel to diversify into supplying products and entertainment to the family unit and to the world of the young."[8] The circus acquisition was the high-water mark of

Ruth Handler's corporate ascendancy. The child of poor Polish immigrants had purchased the most recognizable and beloved icon of American fun.

In 1971, there would be negotiations for a proposed Mattel merger with the Kinney Corporation (then led by the late Steve Ross), which owned the Warner Brothers film studio. On paper it seemed like a good mix, but Handler noticed that she would be left with the toy company presidency while the financial acquisition whiz (whom she neither liked nor trusted) would eventually become CEO of the new conglomerate. Handler was outraged. "Oh no that would never work. I would never go for that. I would never have that man telling *me* what to do."

The handwriting was on the wall but Handler didn't see it. Mattel was no longer an intimate family-owned company where the Handlers knew everyone's name. Wall Street had decreed that the Handlers did not have the business acumen to run a large, New York Stock Exchange–listed company. Other Mattel executives with titles and large salaries were making the day-to-day and long-range decisions. Elliot was still considered a valuable asset for his design capabilities, but Ruth was being bypassed on major decisions. She had become a figurehead, a forgotten has-been whose best work—Barbie—was years behind her.

## Accusations of Financial Impropriety and Stock Manipulation

Janice Lee, executive vice president of Cahoots, the Internet's advertising and awareness research company, remembered that fateful day in 1975 when she was an executive at Clairol in New York City: "I picked up the *New York Times* and the headline stated that my idol, Ruth Handler of Mattel, had been indicted for stock manipulation. No one could believe it. I had heard her give a talk in Los Angeles and I was impressed with her retail knowledge and can-do spirit. All of the women who worked at Clairol were saddened by the charges."

The business events that would change Handler's life forever began in 1968 when a prolonged strike curtailed deliveries. Then, a year later, a fire, weeks before the Christmas toy-shipping season, wiped out Mattel's warehouse on the Mexican border. Ruth remembered these catastrophes: "First there was the strike and then, just as we were gearing up for the Christmas rush, a fire in our Mexican assembly plant in Mexicali destroyed our chance to ship merchandise at our busiest time. It was a total loss that badly affected our cash flow." These two events resulted in losses of millions of dollars.

1969's revenue shortfall increased a practice at the company called *bill and hold,* a standard toy-industry procedure in which sales are recorded at the time invoices are written and then merchandise is placed in inventory for shipping at a later date. This is known as *accelerated revenues,* and it works for small amounts. But much to Handler's surprise, by 1970 the bill-and-hold total had risen to $14 million.

By 1972, Mattel's prior three year of horrors had combined to generate a $30 million after-tax loss for fiscal 1971. Two years later, in early 1973, Elliot Handler issued a public statement that Mattel had rebounded from financial difficulty and would show a profit that year. Two weeks later he was forced to announce that Mattel would in fact show not a profit but another loss. Panic set in on Wall Street, the stock plummeted, and then the stockholder lawsuits commenced.

The Securities and Exchange Commission (SEC) stepped in to look for improprieties, mainly to see if any Mattel executives had profited from the false financial forecasts. The Handlers had to rely on the company's financial executives to deal with the SEC. As Handler wrote in her autobiography: "Elliot and I were being pushed into a helpless position. We were so dismayed at everything that was happening that we just sat back and let others take over. We let them do it to us!"[9]

With the SEC and the U.S. Attorney General breathing down Mattel's neck in 1975, no employee at the company wanted to associate with the Handlers. The sword of Damocles dangled over the owners' heads, and formerly faithful employees started to hide from the team, particularly from Ruth. She had become Mrs. Invisible at the office.

Handler could put up with investigations and loss of corporate control, but she would not stand being ignored. In 1975, she walked out of Mattel forever. She said, "I couldn't tolerate for another minute, the hostility, the snubs, the demoralizing lack of anything constructive to do." Elliot followed six months later.

But looming around the corner was a calamity of Greek tragedy proportions, Handler's very public fall from grace. In most cases, a personal disaster of this magnitude would have blared *the end* of anyone's life's story. The turnaround comeback story was still years away, and Handler first had to undergo horrible legal trials and personal tribulations. She was down but not out and she said it best herself: "There's a still a lot of fight in me, and perhaps fight's the thing."

## Pleading "No Contest"

In 1975, the U.S. Attorney General's office charged that Ruth Handler and four other Mattel financial executives had conspired to violate federal securities, mail, and banking laws by preparing false and misleading financial records in the years from 1969 to 1974. Each count of the 10-count charge was punishable by two to five years of jail time.

Handler's defense was that she was kept uninformed of the financial manipulations going on behind her back (Elliot was never indicted). But this defense proved a dual-edged sword: How could the president of the largest toy company in the world—someone who had been one of its top executives for 30 years—claim she was naive and uniformed about how the company's business finances operated? It was as though the captain of a cruise ship had claimed not to know much about navigation after the vessel crashed upon the rocks. The stockholders—especially those who had lost money in the two weeks between Elliot Handler's two conflicting profitability statements—demanded accountability. The person in charge whose hide they wanted was Ruth Handler—and they also wanted the owners' money.

Over the next three years, this ongoing and public legal case produced a constant stream of headlines and stories in the newspapers and business magazines. Perhaps it generated more coverage in the media than if the company had manufactured a mundane product like brake shoes and the president had been male. Mattel, the toy giant, and Handler, the first woman named and first woman appointed in so many areas, became a series of hot news stories.

The civil case originating from class-action lawsuits against Mattel by its shareholders was settled with a $34 million payout in 1976. The

Handlers turned over 2½ million of their own Mattel shares—approximately 50 percent of their company holdings—to assist in resolving the lawsuit. To the press and the public, the facts of this settlement led to only one conclusion: The Handlers must be guilty of all the charges.

Living under a cloud of doubt about the eventual criminal proceedings caused Handler to experience a living hell. Her self-confidence had already been depleted after the mastectomy; one aspect of that trauma was the feeling of defeminization. Now, she had to deal with the accusatory stares from strangers and friends after the civil settlement had been announced. Even in her own apartment building, she was affected by the feelings of shame: "The elevator ride finally became so intolerable that I took to using the freight elevator instead. By the same token, it became torturous for me to visit the country club. We just stopped going."[10]

In 1978, Handler and three of the other Mattel financial executives pleaded not guilty to the criminal charges and were bound over for trial. She wanted desperately to fight the case, but the lawyers convinced her to plead nolo contendere, a legal term that meant she would not contest the charges. The decision resulted in no trial. But she demanded to plead nolo *and* to plead innocent at the same time. Her attorneys found precedent for this dual plea, and that's what Handler did before the judge.

The head of the U.S. attorney's office was outraged that Handler's nolo plea had included a profession of innocence. Said the official, "Giving credence to such claims of innocence calls into question the integrity of the system and is therefore deeply unfortunate."[11] Handler had won a little victory but now faced retribution for her nolo plea. The result was the largest public service sentencing penalty ever given up to that time: $57,000 in reparations and five years probation on the condition that Handler donate 2,500 hours of public service.

Handler's route to sanity and self-satisfaction would come in the artificial breast business.

## Moving On: A New Business

Flash back to 1970, the year of Handler's mastectomy. Handler went to purchase a prosthesis in a department store. Like most women in her situation, she was embarrassed and slightly self-conscious to be shopping for an artificial breast. She whispered her request to the clerk behind the counter and was shocked when the saleswoman walked away in disdain without saying a word. The memories of that day were still painful when Handler remembered the incident years later: "The clerk huddled with two other saleswomen and the loser of the three got me, got to wait on me. I got the loser because of my condition."

The humiliation of being a "loser" paled compared to the next stage of her treatment in the department store. Handler was shown to a dressing room with a closed curtain. Suddenly, over the top of the transom, came a formless, liquid-filled artificial breast. Again, in her own words, "I looked at this shapeless glob that lay in the bottom of my brassiere and thought, 'My God, the people in this business are men who don't have to wear these things.' "[12]

At first, Handler thought that the problem was size. Her bra size was 36C but she was holding a size 6 breast and asked the saleswoman for a size 5, realizing that the breast sizes were not correlated to lingerie sizes. But neither the 6s or the 5s really fit under her clothing, and there seemed no way to hide the fact of the mastectomy. She said, "I felt defeminized so I started wearing vests, jackets, sweaters, anything to hide the fact that the two sides didn't match."[13]

For Handler the feelings were twofold: not being able to buy herself a product that fit and also sensing that thousands of other women like herself experienced the same indignity every day of their lives. Even two years later with the first sale of silicone products, the egg-shaped breasts were sold in the same confusing size system and also caused problems because of their excessive weight.

Handler had heard about a skilled prosthetic artisan in California named Peyton Massey whose specialty was artificial body parts. She ordered a custom-made prostheses, for which she paid $350. But months later she was disappointed because the new breast had a peculiar odor and the edges were visible outside her bra. After she lost weight, her body shape changed and the breast was too big for her new size. Expensive customizing was not the answer to solving the breast replacement problem.

The fighter lurking under Handler's skin started to emerge: She would start making better artificial breasts for women in her situation. If the marketplace couldn't deliver a product that met women's needs,

Handler would. Instinctively, she realized the problem: The artificial breasts available didn't meet the requirements of women's differing body shapes, didn't come in left or right models, and didn't come in half sizes.

Early in 1978, on the heels of the pending judgment in the criminal case, Handler returned to Massey's office, offering him the revolutionary idea that they team up to manufacture artificial breasts for over-the-counter sale. Originally, he reacted with the same negativity as had the male designers at Mattel who had listened to Handler's idea for an adult doll in the early 1950s. He rejected the idea as impractical, but she was accustomed to breaking resistance—particularly if it was male.

Massey finally assented, and Handler reacted like a spirit reborn: "I felt flickerings of my old resolve and sense of purpose." In a few weeks she had set up an office and had called in former Mattel design and production personnel and Elliot, too. She spelled out precisely what she wanted in the new, ready-to-wear breast. It had to fit into a regular bra, not ones specially made to hold a prosthesis. Most important, she insisted that the products be marketed in standard bra sizes so a woman who wore a 34B would recognize her prosthesis size immediately.

Massey, chemists, and tooling experts finally refined Handler's creation. Eventually, it would be a liquid silicone enclosed in polyurethane with a rigid foam backing. The retail price would be between $140 and $200. The prototype version was made in her 36C size. She would become the model on the runway showing off the new creation. Now, all that remained was to choose a name for the company. The old formula of combining the two founders' first names was resurrected. It would be named *Ruthton* after *Ruth* and *Peyton*. Handler believed that this reward had been a long time in coming: "At this time, having my name in the company name was very important to me. I'd been cofounder of Mattel and never complained about my absence in the name of that company that I helped nurture and build. But the times were different now. And so was I. *Ruthton* was my declaration that this was something that I was going to do *my* way."[14] And she did.

The product was called Nearly Me, and the first person Handler hired was a former Mattel marketing specialist named Alexandra Laird, who had also had a mastectomy. In the formative years of the company, the only personnel hired were women who had had mastectomies.

Handler realized that each new hire would become a spokeswoman for the product and the company. She said, "I trained a whole crew of women who had also had mastectomies and I went around with them all the time."

Handler's name could still call in some department store chits, and she headed for Neiman-Marcus in Dallas, the premiere department store in the United States, to launch the line. The first Neiman sale proved promising. Handler learned that presale promotion was the key to informing women about the product. Henceforth, she and her employees—eight middle-aged women who had all lost breasts to mastectomies—would send handwritten invitations to breast cancer victims, conduct seminars in the host stores, and appear on television talk shows.

## Success Again! The First Million

By 1980, the company's sales exceeded $1 million. When Handler entered the market, there numbered only a few companies that manufactured artificial breasts. She delighted in saying, "I took the old-time companies that were self-satisfied and smug and shook them up." Not stated was the fact that she believed those "old-time" companies were run by men.

She would do anything to promote the product, even baring her brassiere to photographers to demonstrate that no one could tell the difference between a real breast and a Nearly Me replacement. Handler also traded off Barbie's fame for appearances on television. Soon, she became the acknowledged spokeswomen for breast cancer and even fit former First Lady Betty Ford with a Nearly Me breast.

The key to her recovery as a women and as a businessperson was helping others. "Helping other women became the answer to helping myself. I regained my self-esteem," she said. She recalled a moment when she stood in a fitting room and in walked a dejected and angry woman who had recently had a mastectomy: "When this women buttoned her blouse and saw that the two breast sides matched, she smiled and stuck her chest out. That was my ultimate satisfaction. That was the biggest charge I ever had."

In 1991, at age 75, she sold Nearly Me to a health and beauty aids division of Kimberly Clark. It was a smart move because the giant retailer could make the product accessible to many more women through its vast distribution system. Through more efficient production methods, the price dropped to $115.

By risking failure with a radically new product, Handler had restored her reputation, relying on the inner reserves of strength built up from years of hard work. At Mattel, she had fought hard to reach the pinnacle of business success, and she battled again with Nearly Me to restore her good name. This immigrant's child had not struggled to get to the top and be cast aside as a pariah. As she would later say, "I rebuilt my self-esteem and I rebuilt the self-esteem of others."[15]

## "Find Something to Do to Help Others"

Ruth Handler could have rested on her laurels after her success with Nearly Me. She could have stayed at home playing bridge and mah-jongg and reading. American women had responded positively to her brave and forthright stance on breast cancer. She could have taken one last bow and exited from view. But there was one small voice that called from her past: It was Barbie. The doll had become one of the most powerful twentieth-century icons of American culture—a toy that some women considered to be the nation's first feminist. M. G. Lord, author of *Forever Barbie,* wrote, "She's [Barbie] something upon which little girls project their idealized selves. For most baby boomers, she has the same iconic resonance as many female saints."[16]

The emerging world of Barbie nostalgia and Barbie collectables did not go unnoticed by Mattel. Dolls from the 1950s in their original boxes were selling for over $5,000, and the publicity was great for business. Baby-boomer mothers and their daughters shared in the Barbie magic. At convention events throughout the country, everyone wanted to hear about the "birthing" of their favorite doll. Mattel hired Ruth Handler to attend these Barbie festivals and speak about the early years.

At home, Ruth Handler keeps a gold-plated Oscar-looking Barbie that was awarded to her at a festival by grateful fans. Two porcelain Barbies are nestled in a display case, and five early Barbies are set in a drawer. It's no surprise that Barbie's mom still cares after all these years.

Handler is retired these days, heading out weekly for an enjoyable game of poker at one of the nearby California poker parlors. She also does some stock trading via the Internet. She remains optimistic and upbeat. Her advice to people who experience a downfall is simple: "Don't dwell on what happened, no matter how bad it was. Find something else to do. Find something to do to help others."

In 1996, Handler returned to Denver, where it all began, to speak at a luncheon sponsored by the Allied Jewish Federation Women's Department. "I like to think of my life as an impossible dream," she told the audience. "I've had a lot of nightmares, but I've always been able to pick up and move on."[17]

Ron Popeil

## CHAPTER 5

# Ron Popeil

*Founder of Ronco*

*"You might as well go for it."*

$\mathbf{F}$ OR ALMOST 30 YEARS, Ron Popeil's commercials flickered across
television screens and into American living rooms, making him
not just an icon of advertising but a fixture of U.S. popular culture—a
phenomenon as inescapable as weather. He wasn't merely telegenic.
He was a commercial force. Within the solar system of television, he
occupied his own planet. What Johnny Carson was to golf swings and
nervous tics, Popeil was to odd yet compelling kitchen appliances—
gadgets you didn't know you needed, until he sold them to you.

There was the Inside-the-Shell Egg Scrambler, which, by use of a
spinning needle, penetrated and prescrambled eggs before their shells
were cracked. There was the Tidie Drier, a combination pantie, bra,
and hair dryer. There was Mr. Microphone, which let people broadcast their own voices over ordinary radios. Teenage boys, especially,
loved Popeil's commercial for Mr. Microphone, which showed how
they could hail girls with it while cruising in Dad's car. There was the
Miracle Broom, the Ronco Rhinestone and Stud Setter, the freon-
spritzing Glass Froster (which chilled one's glassware at the expense of
the ozone layer, though no one knew that at the time). And finally
there was Popeil's fabulously fecund O-Matic family, whose progeny
included (but were not limited to, as lawyers like to say) the Chop-O-
Matic, Dial-O-Matic, Whip-O-Matic, Mince-O-Matic and, most especially, Veg-O-Matic, which did for celery and carrots what the guillotine
had once done for the nobility of France. The Veg-O-Matic alone sold
11 million units at $9.99 each. But wait! There was more! There was,
for instance, the Popeil Pocket Fisherman—an abbreviated rod-and-

reel so compact you could clip it to your belt. Still later, there was the product many consider to have been his crowning achievement: spray-on hair.

Today there are Popeil collectors and Popeil scholars. At least one museum has devoted lectures to the man's oeuvre. No less an institution than *Saturday Night Live* has given him what amounts to its official seal of approval: Comedian Dan Ackroyd once burlesqued Popeil's gadgets by demonstrating what *SNL* called the "Bass-O-Matic"—an appliance that diced, sliced, minced, mulched, pureed, and ultimately *liquefied* a whole fish—bones, head, tail, scales, and all. ("I loved it," says Popeil, who considers parody the sincerest form of flattery.)

It seems impossible there ever was a time when Popeil *wasn't* on television. But there was one: a dark spot in the late 1980s. One minute Ron was dicing and slicing happily, a warm glow on picture tubes from coast to coast. Then—*poof!*—he disappeared. The whole Popeil empire flickered and went dark, as Ronco, his namesake company, subsided into bankruptcy.

Popeil calls this period his "semiretirement." Bankruptcy yanked the Rug-O-Matic out from under Ron, and he fell hard. The biggest bruise he suffered wasn't to his wallet. His personal assets remained intact, and he continued to lead a comfortable enough life. But losing his television exposure deprived him of something more elemental and more satisfying than money—the pleasure he got from connecting with a mass audience. Trite as it may sound, Popeil had gotten into sales originally because it filled an emotional void: He was looking for love.

## A "Miserable" Childhood

Popeil had gotten precious little love growing up, as he relates with disarming candor: "My childhood is a blur. I recall very little of it. Most of the early years were so painful that I blocked much of it out."[1]

Though he says he can't recall anyone ever celebrating his birthday, he was born May 3, 1935, to Julia and Samuel Popeil of the Bronx. When he was 3, Ron's parents divorced, and he and his half-brother Jerry were sent to a boarding school in upstate New York, where they lived for the next five years. Not once in those years did his parents visit. Not for school events. Not for holidays. Never.

When Ron turned 8, his grandfather and grandmother appeared at school and took the two boys to live with them in Miami. The reason Ron and Jerry weren't living with their father, they were told, was that Sam was busy running a kitchen products company in Chicago—Popeil Brothers—and was living in a hotel.

Popeil is as unsparing and unsentimental about his grandparents as he was about his parents: "I have blocked almost all the memories of my miserable life with my grandparents. They had a terrible relationship and fought all the time." They ate frugally, subsisting "on peasant dishes—chicken feet, bean soups, and things like that."[2]

His grandfather Isadore was "a mean, unhappy man who didn't believe in anybody or anything. He was an immigrant from Poland and he graduated from the school of hard knocks. I don't think he ever told a joke—or laughed at one—in his life. I never called him Grandpa, Granddad, Izzy or Isadore. In fact, I didn't call him anything. He never had a name, as far as I was concerned."[3] The grandfather did have one pastime, though, that brought him pleasure: He enjoyed telling young Ron, every chance he got, that Ron's mom had been "a tramp."

Mary, Popeil's grandmother, was on the other hand, "a wonderful woman. She spent most of her time in the kitchen cooking, and what I do remember fondly is hanging out in the kitchen and watching her cook." He thinks his fascination with kitchen gadgetry started there. From Mary he learned how to cut onions and how to get into "the nitty-gritty of vegetables and fruits."

In 1948, the grandparents and the two boys moved to Chicago, where Isadore had been hired by Sam Popeil to run Popeil Brothers' factory. The factory ("cold, dark, dingy" recalls Ron) made such gadgets as the Citrex Juice Extractor, the Slice-A-Way cutting board, and the Popeil Donut Maker, all of which were sold by pitchmen via live demonstration in dime stores and at county fairs. Though Ron worked weekends at the factory (unpaid), he never saw his father. Sam took weekends off.

This Dickensian idyll ended three years later when Ron, then 16, experienced what he calls "a revelation": He could sell.

## Selling at a Street Bazaar

The moments some great artists discover their true callings are lost to history. The young Nijinsky's first twirls and hops, the tunes hummed haltingly by little Liszt—of these we have no record. But Popeil himself supplies us with a picture of his debut as pitchman: The year was 1951, and the stage on which he opened was Chicago's Maxwell Street—a gritty, smelly, multiblock bazaar where bargain-hunters sought out cut-rate kitchenware, clothes, and sundries.

Popeil had bought an armload of products from his father (who'd sold them to him wholesale) and taken them to Maxwell Street one weekend. Then he did what just came naturally: "I pushed. I yelled. I hawked." It was *veni, vidi, vici* all over again, but in a retail setting. Popeil found himself launched upon a new and boundless sea. Selling was exciting. It was profitable. And what was more, it *felt* good. After living 16 years without love, Popeil had discovered in sales what he calls "a form of affection"—an immediate, powerful, and visceral connection to other people.

Every weekend he attacked Maxwell Street afresh, arriving at 5 A.M. with all the props he needed for his product demonstrations: a portable microphone (he hadn't yet invented Mr. Microphone), flat-topped tables, and several hundred pounds of vegetables in different colors. It was nothing for him, he says, to cut up 100 pounds of potatoes in a single day, plus 50 pounds each of onions, cabbages, and peppers.

At the same time that his young friends were out enjoying themselves at movies or at malt shops, Ron was chopping, yelling, selling. The work, he says, was physically demanding not just on his voice but on his feet and back. Sometimes he stood for 10 hours at a time: "In summer, it was hot. In winter, it was freezing. The tables I used were housed at a fish store, and you know what that could smell like." Still, he found the work was satisfying. Though no one had ever taught him the first thing about selling, he discovered he had a natural gift for immediately grasping a product's "hot buttons"—the features that, when stressed with proper showmanship and patter, could send previously blasé shoppers reaching for their wallets. Soon he was grossing $500 a day—big money in the 1950s for an adult to be making, let alone a kid.

By age 17, he was making enough money that he could afford to move out of his grandparents' house. He spent a year attending the University of Illinois. But impressed by how much money there was to be made from selling, he quit college and never returned. He had already learned, he says, an important fact about money: The people whom he spent it on didn't care how he'd made it—whether he was a doctor or a lawyer or some other type of professional. "Nobody ever asks you where the money comes from. They just take it. Money is money. It all looks the same when you're spending it."[4]

## Developing His Sales Pitch

Educationally, his biggest break came not at the University of Illinois, but at Woolworth. He talked the manager of Chicago's State Street Woolworth into letting him sell freelance, on the main floor. This wasn't just any Woolworth but the biggest and most profitable store in the whole chain. It covered most of an entire block. From the manager's perspective, the deal Popeil offered was a no-lose proposition: Woolworth paid him nothing. They just let him sell, and, at the end of every week, they collected 20 percent of whatever Popeil had brought in. The remainder—which usually amounted to about $1,000 a week—Ron kept. That was more money than the store manager himself was making, and it was twice the average worker's *monthly* salary. College dropout or no, Popeil was doing nicely.

Working day after day at Woolworth, 10 and 12 hours at a stretch, he learned to master the same challenge later posed him by television: Every single moment, a mass of people passed by, none of them having any preexisting intention of buying what Popeil had to sell. It was Ron's job to stop them cold, grab their attention by its lapels, and persuade them—entertainingly, irrefutably, and quickly—to buy whatever he was selling. It didn't hurt, of course, that Ron at this age looked like a young Paul Newman, with white teeth, chiseled features, and blue-green eyes. Women, especially, lingered longer as he got better at his craft. Fewer and fewer shoppers of either sex were able simply to pass him by (figuratively speaking, to change the channel) without staying to hear him out.

He began experimenting with some of the memorable catchphrases and tag lines that later would cause generations of television viewers to laugh, smack their foreheads, and exclaim, *"Oy!"*:

- One gadget, he told shoppers, sliced onions so effortlessly, "The only tears you'll shed will be tears of joy."
- Another sliced a tomato so thin "It had only one side."
- Still another chopped ham for ham salad, chicken for chicken salad, or "horse for horse radish."
- A Popeil-brand knife was so sharp it "could shave the eyebrows off a New Jersey mosquito." (Why a *New Jersey* mosquito? Who knew! Who cared! The line worked, so he kept it in the act.) The same knife could "cut a cow in half, and that's no bull."
- He waffle-cut potatoes, then held the slices underneath his ears: ". . . and if you don't want to *eat* them, they certainly make beautiful earrings."
- Products that required batteries were never, in Popeil-speak, *battery powered.* Rather, they were *cordless electric,* which implied both power and mobility without ever suggesting owners might be put to the inconvenience of having to buy new batteries.

In summers, he branched out into the county fair circuit, selling alongside more seasoned carnies. From the best of these—the pros—he learned new techniques. There was Frenchy Bordeaux ("my favorite— probably the greatest pitchman ever") who made money by *giving* stuff away. "Who out there would like a free lighter?" he'd yell, throwing handfuls of lighters out willy-nilly. "Who needs a pen?" He'd throw pens out. A crowd would gather. "Now . . . who wants a radio for a dollar? I can sell only fifty. Who wants one? Put your hands up, with your dollar." He'd collect the money, wrap each bill around a radio, then hand back both the bill and the radio. The radios, too, were free! On it went. Eventually, once he had cemented his rapport with the audience, he'd begin to offer even "better" deals, building up to a sewing machine "worth $600" that he was selling for just $200. If he got, say, 15 takers, he'd not stop there. He'd offer to throw in a fine "Bordeaux Geneva" watch valued (by him) at $69.95, *plus* a pair of $30 earrings. Jeeze, the guy was just giving the whole store away! Eventually, 70 people might each pay the $200 for the sewing machine-watch-and-earring combo. Popeil figured that the $200 package had cost Frenchy exactly $100, meaning Frenchy made $7,000 every time he sold to 70 people. And he did that every 45 minutes. *Vive la France!* (If this all sounds a bit familiar, it's because Popeil himself has used the same "but wait, there's more!" technique countless times.)

From the battlefield of Woolworth and the fairgrounds, there emerged a young salesman both brash and indefatigable—a maestro cloaked in bulletproof self-confidence. He was ready for larger worlds.

## Selling on Television

A second big break came Popeil's way in 1958: television. A pal told him of a station in Tampa, Florida, where anybody could make a television commercial for just $550. Popeil was interested. But what product would he advertise? At around the same time, another friend told him of a garden accessory that sounded suitable: a spray nozzle for hoses that contained a compartment into which the user dropped a tablet. Depending on what kind of tablet was put in (detergent, wax, fertilizer, herbicide, or insecticide), the gizmo was variously a window washer, car washer/waxer, fertilizer, or weed-and-bug killer. Better yet, as customers exhausted their original supplies of tablets, they had to buy more. The thing seemed like a natural, so Popeil bought a quantity of nozzles, taped a commercial, and then bought advertising time—first in Chicago, then in other markets. Pretty soon he was playing to hundreds of thousands of viewers—a bigger audience than he ever had pitched to at Woolworth. In four years he sold nearly a million nozzles.

The business worked like this: Popeil would approach a store's owners and offer them a quantity of nozzles on a guaranteed-sale basis. That meant the owners paid Popeil up front for the whole shipment, but that Popeil would commit to buy back (after a certain period) any product that remained unsold. The owners couldn't lose. Plus, Popeil promised that his ads would direct buyers to the owners' stores where, presumably, they'd buy other merchandise as well.

In 1964, Popeil formed Ronco, his namesake company, and began advertising more aggressively. At first he pitched products originally dreamed up by his father, including the Chop-O-Matic, Dial-O-Matic, and Popeil Pocket Fisherman. The Fisherman, Ronco's first runaway hit, sold 2 million units at $19.95. Later, he added products he himself originated, including the Ronco Smokeless Ashtray; Ronco Bottle and Jar Cutter; the Buttoneer (which reaffixed popped shirt buttons); the Feather Touch Knife; the CleanAire Machine (a household air cleaner); Mr. Microphone; and a hand-held vacuum, the "cordless electric" Miracle Broom.

Contrary to what readers of a certain age may think they remember from these ads, Ron seldom appeared full-figure on the screen. What you saw of him, mainly, were his hands. As he used these, deftly and gracefully, to demonstrate a product, viewers heard his smooth and pleasing voice tolling off its virtues. Every so often he'd pause rhetorically to ask, "Isn't that amazing? Isn't that sensational?" No matter how amazing or sensational it was, the deal only got juicier as Ron piled on more and more free extras—all included in the same low, low price. (It was the Frenchy Bordeaux technique, writ larger.) If you bought the slicer, you got the knife set—free! Isn't that incredible? And if you hung in just a little longer, you could be assured that, come the kicker, you'd get some additional reward. He was a suitor whose bouquets kept getting prettier and prettier, a troubadour whose troth could be summed up in four sweet words: But wait! There's more.

All of which is not to say he didn't sometimes meet rejection. What's not well known about Popeil is that he's had his share of flops and marketing misfires, including, for example, the Inside the Outside Window Washer. The Washer consisted of a pair of magnetized handles, each holding a specially impregnated window-cleaning paper. The user put one handle inside the window, the other outside. The magnets kept them aligned—as one descended, so did the other. Popeil decided to test the prototype on the windows of his Chicago high-rise office. The outer unit somehow became detached and plummeted 16 floors straight down onto Michigan Avenue, where it narrowly missed hitting the father-in-law of a Popeil executive. There were other duds besides this, including the Prescolator, a Mr. Coffee–type coffee brewer that was too far ahead of its time, and the Hold-Up bulletin board, which was sort of a Post-It note in reverse: Instead of the note being adhesive, the whole board was.

Despite its failures, Ronco scored more hits than misses, and sales mounted rapidly—from $200,000 the company's first year, to $4 million, to $8 million, and up. Vacationing in Aspen one day in 1968, Ron found himself seated in a Jacuzzi next to an old friend from his University of Illinois days—a guy who'd done very well in the stock market. The friend asked if Ron had ever thought about going public. "What's that?" asked Popeil. At 34, he knew plenty about selling but not much about high finance. Ronco—renamed Ronco Teleproducts—went public in 1969, with Ron pocketing millions—a windfall that, he says, was "a pretty nice thing for a guy who grew up on chicken feet and bean soup." By the early 1970s, the company was reporting annual sales of $20 million.

For a decade, Ronco hummed along so smoothly it might as well have been a Cash-O-Matic: Product followed product, commercial followed commercial, sales increase followed sales increase. Popeil enjoyed the good life, becoming not just a pal of Las Vegas mogul Steve Wynn but a member of Wynn's Mirage Resorts board.

## Bank Troubles and Bankruptcy

Then suddenly in 1983 there came a hiccup—an event that at first seemed to have nothing whatsoever to do with Ronco: Continental Bank of Illinois got itself into big trouble with some spectacularly bad loans and had to be bailed out by federal regulators. Ronco had had no dealings with Continental Illinois. But Continental's troubles struck fear into other Chicago banks, including Ronco's lender, First National. Relations between Ronco and First National had never been anything less than chummy. The bank had periodically lent Ronco money for expansion, and by the early 1980s Ronco had what amounted to a $15 million revolving line of credit with First National. Ronco simply paid the interest and rolled the rest over.

But as Popeil explains, Continental Illinois' debacle changed everything. First National "got nervous," he says, and decided to reevaluate all its loans, including Ronco's. Executives who had managed Ronco's loan for years were summarily replaced with a new crew, whose view of Ronco's business was more critical, less friendly: "They saw that they were loaning us this $15 million, and they asked, 'So, okay . . . what's our collateral?' Their collateral was our inventory plus our accounts receivable. And when they looked at our inventory, they saw stuff like the Inside-the-Shell Egg Scrambler and the Food Dehydrator. Their reaction was, 'Are you kidding? We've got $15 million out, and we could end up with *egg scramblers?* Wait a second!' " So, in the late fall of 1983, First National told Popeil they were sorry, but they'd have to call his loan before the end of January.

This posed a major problem: Most of Ronco's receivables didn't come in until after January. Says Popeil, "If yours is a Christmas business—as mine was, with the bulk of sales coming in the fourth quarter—there's no way you can get your money by the end of January. It wasn't like today, when people just charge stuff to their credit cards. Ours was a business that worked by our making TV commercials that directed people to a retailer to buy our products—to Sears, Woolworth, Walgreen, Thrifty, or to places like that. And retailers do not pay vendors in a timely fashion. We didn't get paid fully until April or May." So, when the loan came due in January, Ronco couldn't pay. Even though Popeil says he hoped somebody would appear to rescue him, no one did. "Come the end of January, the bank stepped in and took over our accounts receivable. They started pocketing the money that should have been going to our suppliers. And one of my major suppliers, who was owed $500,000, forced us into a Chapter 11 position."

Around the same time all this was happening, Popeil's father died. It's an indication, perhaps, of the relationship between father and son that Popeil, in his account of this period, makes no mention whatsoever of his father's death. It's not that Sam had been quiescent. After his divorce from Ron's mother, Sam remarried. He and his second wife, Eloise, had briefly made headlines in 1974, when Eloise was convicted of having hired two hit men to try to have Sam killed. She served 19 months of a longer sentence. She and Sam divorced. Then they remarried. (As for Ron's mother, she and Ron met only once in Ron's adult life: They had lunch together in a New York restaurant when he was in his twenties. Though they spent an hour chatting, he never asked her why she had abandoned him. It seemed to him she needed money, so he gave her some. They never spoke to or saw one another again.)

In 1984, with Ronco in Chapter 11, Popeil was too busy fighting for his financial life to dwell on family or personal matters. Things at Ronco were, in his words, "a mess." First National was taking most of the money coming in, so he didn't have enough cash to buy television time. Nor would his suppliers sell to him. Ronco managed to limp along in this condition another few years. "Things," says Popeil, "dwindled down." Then in 1987 the unthinkable finally happened: Ronco Teleproducts—as much a fixture of the consumer scene as television itself—flickered its last flicker and went completely dark. The Popeil gadget empire subsided into Chapter 7 bankruptcy, and went out of business.

First National was now forced to confront the question it had dreaded: What to do with all those egg scramblers? Its answer: Hold a public auction. The inventory consisted at that time of about 10 or 12 different products. The bank's plan was to let buyers bid on each one separately. Popeil, however, made a counteroffer: He'd buy the whole thing for $2 million. The bankers said thanks, they'd consider it—but only after they'd seen how much they could get collectively from single-product bids.

Popeil waited until all these bids were in. "I'm guessing they totaled something like $1.15 million," he says. "At that point, I literally could have bid one dollar more and gotten everything. But the bank said, with a smile on its face, 'Hey, Ron. You said you'd buy it for $2 million.' Now, I have a code of ethics: If you make a statement, you have to honor it. So when the bank said, 'Are you still going to give us the two mil?' I said yes; yes I am."

So he paid the $2 million and got back his entire inventory, including not just the Scrambler, but a few products he believed still had great unrealized potential—most especially the Ronco Electric Food Dehydrator. "I ended up owning everything myself—not just the inventory, but the intellectual property and all the tooling—the whole kit and caboodle."

As he retells this, he sounds pleased, emphasizing what a coup it was in business terms. But you have to wonder—how did he feel? How did it feel to be Ron Popeil, who had gone pretty much overnight from slicing and dicing his way into a million hearts to being bankrupt and off television?

"Bad," he says. "I felt really bad that it had to end this way. It wasn't a comfortable feeling knowing that I had lost all the equity in my stock." But since he'd never guaranteed any loans personally, his own assets remained untouched by creditors. Apart from having lost the value of his stock, he was materially okay. It was the intangible losses that weighed more heavily on him. "Embarrassment," he says, "that's the big thing that hit me." He felt his good name had been tarnished by the bankruptcy. And he felt the censure of Ronco's angry, disappointed shareholders. "I'd run into them every now and then, and they'd say, 'Ron, I trusted you, and now I'm going to lose most or all my money. You have a responsibility.' And they're right. You have to bear the brunt of that."

On top of that, Ronco's troubles had appeared so suddenly and unexpectedly—"out of left field," says Popeil. There was an element of shock. One minute he'd been pitching; the next, *blamo!* He was out of business. "It wasn't fair," he says. "It disrupted my business and, to some degree, my personal life. You don't know the ramifications when somebody tells you they're taking your business away. There are a lot of I-don't-knows. Someone else is controlling your destiny. You have to take everything one day at a time, one step at a time. That's all you can do. It's an odd experience." Events, he says, felt like they were unfolding in slow motion.

During this tough time, on whom could he rely? Were there people who reached out to offer him comfort or support? Were there friends who phoned every now and then, perhaps, to say, "Hang in there, Ron"?

No, there weren't. Nobody did that.

Popeil's theory is that to most people he still looked as if he were getting along just fine. The bank, having taken over Ronco, was paying him a salary of $1,000 a week. "That was far less than what I'd been getting," he says, "but it was still better than most people's standards." In the world's eyes, he thinks, he still qualified as well heeled. "When people see you're making money—far more than a normal wage—you're not going to get the sympathy of family or friends." At least he didn't from his.

Maybe this explanation is sufficient, because Popeil's life, in superficial ways, did continue on virtually as it had: He lived in the same house. He ate the same food. He wore the same clothes, which never had been especially fancy, not even at Ronco's height. ("I'm a Gap man," he explains.) He adhered to all his same routines.

But it would be false to say he felt no loss, as he himself is first to admit. "Anyone who's ever been a chairman or a CEO of a public company, you miss the perks—everything from the cars you drive to the way you travel. You're the head of a company listed on the American Stock Exchange. You've got a nice office, lots of amenities." Now, as he struggled to get his affairs reorganized, he found himself working in office space he'd rented in a warehouse on the outskirts of Los Angeles. "It was . . . a horizontal move," he says, describing his change of venue. "The new office certainly wasn't in the same style. It was lower key, a lot more bare. A lot more like Wal-Mart. I was in a room with no pictures on the walls. But I still had telephones that worked, a secretary."

## Starting Over—Selling at County Fairs

From this redoubt, Popeil began liquidating Ronco's inventory. It was lonely work, he says, because there wasn't anyone to whom he easily could delegate it. Nobody had a better understanding than himself of what was salable, and what was not. Years earlier, when Ronco first went public, he'd had to rely on experts whose knowledge of finance, for example, had been far greater than his own. But now that the business had been pruned back to its roots, the challenge facing him was one of salesmanship, pure and simple: How to unload a $2 million inventory. And who knew more about selling Popeil products than Ron Popeil? Armed with inventory, he hit the county fair circuit.

Focusing on the positive side of this huge step backward, Popeil says, "It was great to come in contact with people again, one on one, at a live show." A lot of them would recognize his name immediately at these fairs, or at other events he worked—flower, home and garden, auto, and gun shows. This was 1987 to 1989, when Ron Popeil was more familiar as a name than as a face. "In my old commercials, you saw mainly my hands. Today, of course, I'm in everyone's face! *My* face is in *everyone's* face! Today I can't go anywhere without being recognized."

Still, returning to the hustings was depressing: "I had gone from being the CEO of a publicly traded firm to working in hundred-degree temperatures in buildings that weren't even air conditioned, and I was there for 12 or 13 hours a day, every day." He was back to doing the kind of selling he'd done when he was just starting out. Only now he wasn't just starting out—he was 50 years old. "Who wants to get up at five A.M. at that stage of their life?" he asks.

He'd get up before dawn, in order to prepare vegetables and other foods so that they'd look appetizing. "A fair opens in the wee hours," he says, "and it stays open until 11 o'clock at night. If you pay a flat fee for your booth and leave early, you're paying for nonutilization. Close up my booth early? No. I would spend as much time as I possibly could, to prorate the time—12 hours, rather than 8. It was a lot of hard work, a lot of uncomfortableness sometimes, because of weather." And it was unremitting. "Big fairs, like the Sonoma County Fair in California, run 30 days in a row. Most of them in the Midwest run 10." All that standing and shouting, he says, taxed his stamina. "It takes its toll on your body and your voice. You don't have any time, during a fair, to exercise properly. You work 12 hours and get to bed at 10, after grabbing a quick meal at Denny's. Then, the next day, you start the cycle over again. There's no vacation."

His living conditions were none too plush. "If you're at a fair in Podunk, Iowa, you take whatever accommodations are available. It might be Motel 6. Yes, there were times I could have stayed at a much nicer hotel farther away; but I chose not to. I always try to keep expense down, revenue and profit up. It has nothing to do with your stature in life."

How did he manage the small domestic details of life out on the road? Did he, for example, do his own laundry? No, he says, he usually had it sent out. "But it's nothing for me to do my own clothes, even today. I sometimes wash my own underwear out. I was in Florida two weeks ago and found I wasn't traveling with the right clothing. I ran out, so I had to do my laundry in my room."

He worked on and on, alone. It took him only a year to liquidate enough of the inventory to get his $2 million back. And by 1989, two years later, he'd unloaded the whole thing.

Did this three-year sales marathon get any easier, as it went along? "No."

Did it, maybe, teach him something *new* about selling—some subtlety he hadn't grasped before? "No."

Was the ordeal perhaps *necessary*, in some larger, metaphysical way, to his subsequent phoenixlike comeback? Was he paying some sort of penance, possibly? "No."

Well, okay, then—why did he do it? He didn't *have* to do it—at least not for financial reasons. He still had plenty of money after the bankruptcy. And in terms of professional achievement, he had more than proved himself already. No other pitchman had ever done what he'd done on television. Why didn't he simply lapse into a decorous retirement and veg out? Another person might reasonably have packed it all in after 1984—or, if not then, after 1988, once he'd liquidated all $2 million in merchandise, thereby proving to anybody's satisfaction that he still had the old moxie, the old razzmatazz, the old megillah. Another person might indeed have done that, but not Popeil. Retirement, he says, is a step he could have taken even earlier—after he'd made his first million. "But retirement would have been boring. The truth is, I'd work for nothing. I enjoy it. And I'm good at it. It's a kick in the ass."

## Back on Television: Making "a Million Bucks on QVC"

Popeil, congenitally, is just a never-say-die kind of guy. So rather than give the world the raspberry in 1989 and decamp to some alpine lake with a gross of Pocket Fishermen, he instead began plotting a new chapter in his romance with the public, a new way to woo and win consumers' hearts. It would be a commercial, but one that had the look, feel, and length of a full-blown feature program. With 5 minutes, he knew he could do okay. With 10, he'd be twice as good. And with 30, he'd be absolutely irresistible. Figuratively speaking, he hitched up his pants, stared the camera in the eye, and again proclaimed, "But wait, there's more!"

Like Napoleon on Elba, Popeil spent 1989 to 1991 plotting his return. He knew he needed the right product and the right format. Advertisers already had pioneered the 30-minute infomercial—which, by virtue of its length and its reliance on an entertaining host, seemed tailor-made as a showcase for his talents. And as for product, he still had the Electric Food Dehydrator. Initially, he had a deal with the catalog sales company

Fingerhut that called for him to sell the Dehydrator on television. But when this failed to pan out, Popeil seized the initiative and forged ahead on his own. He spent $33,000 to produce a half-hour Dehydrator infomercial. Script? He didn't need one. He could recite the pitch from memory.

The infomercial, which took the form of an audience-participation show called *Incredible Inventions*, debuted in 1991. It opened with a best-of roundup of Popeil's past hits, including the Pocket Fisherman, Veg-O-Matic, and others. Then his female cohost introduced him and asked what new inventions he'd been working on. Popeil was off and running. It was just like the old days, only—but wait!—it was better. Now, by using an 800 number and credit card billing, sales were instant. There was no delay in getting paid. Money literally was coursing through the phone lines.

Popeil was back—and with a vengeance! In the early 1990s, he made $19 million with the Dehydrator alone. Not that the Dehydrator remained alone for long. Popeil knew he quickly needed a second product to follow up the first's success, something genuinely novel that would goose sales even higher. What should it be? It needed to have wide appeal to both men and women. It had to be relatively cheap. It had to be surprising, entertaining. A friend happened to tell Popeil about an aerosol hair-care product he'd seen in Australia that, when sprayed on people's bald spots, left behind a kind of furry hydrocarbon. *Bingo:* spray-on hair!

Popeil bought the U.S. rights to the product, tinkered with its chemical composition and packaging, rechristened it GLH (for *great-looking hair*) Formula No. 9, and sold 900,000 cans in one year. In many ways, spray-on hair was the quintessential Popeil product—novel, silly, and unimaginably popular. With it, he got huge publicity.

He was on a roll. The former Ronco Teleproducts gave way to Popeil Inventions. The Food Dehydrator and GLH gave way to the Ronco Rotisserie and BBQ, the Popeil Pasta and Sausage Maker, and eventually to Ron's most personal of products, his 1995 autobiography, *The Salesman of the Century* (Delacorte Press).

His current success, he says, is beyond his "wildest dreams" (and for Popeil, *wildest* means something). "On the Rotisserie alone, the numbers are gigantic—over $200 million in sales in the last 12 months. It's awesome. I can't even devote all the time to it I should." With just a few short concentrated bursts of personal selling on QVC, he can (and does) move $800,000 worth of merchandise in a single 24-hour period. "From that my profit is $200,000. Not bad for a day's work." That's not even counting additional profit he gets at retail from units sold to shoppers attracted by the airplay he's gotten on television.

"This weekend," he says, meditatively, "I'll make a million bucks on QVC. I will stay in a little tiny hotel over there, near their studio—not like some other places I'm accustomed to. Yes, I could stay at a much nicer hotel and use a limousine, but I choose not to. I keep expenses down, revenue and profits up. That much hasn't changed."

And the future? What's ahead for Ron Popeil? His confidence seems boundless. He's got stuff in the pipeline, he says, you just would not believe. (Who among us would want to challenge him on that?)

## "If You Snooze, You Lose"

The only thing Popeil is the least bit shy on, really, is advice—the kind you're no doubt looking for right here—advice on how to become successful—and stay successful. Oh, he's got some, but it isn't very touchy-feely. Nor does it come from self-help books. "I haven't read any books that have spurred me on to a different way of thinking," he says. What he's picked up, he's picked up by osmosis.

- *Tip 1: It helps to be well heeled.* This sounds silly, but he means it: Being rich made it easier for him to get through bankruptcy and his hiatus from television.
- *Tip 2: Never guarantee loans personally.* "I can tell you that the smartest move I ever made in my life was not personally guaranteeing anything myself. Personal guarantees can wipe you out."
- *Tip 3: If you (unlike Popeil) need to hire experts to bail you out, don't cut corners—make sure you've got the best.* "A friend of mine a week ago was going to use this lawyer because the lawyer was his friend. I said, 'You're going about this ass backwards—you think that because the guy's your friend you're going to get a better deal? What you want is the best legal counsel you can get, period. Don't settle for second best.'"
- *Tip 4: It helps to have a stoic attitude.* Much of the good that came his way, he thinks, was purely the result of luck, such as

going public at the right time (1969). So was much of the bad. "Outside forces over which you have no control can control your destiny." He doesn't believe you can guard against these forces. They just hit you. The only blessing (if that's the word) is that *big* misfortunes don't hit you very often. He counts bankruptcy as his only one so far.

Truth is, Popeil's story has little in it to warm the heart of an advice guru or professor of self-improvement. It's kind of thin and cold, measured by conventional standards of the uplift industry: He didn't draw strength from his wonderful family or friends. He didn't cast his eyes upon a higher power and receive comfort. He comes across as a person who, when trouble came, reached way down deep inside himself and found exactly . . . zilch.

"Who can think about religion?" he asks. "When the plane is crashing, you're not thinking about praying, but about fixing the problem. You push on, focused on what you're doing. You can't take time to look outside. I was so busy moving in a forward direction that I didn't have time to pray."

Moving forward is the big thing—maybe the only thing. That, and staying focused. The game's not over, he stresses, until you lie down and quit. (His favorite maxim: "If you snooze, you lose.") Stay in the game, and there's at least a *chance* you might prevail. So your window magnets plummet to the street! So what? Keep on pitching.

He first learned this lesson way back in his Woolworth days, in a way that imprinted the message forever after on his brain. His product-du-jour, then, was a spray-on shoe wax called Instant Shine. Why be content, he reasoned, with selling it one can at a time, when by finding one large customer he could sell thousands all at once? And what institution's need for shiny shoes was especially acute? The National Guard. So he secured an in-person interview with the ranking general. Popeil asked if he might have a pair of the general's black boots, on which to demonstrate the product. An adjutant complied, and Popeil, with the general watching, sprayed. To Popeil's private horror, the boots turned white. He vamped a bit, then asked if he might try a second pair. He sprayed those. They turned white. The general now regarded him with the kind of expression that, in silent movies, is accompanied by a card reading, "*Well???*" Popeil summoned up his nerve, looked the general in the eye, and said: "So, okay, General—do I get the National Guard account or not?"

Neither the general's reply (which, for reasons best known to him, was yes) nor the reason for the product's malfunction needs concern us here. What matters is the moral Popeil took away: When all looks lost, "you might as well go for it." How did he manage to rebound from bankruptcy? It may not sound inspirational, but he did it of necessity and by sheer moxie. Spiritually speaking, he did it on a diet of chicken feet and bean soup.

Emma Chappell

## CHAPTER 6

# Emma Chappell

## Founder of the United Bank of Philadelphia

*"I had this awful inclination to give up."*

"**F**IRST OF ALL," says Emma Chappell, known throughout her native Philadelphia as "the people's banker," "you have to understand that my whole life has been a series of crises. I'm not someone who was born with a silver spoon in their mouth." To look at her, you might easily think otherwise: Dressed in a gray pinstriped wool jacket, seated behind a heavy desk, gold and silver jewelry accenting her neck and wrists, Chappell radiates not only prosperity but the kind of confident, relaxed authority one might expect from a Rockefeller, a Mellon, or some such old-line financier.

She herself, however, is neither male, nor white, nor to the manor born. She's a big, robust African American woman, exuberant, and alive with far more humor than one would expect from the average bank's CEO. The bank she founded and still heads, United Bank of Philadelphia, ranks eighth in assets ($140 million) among U.S. black-owned lending institutions. (The only color United cares about, says Chappell, is green.) It's no less a part of Philadelphia than the Liberty Bell or Betsy Ross's house—both of which are near United's head-quarters. The bank's birth, however, was anything but easy, and there came a time in the late 1980s when Chappell's fight to win financial self-determination for Philadelphia's minority community came close to failing. In that one instant—on the eve of the Fourth of July, 1989—her obdurate self-confidence, which previously had seen her through many a challenge, broke. For days the bank's future (and her own) hung suspended.

That crisis, says Chappell, was the single worst one she has ever had to face in her 57 years. But it was hardly the first.

## First Mentor: Her Minister

When she was a kid, Chappell says, "I thought I wanted to be a doctor. I thought I would help people, so they wouldn't have to die." Then, when she was just 14, her mother passed away. "I was with her the night she died. And after that, I was afraid of dead people for a while—definitely afraid of blood. So I thought maybe being a doctor was not for me." A smile crosses her face, and she laughs. "I was not very big on being a doctor anymore."

After she lost her mother, the single biggest influence in her life—apart from her father, George, a chef at Horn & Hardart—was her minister. "We used to spend a lot of time in church when I was growing up," she says. "My minister was very strong, and he'd always preach the gospel." This wasn't just any pastor, but Dr. Leon Sullivan, head of Philadelphia's Zion Baptist Church, who would later become famous for making moral forays from his pulpit into the world of business.

In 1959, Sullivan led 400 fellow ministers in a boycott of Philadelphia companies that refused to hire African Americans. In 1965, he persuaded his parishioners each to invest $10 a month in a church-affiliated corporation whose mission was the creation of black-owned businesses. The corporation eventually built and managed an apartment complex, a shopping center, and a garment factory, among other ventures. In 1971, Sullivan became the first African American board member of General Motors. And six years later, he propounded what would eventually become known worldwide as the Sullivan Principles—an antiapartheid code of conduct governing U.S. corporations doing business with South Africa.

Sullivan preached that his parishioners ought to serve God not just in church but in their daily lives, in any way they could. "He would say, 'Use what you have in your hand,' " remembers Chappell. " 'If you find yourself doing what you enjoy doing, you should always do that—make it your life work—do what you *enjoy* doing'. Little did I know I'd have a chance to experience his teaching first-hand."

When Chappell turned 16 and was about to graduate from high school, Sullivan asked her what she intended to do with her life. "I told him I was going to get a job, because I couldn't go to college right away." He asked what kind of job she wanted. "I said, 'I can do anything'— because when you're a kid you think you can do anything, take the world by storm." Sullivan decided she should first take an aptitude test, administered by him personally. When she sat down to take it, she recalls, the moment felt portentous: "This was the pastor of my own church giving me this test, right there in the church basement. He said, 'I want to see what you can *really* do.'"

Chappell aced mathematics, and Sullivan said, "Whoah!—I know *just* the job for you!" He asked her to consider banking—a field that then employed few, if any, African Americans in Philadelphia. He offered to make all the necessary introductions and arrangements for her, asking one thing in return: She must agree to stay in banking for at least five years. Chappell complied. "And the rest," she says, with a laugh and wave of her hand, "is history!"

## "I Had This Great Job of Counting All This Money"

She began work as a $45-a-week clerk photographer at Continental Bank, taking pictures of customers' checks and deposits. She was 18, and from her very first moment in the bank, she says, she loved everything about it. What aspect appealed most? "I remember seeing . . . *all this money.*" She liked handling the money, counting it, watching the expressions on people's faces when a teller put money in their hands. Most of all, she liked its power to do good: If someone needed education, money bought it. If someone was sick, money could help them buy the medicine to get well. Her thinking about her life's vocation changed. "I thought: What better way to be a 'doctor'? What better way to heal people than by gaining control over money and helping them to be able to get *more* money for themselves?"

She quickly graduated to teller, where, she says, she loved the social interaction with her customers.

> That's the first line when you come into a bank—you go to the teller to cash your check or make your deposit. Here I was, the only African American in banking in Philadelphia at the time. I got to meet very few other African Americans; the customers were mostly white. But no matter what, each of them got to know me, and I got to know them; I knew their signatures. When they came into the bank, it was like we had this great fraternity where everyone was always happy: "How are you today? How's your brother, and what is your sister doing?" All in the family. And, at the same time, I had this great job of counting all this money. And I had all this money in my drawer. I loved it! I loved being in an environment of handling money.

Being a teller, she says, "was my favorite job of all time."

As I rose up the ladder, in each job I had an opportunity to see how money could influence people in a positive manner. So when I got into the loan department, we made loans to people who either wanted to buy a house or remodel a house, pay for their education, pay medical bills. I wanted to learn all there was to learn about having money and controlling the outflow and inflow of dollars. And that's what happened. They were very wonderful people at Continental Bank, and they more or less adopted me as if I were a kid. I must have been "a kid" to them until I was 30 years old. In their eyesight I never grew up, so that allowed me to learn everything. They just sort of took me under their wing and raised me up through the ranks. I was the youngest kid ever working in a bank and had an opportunity to be exposed to banking and finance at levels that were unheard of at that time.

Outside the bank, Chappell got involved with such organizations as the National Association for the Advancement of Colored People (NAACP) and the Southern Christian Leadership Conference. Initially, the bank was at best neutral towards these affiliations. But with passage of federal legislation requiring banks to improve their lending and other services to minorities, her connections to advocacy groups became an institutional and political asset. In 1971, Continental gave her the go-ahead to establish a program to make business loans to moderate- and lower-income borrowers. Shortly after that, she took a leave of absence (with the bank's blessing) to help organize what today is known as the Philadelphia Commercial Development Corporation, an entity that finances economic development projects. After her return to the bank in 1975, she was named liaison to the Small Business Administration and helped make some $30 million in loans to minority-owned and woman-owned businesses.

During these same years she married, had two daughters, separated from her husband, and almost died from meningitis. (Never a dull moment.)

I was bitten by a mosquito. And a week later, I was in a coma that lasted for 10 days. My heart stopped. They gave me up for dead. And I overcame *that*. This was right after I'd separated from my husband. My life has been so crisis-oriented and so successful. I felt the mosquito's bite. It shot straight to my head. Then one day, I just couldn't get up. I had this high temperature— 108 degrees—perspired like mad. I was taken to the hospital and given a spinal tap. That's when I lost consciousness—the pain was too excruciating. They put me in a room with this 90-year-old woman. A priest came to pray for her. And as the priest was praying, I started praying with the priest. All of a sudden, I didn't have any pain. And I could look down over my bed and see these doctors around the bed working on this patient—and I kept wondering what they were doing. I remember racing through a tunnel of light, looking for my mother and my mother's face. They tell me if I'd seen her, I'd probably have died. There were all these people with white outfits on. And I remember looking for Jesus, and seeing Him at a distance. I never did see my mother. I technically died—stopped breathing. And they hit me with the paddles, to shock me back to life. Then, all of a sudden, I'm back in my body. They wrote my story up, later, in the medical journals. I'd been so sick, but the doctor said he'd had nothing to do with my recovery.

This experience convinced her anew that God had put her on earth for some purpose, and that He wasn't finished with her yet.

Chappell became the first African American vice president in Continental's history (and the first woman to hold such a position in finance anywhere in Philadelphia) in 1977, at the age of 34. She began to dream of one day starting a bank of her own—one dedicated to the needs of minorities. Her ambition wasn't unprecedented, she knew, but examples of African American women who had carried it off successfully were few. In fact, there was only one: In 1903 Maggie Lena Walker—executive secretary-treasurer of an African American fraternal organization called the Grand United Order of St. Luke—founded the St. Luke Penny Savings Bank in Richmond, Virginia, with herself as president. No African American woman had formed a bank before or since. "She—her example—definitely was an inspiration," says Chappell. "Obviously, she was my idol. I had always wanted to be able to do the things she did. The fact that she was able to do what she did back in the early 1900s was a miracle in itself. At least today we have all kinds of technology. They didn't have anything of the kind back then. I was very impressed with her accomplishment."

## Financing and Fundraising for Jesse Jackson

Before Chappell could take action on her ambition, though, she got an offer she couldn't refuse: In 1983, Jesse Jackson asked her to be the national treasurer for his presidential bid.

Here again, Chappell says, she had a chance to observe, close up, the constructive power of money: It was the fuel that made possible every initiative of the Jackson campaign.

> What I did there, as national treasurer, was first, I read the regs on campaign finance. I'd come home every night and read them; then, next day, I'd apply them. I handled all the financing and fundraising. We raised something like $11 million, and in 1983–84 that was a *lot* of money. We ran one of the best-kept campaigns ever, because, as national treasurer, I made sure all the money was accounted for in every city. I handled all the books and records, arranged for sale of all the political paraphernalia, traveled all around the country. While he was out there making the speeches, I was back in the office, taking care of the money, making sure all the records were so clean that afterwards, when it was all said and done, Reverend Jackson could not be tarnished. In that way, what I did was very important.

She was able to give jobs to people, to personally see to it that all the vendors were paid. "I made sure Reverend Jackson was happy as a lark, because he never had to worry about the money aspect of his campaign. I could account for *every penny.*"

The experience proved invaluable. "It exposed me to politicians I never otherwise would have met. Today I know them—people who are mayors of cities, people in the current administration or the previous one. Mayor Brown in San Francisco? He has the *best* parties!" she laughs. "He's a great guy! I met most of anybody who's anybody in politics." Even at the time, though, she says she recognized that politics was not "the scene for me . . . because I'm a banker. A lot of people have asked me to run for office, but I've just never had a burning desire to do it."

After the 1984 election, once she'd paid off all campaign debts, she helped Jackson launch the Rainbow Coalition. "I became the first vice president for administration for the Coalition," she says. "We helped to get the Rainbow started in some 30 or 40 cities. Here again, I went to each city to make sure all the books and records were correct, because these local organizations were led by ministers, and oftentimes they didn't see the importance of keeping the financial records straight."

Finally, in 1987, she returned to her vice president's job at Continental Bank, having concluded that banking—not politics—was the arena where she could do the most good for the most people. Reverend Jackson agreed. He felt the contribution Chappell still stood to make in finance—helping minority borrowers and business people get access to capital—was potentially as great as any he himself might make in politics.

## "We Could Create Our Own Bank"

A group of lawyers and investment bankers soon approached her. They, too, wanted to start a bank whose focus would be lending to minorities, and they saw Chappell as just the woman to head up their effort. Their plan had been inspired by a piece of legislation that gave investors certain credits for backing minority-owned businesses—in much the same way that the Community Reinvestment Act (CRA) gives banks incentives to lend to low-income and moderate-income communities. "They told me," says Chappell, "that if I'd take on the leadership, I would not have to worry about raising the money—because they already had money set aside." This was in July 1987. "Then in October '87 the market crashed, and money dried up. People were not investing in anything, let alone banks, at the time."

Financially speaking, she was back to square one. Worse, though, she was now out on a limb:

> By then I had begun to talk about creating a bank with people who knew me in the community where I'd grown up. People had already espoused the idea that "if anybody can pull it off, Emma can, and we're going to support her." The ministers in the all the churches and the leaders of all the nonprofit organizations had already begun to talk about it. There was coming to be this groundswell of support for the idea that perhaps we really could create our own bank.

After the market crash, she didn't want to have to go back to those same supporters and tell them their dream—and hers—was dead. So she started working on an alternative plan—one that drew on community support. It was predicated on small investors contributing a large part of the necessary money. Meanwhile, the fears that had followed in the wake of the market crash subsided, and big investors once again seemed interested in helping her get started.

In 1990 she left Continental to devote herself full-time to getting her bank off the ground.

In the course of researching her business plan, she found numbers that showed how difficult it had been for minority borrowers to get funds from established banks. Though the population of Philadelphia was roughly 40 percent minority, only $8 million in loans—less than 3 percent of the amount lent in 1987 ($292 million)—had gone to minority borrowers. For small business loans, the percentage was even lower. There had been, she says, a lot of redlining: A disproportionate number of people in certain neighborhoods had been denied access to mortgage money. When, despite this, they somehow managed to acquire homes, they couldn't get the equity loans they needed to fix them up. Small businesses were having difficulty getting loans to start new businesses or to expand existing ones. To Chappell's mind, there was a clear need for a bank that would focus on the needs of thse minority customers—not just African Americans, but Hispanics, Asians, women, and other constituencies underserved by existing banks.

## Raising $3 Million—and Finding It's Not Enough

Chappell's research further showed that over the years there had been at least five attempts to start such a bank in Philadelphia. Yet each one had failed, most because they'd had difficulty raising money. "But there was also," says Chappell, "a mind-set against having a financial institution that focused on the minority community. Each time a proposed bank would get to a certain level, there was some kind of roadblock put in its way, so its backers were not able to move forward." A warning bell began to sound in her own mind, quietly at first, then louder as she began fully to appreciate the odds against her success. She began to expect resistance, to anticipate problems. "In a sense, I guess, I braced myself for *something*. I just didn't expect it to happen when it did. And I didn't expect to be of the magnitude it was."

Undeterred, Chappell kept meeting with supporters and advisors all around the city. "The conversation," she says "was getting louder—the public was getting excited. In 1989 I thought it was the right time to start raising the capital." So, with her lawyers' help, she put together an offering circular. "I went back out into the community, making speeches and selling the stock at $10 a share, in blocks of 50 shares each. $500 was the minimum investment." Many of the 3,000 people who bought had never bought stock before. But they parted with their money because they believed in Chappell's cause and in her personally. "What they wanted was somebody they could put their faith in." Besides selling stock, she says, "We did all kinds of things to raise money. Young people—children even—

organized bake sales or cleaned cars." By such means—and by appealing to larger investors as well as institutions—she eventually raised $3 million.

All that remained now was for her to file the necessary paperwork with the state banking authorities in Harrisburg, who would then grant her the charter she needed for the bank to begin doing business.

"I had a specific date by which I wanted to get this done," she says—"July Fourth. I wanted to be able to say we'd filed by that date, because it signifies freedom, self-determination, independence—everything we wanted." So taking her business plan and all her other documents, she got into her car the Friday before the holiday and set off for Harrisburg, the state capital, where the secretary of banking—a woman at the time—had her office. "I remember personally driving up the turnpike to Harrisburg," she recalls. "And as I got there, I was starting to get nervous. It was getting close to five o'clock, closing time, because my lawyers had taken so long to give me these heavy packages of business plans and feasibility studies. I drove so fast that when I got out of the car I ran up the steps of 333 Market Street. There must have been 40 steps. I ran up the steps, I got on the elevator and raced into the secretary's office." It was five o'clock.

"You'd think," she says, "That I would have calmed down by the time I'd got on that elevator to the twelfth floor, or whatever floor it was." She hadn't. She was still moving fast, and gathering momentum. She cleared the threshold of the secretary's office and barreled on in to the boardroom, where the secretary was waiting. "Apparently I must still have been moving when I hit the table, because when I sat down, I just hit the table with my hands, and it broke in half—this big glass table. It was the boardroom table."

The secretary—whom Chappell describes as "a white woman, thin, with a severe kind of a face; she had a suit on, a young woman, probably younger than me"—made a little gasp, a noise like "*Uh!*" as if she were sucking in air.

"I just hit the table, and I broke it right in half. Well—" She pauses. "I knew I wasn't going to get anything good from that moment on!" She laughs expansively. " 'This is *not* a good sign'—that's exactly what I thought." By now the secretary was looking "very cold, very unreceptive." Chappell decided to press on.

I sat down, and I said, "Okay, Madame Secretary . . . I'm ready . . . I'm here. The Fourth of July is so important to us, because it means independence, freedom, financial freedom for our people. And I need to get my charter. Here's my plan." And she said "Oh? . . ." She was *very* cold by then. And she says, "Well . . . I don't know. How much money have you raised?" I said, "I've raised the required $3 million." In the charter, in the books, in the regs, it said we needed $750,000, but they [the Department of Banking] had told me, in the process, when they heard about us creating the bank, that it was $3 million. I'd come there with the full $3 million. The whole amount was ready, waiting in escrow. Not a dime of it had been touched.

The secretary told her $3 million wouldn't be enough. Chappell, she said, would need $5 million.

Was Chappell surprised?

I wasn't surprised. I was *shocked.* At the time I put this bank together, there were no books on how to create a bank. We were not able to find a book anywhere. I had to learn everything from scratch. But it hadn't been just me talking to the regulators. We'd had a top-flight attorney.

This setback was the worst of any she had suffered—especially devastating to her because it had come in her own chosen field.

*Why* had the secretary denied Chappell's application? "There just wasn't enough capital. They'd looked at situations that other banks were having, and they felt that we were undercapitalized, and that the economy just called for $5 million." The reason failed to satisfy Chappell, who found it less than convincing.

The decision seemed casual to me. And there was *nothing* to support it. Nothing in writing. This was the first we'd heard of it. She knew we'd been working to get the bank going, and she had not been very positive about it at any point along the way. The truth is, I felt this decision was almost . . . what would you say? Subjective. *Suspect* is the word I'd use.

Chappell couldn't help thinking it was partly personal, too.

What had happened prior to this is we both, she and I, had been candidates for the secretary of banking's job. I didn't know her, and she didn't know me. But we both lived near each other—about three blocks away—and it had been announced to me that I was going to be the secretary of banking. The next day, though, in the paper, it came out that it was her. I didn't hold that against her. I went on working on my plan for the bank. But I believe she was told that she and I had been in competition. To me, since she won, she should have been happy.

Apparently, she wasn't.

"You know what I've found in life?" asks Chappell philosophically.

I've found that what's meant for you, you'll get. But you often times have to overcome a lot of obstacles in order to get it and to be successful. At least that's been my experience. I'm so grateful now I didn't get to be secretary of banking, because I might never have taken this other route. You know? The very fact that it didn't happen made me go further on this. So when I went up there to Harrisburg and dealt with this woman who was looking so very cold and unreceptive, I just left things there and came on home.

## "Nothing in the World Can Take the Place of Persistence"

Her mood, though, was anything but philosophical on her long drive home from Harrisburg that Friday evening. The secretary's refusal to grant a charter had hurt her deeply.

I could hardly see, I was so distraught. Did I think about giving up? Packing it in? Yes I did. I seriously thought about it. I always tell people I'm a Christian banker, and I prayed all the way back home. I thought about our 3,000 shareholders, and I wondered: How could I go back and tell those same people who were so excited about me getting my application ready, who I'd talked to on the radio and told them I was ready—how was I going to tell the public that I couldn't do it? All the way home I thought: Here we are again; we're going to fail. I had this awful inclination to give up.

Next day, at home, she prayed some more. It was now the weekend, so she had two whole days to think things over. "I remember sitting in my bedroom wondering, Do I give up? I've never given up on anything in my life. Why start now?" One of her daughters, knowing what Chappell was going through, brought her a special gift. It was a framed piece of writing—"this beautiful saying, based on something said by President Coolidge"—which since then has become a part of Chappell's personal creed:

Nothing in the world can take the place of persistence. Talent will not; nothing is more common than unsuccessful people with talent. Genius will not; unrewarded genius is almost a proverb. Education will not; the world is full of educated derelicts. Persistence and determination are omnipotent.

She thought back to the many other crises she had weathered: to her mother's death, and to her own near-death experience. "I figured that the Lord hadn't brought me this far to leave me," she says, smiling. In the end, though, it was the seeming *injustice* of the secretary's decision that proved to be Chappell's greatest motivator.

I think probably the very fact that I got turned down made me continue. Because I felt like it was just one person—just one person who was trying to block an institution that was being created to serve the underserved. I really felt I should not let that happen. Especially since banking was my background. Who else would come along and do this? There weren't that many people who'd been blessed to have the experiences that I had had. It's easy to walk away and say "we didn't make it."

She decided she wouldn't say that. She would carry on. But now, how was she to raise another $2 million?

"I said to myself, *I'm a banker.* I started looking at what other bankers had done in situations like this. I did some research." She found out that a number of small community banks had been created by bigger banks investing in them—using them as vehicles for their own purposes, such as meeting their own CRA requirements. "So, I started going back to my fellow bankers and telling them of my problem." The results were gratifying: The first check she got—$100,000—came from her old employer, Continental Bank. Other banks contributed like amounts.

The other thing she decided she would do was tell the truth. "When I came back from Harrisburg, the press called me up and asked me, 'Well, did you get your charter?' " She'd anticipated this moment and knew that, if she'd wanted, she could have cooked up some excuse—some eloquent and persuasive way of saying, "You know, on reconsideration I decided not to go through with our plan after all." Instead, she gave reporters an unvarnished account of exactly what had happened. And they, as a result, helped tremendously. They started calling the Department of Banking and asking where this new requirement—for

$5 million—had come from: "The media called everybody up, and turned out to be my greatest asset." Many reporters felt, just as Chappell did, that the stipulation was unfair.

Meantime, however, as controversy about the bank's application bubbled in local newspapers and in government offices in Harrisburg, Chappell hit upon a new strategy: She would take to the pulpit, making her appeal for funds directly to congregations of the city's churches.

Chappell became a financial evangelist. From 1989 to 1991, there was hardly a church in Philadelphia she didn't visit. "Some Sundays, I'd be in four or five," she says. Her money-raising appeal to parishioners culminated in an event called Black Bank Sunday in which 200 churches participated. "The governor came in, the mayor, the heads of all the clergy—black *and* white. They came and spoke about the need for the kind of bank I wanted, and the importance of its getting chartered. That was an exciting time." Her one frustration: "I was only human. I could only get to so many of the 200 churches in one day."

Another best moment from that period was the visit of a Catholic nun. "We got to this plateau where we didn't seem to be able to get past $4.5 million," explains Chappell. "All we needed was another half million. But we were stuck there, on that plateau. The mother—the head sister—of the Sisters of Mercy came to see me. She brought her finance person with her. I explained what we were trying to do—and that this was such a critical juncture in the raising of the capital." The very fact that the mother visited, says Chappell, provided a huge lift. But the fact that she brought a $50,000 check with her and invested all of it in bank stock "made a huge difference. It came at a time when I really needed it."

During these three years, Chappell admits, she continued to suffer episodes of private doubt. "Why am I doing this?" she asked herself. "What is this about?" She became physically tired, and her appearance changed.

> My friends teased me. They said "Emma, we've never seen you like this." I literally wore a hole in my shoes walking around, going to see people, getting them to understand why we were doing this, trying to convince them to help. There were still a lot of people in the community who didn't believe that it could happen. That meant I had to change a whole mindset. It wasn't just in the corporate community. It was in *my* community, because there had been so many previous attempts that failed, and because they'd heard about all the hurdles I was having to overcome.

A deadline loomed: December 31, 1991. If she hadn't raised the full $5 million by that date, state authorities had warned her, she wouldn't get her charter.

As the date approached, more investors, hearing of her latest plight, came forward. What began as a mere trickle of new money quickly grew. "The people just kept lining up," she says. "They came out in snowstorms. I had people say to me, 'I don't even want to read your prospectus. Just take my money. Get that bank open. You go, girl!'" By the time it was all over, she'd not only raised the $5 million—she'd raised $6 million—$1 million more than the state requirement.

She herself, meanwhile, was going broke. All this while, she'd been living off her own savings, refusing to pay herself a salary out of the monies she had raised. During the six months between meeting the December 31 deadline and the bank's opening in 1992, she started running out of money for personal expenses. "It was getting mighty low, and I was starting to worry. The longer it took the regulators to approve us, the scarier it got for me. At one point I started thinking, 'I'm not going to make it.'" Friends lent her money to live on. "Fortunately for me," she says, "I didn't have a lot of bills. But I had already identified my vent." Her vent? "My vent—in case I became homeless." She laughs. "You know how you see people on the street, lying on top of a vent to keep themselves warm? I had identified this one vent, right out in front of the place I had chosen to be my bank—where the first bank was going to be located. I saw a lot of steam coming up there, so I figured it might be warm."

She'd raised the $6 million. She'd met the Department of Banking's deadline. She'd risked both her reputation and her own financial solvency. Wouldn't you expect that now the worst would be over? That everything else would be pretty much clear sailing? "For me?" asks Chappell with mock surprise. "Oh no! Not by any means."

The Department of Banking finally approved United's charter. That hurdle, at least, was cleared. But the next proved to be getting Federal Deposit Insurance Corporation (FDIC) insurance, without which the bank couldn't open. Months passed. What was up? "I don't know," says Chappell. "They just didn't seem to want to give us the insurance. Nobody ever told us anything was wrong. We knew our applications were all in place." More time passed. Still no insurance. "I hired staff. We had our offices all selected and decorated. We were ready to open the doors. So, finally, I called them." And what she said was this: "If you don't give me my insurance—and those FDIC stickers to put on the doors—we are going to open up our doors anyway. And we are going to tell all 3,000 of our shareholders they should go up to New York themselves, to your offices, and get their insurance, 'cause there's no reason we shouldn't have it." Bingo! "They Federal Expressed it. I got my stickers, and we opened up the doors. We had so many FDIC stickers you wouldn't believe it." (She laughs.) "I think they just could just imagine all 3,000 of these African Americans coming up to their offices and asking for that insurance."

## Open for Business at Last

United officially opened for business on March 23, 1992, in offices on Market Street, near Independence Hall. Reverend Jackson spoke— "beautifully," recalls Chappell. The governor attended, as did the mayor, Edward Rendell, members of the city council, and various celebrities. Finally, there were the bank's real guests of honor—the small investors who'd put their money behind Chappell's dreams. "We must have had all 3,000 of them trying to get in at once, to make deposits," she laughs. There was someone else present that day as well: The secretary of banking, whose conference table Chappell had smashed in two. She professed herself proud of Chappell and her accomplishment.

In the years since then, honor upon honor has come her way. She holds honorary degrees in law, civil law, and humanities. In 1999, Mass-Mutual and the U.S. Chamber of Commerce conferred on Chappell their prestigious Blue Chip Enterprise Award, which recognizes business people who have shown courage in the face of obstacles.

Toward the end of *Forbes'* visit with Chappell, she pulled out an album of photographs taken during the bank's opening party, narrating each image with the sort of satisfaction and bemusement a woman usually reserves for pictures of her children and grandkids:

See that? That's when the office was *clean*. I had nothing on my desk. The sink was clean. There's the governor. There's Jesse Jackson. There's Jesse again. This guy, here, was CEO of Strawbridge and Clothier, a big department store across the street. He came over here to be with the rest of the crowd. He said to me, "I can't stay in my store anymore. I've go to come over to where all the *action* is." There's Patty Labelle. She came up and sang. It was fabulous. There's the cake. This was the place to be!

A rare thing happened during her narration of these photos: She wasn't interrupted. Usually, depositors and other customers—including the very smallest ones—call nonstop, knowing Chappell prides herself on being personally accessible. "They call and they say, 'I want to speak to Emma.' And they know my voice, too, so there's no fooling them. I got a message just the other day from a woman who says she wants to make a deposit but only if she can talk about it directly with me. She has only a little money, but she wants to talk to me first." On a different occasion, another woman called from her hairdresser's, taking Chappell to task for not having enough deposit slips on the counter of her local branch. As Chappell herself often points out, the bank figuratively and literally is a family affair. Not only has she remained close to her original supporters (now her depositors), but her own two daughters have taken on roles at United: Verdaynea, a graduate of Wharton, helped organize and open the bank, and sat on its board. Tracey heads up the bank's nonprofit Philadelphia United Community Development Corporation, which offers consumer-education programs promoting home ownership, financial literacy, credit repair, and small-business start-up.

Chappell thinks that United's keeping close ties with the minority community allows it to capitalize on opportunities that a bigger, more distant institution might easily overlook. Two examples: home improvement loans and loans to small businesses. Fewer than 1 percent of United's loans currently are delinquent, and, for three years running, the Federal Reserve has awarded the bank outstanding CRA ratings. Assets, as previously noted, stand at around $140 million, placing it in the top-10 largest black-owned lending institutions in the United States. "Black-owned" really has become something of a misnomer, because many of the bank's customers and depositors, at this point, are Hispanics and Asians. ("The only color we care about," Chappell says again, "is green.")

## "Be Determined to Accomplish Your Goal"

Chappell's advice for other people waging battles is short and to the point:

> First of all, I would say: Be willing to talk to God during your most difficult moments, to look for Him for direction.
> Second, believe in yourself. I believe I can do almost as much as any-

one else can do, if I put my mind to it. Be able and willing to take what comes with leadership. Often times, during the most difficult moments, I remember that I cannot afford to look like I'm struggling or suffering, because I need to inspire the rest of my staff to follow me. They expect me to be strong and to work out the solution, whatever it might be.

Thirdly: Persevere. Be determined to accomplish your goal.

Beyond that, cultivate your own mentors and heroes. How different life might have been for her, had Dr. Sullivan not originally guided her into banking. In recent years, Chappell has sought guidance from Hugh McColl, CEO of Nationsbank. Shortly after she persuaded Nationsbank to make a $300,000 investment in United in 1995, Chappell recruited McColl as a mentor, getting his advice on what she could do to attract larger corporate customers. United now offers *sweep* accounts, which allow corporate depositors to make money overnight from deposits sitting in non-interest-bearing accounts.

Chappell might easily have cited a last bit of advice, so simple it's easily overlooked: Tell the truth.

The single best think I ever did was tell the truth to people and be honest along the way. That was one of the best decisions I ever made. Because that way, people see the human side of what you're up against. All too often people try make things look too easy—like it just "happened." I bet there isn't one person who would tell you, whether they liked me or they don't, that I didn't work hard to pull this off. People always understood what I was up against. They appreciated all the sacrifices that I made and that my board members had to make. I think that's why we were so successful and remain successful.

Remember the time I was driving back down the road from Harrisburg? I was torn between telling the truth and saying something different from what had happened. What could I say? Naturally, you would want to make it sound like you're so great—"What really happened," I could have said, "is just that I changed my mind and decided I didn't want to do it." When, in fact, that wasn't it at all. I was about to fail, but through no fault of mine. I mean, I had done everything I knew had to be done.

Happily for her and her investors, "everything" turned out to be just enough.

Donald Trump

C H A P T E R  7

━━ ≅◆≅ ━━

# Donald Trump

*Chairman of the Trump Organization*

*"Fight back. Always fight back until you win."*

DONALD TRUMP IS MANY THINGS—as Trump himself would be the first to tell you: real estate mogul, best-selling author, self-promoter, wheeler-dealer, ladies' man, and, most recently, presidential aspirant. Moreover, Trump *has* many things—yachts, golf courses, estates, international celebrity and a seemingly endless string of young women eager to be photographed clinging to his arm. It's hard, in fact, to find anything Trump has ever lacked—except, perhaps, a sense of irony about himself.

He has bragged that his book *Trump: The Art of the Deal* (Random House, 1988) was not only one of the best-selling business books of all time, but had also ranked, "along with *Bonfire of the Vanities*, [as] the best-selling book of 1988."[1] Yet while Trump's book was an unabashed celebration of the era of affluence later dubbed the Me Decade, Tom Wolfe's book (Farrar, Straus & Giroux, 1987) was a critical, highly satiric send-up of that same decade—and of people like Donald Trump.

The two books were almost polar opposites in their depiction of the years that had seen Trump's rise to wealth and business stardom. If Trump's book was a boast, a celebration of his achievements, then Wolfe's was an insinuation that those achievements were somehow suspect, built on morally wobbly foundations. The Wolfe book caused readers to question their admiration of the rich. In 1989, columnist Pete Hamill, writing in *Esquire,* went so far as to suggest that Trump might as well have been a Wolfe character: "If [Trump] hadn't existed, Tom Wolfe would have had to invent him."[2] To the full extent that public attitudes toward the 1980s came up for reevaluation, so did Trump's image and reputation.

All of which is to say that the type of challenge faced by Trump was different, in kind, from any other treated in this book. He didn't just have to contend with a tangible and concrete problem—a downturn in the economy so severe that it nearly bankrupted him. On top of that, he had to wiggle out from under the rubble of an era he himself had symbolized.

Like other figures who loomed large in the 1980s—most notably junk-bond king Michael Milken—Trump hit setbacks that could easily have done him in. But Trump seems to have emerged, if not unscathed, then certainly *less* scathed than most of his contemporaries—and definitely in better odor than his critics would have predicted around 1990, when his fortunes hit rock bottom. Trump, by surviving these travails, has become a new-and-improved Trump, one who is subtly yet noticeably more conservative in his purchases and investments; one who has learned (by having been forced) to cede a certain amount of power to seasoned financial and business professionals within his organization; and one who now answers to public shareholders in some of his most highly prized properties.

The story of Trump's comeback and success is not one of self-flagellation and penitence, of public apologies and fire sales. Rather, it is the story of person coping with a new age, a new economy, and the need to make business decisions based on a different set of exigencies. In making this transition, Trump has begun once again to thrive—this time in an era he neither dominates nor defines. That should be okay with him, though, so long his investments and properties continue to mint coin—as most, if not all, of them were doing at this writing.

Not that business is Trump's sole concern these days. He considered a possible presidential run in 2000 on the ticket of the Reform Party (which supported diminutive Texas billionaire Ross Perot's bid in 1996). For a time, he thought he stood a realistic chance of winning: "Let's cut to the chase. Yes, I am considering a run for president. The reason has nothing to do with vanity, as some have suggested, nor do I merely wish to block other candidates. I will only run if I become convinced I can win, a decision I will make late this year."[3] Minnesota Governor Jesse Ventura (another Reform Party success story) at one time thought Trump should go for it. But not everyone applauded the 53-year-old

Trump's presidential aspirations. "The flirtation of the Trumpster, as he calls himself, is the apotheosis of our Gilded Age," wrote *New York Times* columnist Maureen Dowd disapprovingly. "Our politics is warped by money, celebrity, polling and crass behavior, and our culture is defined by stock-market high-rolling, boomer narcissism, niche marketing mania, rankings and a quiz show called 'Who Wants to Be a Millionaire?' "[4] In other words, Trump—in her view—was a horrible guy, but a horrible guy ideally suited to the mood of the nation.

Trump himself never doubted he was the ideal tenant for 1600 Pennsylvania Avenue. One of his main campaign proposals would have been the implementation of a one-time 14.25 percent tax on individuals and trusts worth in excess of $10 million in order to "pay off the national debt in a single year."[5] Despite the fact that he claims he personally would have had to fork over some $750 million in taxes under such a plan, Trump figured it would appeal to the vast hordes of working men and women in this country and make him a kind of populist hero. This, too, is ironic, because Trump has made much of his name and wealth backing superluxury projects that can be marketed solely to the upper reaches of the opulent. Ultimately, Trump concluded that the Reform Party was "a total mess" and shelved his presidential ambitions in February, 2000. Perhaps. But maybe his stepping back from the role of presidential candidate suggests the emergence of a new Trump, one who is trying to be more realistic in picking his projects—and perhaps even humble enough to know where not to tread.

Would Trump have made a viable president? Who knows? What's certain is that he has come a long way from the dark days of the late 1980s and early 1990s, when he seemed to be within spitting distance of bankruptcy and when his empire, by many accounts, was on the verge of crumbling. The media, which had built Trump up into a real estate wunderkind whose very touch ensured success, turned on him with a ferocity matched perhaps only by his former wife Ivana in their divorce proceedings. "For a high-rolling decade, Donald Trump was the King of Glitz. He built sumptuous casinos and gleaming apartment buildings, bought world-famous hotels and a fleet of planes—and plastered his name on everything," wrote *Time* magazine in a story called "Trump: The Fall" in 1990. "Now, just as suddenly, he's become a national object lesson in how fast those heavily borrowed fortunes and the fame that came with them can fade."[6] The *Wall Street Journal* jumped into the Trump-bashing game with a similar zeal:

> On paper, developer Donald Trump could be a perfect candidate to seek formal protection from creditors under Chapter 11 of the federal Bankruptcy Code. He owes money to a dizzying array of suppliers, banks, and bondholders, and hasn't any prospect of paying them off in full this year. Restive bondholders and casino suppliers have filed lawsuits and more are expected. If one bank should move to foreclose on Mr. Trump, others could follow in rapid succession. Bankruptcy court could provide an orderly way to keep creditors at bay while Mr. Trump attempted to put his financial affairs in order.[7]

1990 was indeed a grim year for Trump. "It's usually fun being The Donald," he recalls, "but in the early 1990s, trust me, it wasn't . . . I was many billions in the red." It was during 1990 that Trump suffered perhaps his most stinging moment of truth—a moment that by now has become the stuff of legend. Trump was walking down Manhattan's Fifth Avenue—site of his flagship development, the Trump Tower—with then–love interest Marla Maples. Trump spotted a blind beggar with a seeing-eye dog and pointed him out to Marla. "He's a beggar," Trump told Maples, "but he's worth $900 million more than me today." At the time, Trump was nearly $1 billion in the hole on debts he had personally guaranteed. As he put it, "My world began to tumble."

What had happened? How had the man who, perhaps more than any other single figure, had personified the go-go 1980s come to such bleak pastures? How had he let himself fall to a place where creditors were biting at his heels and the possibility of *personal* bankruptcy seemed not far off? For the answer, we need to look at Trump's life before the fall.

### An Early Role Model: Norman Vincent Peale

Donald John Trump was born on June 14, 1946, to Fred and Mary (MacLeod) Trump. Fred was the son of a hard-drinking Swedish immigrant who died when Fred was 11, leaving the boy an orphan. Fred Trump eventually began developing middle-class housing in New York City's outer boroughs (primarily Brooklyn and Queens) and in time put up some 24,000 apartments. This permitted him to amass a fortune of some $20 million and a 23-room house in the exclusive Jamaica Estates neighborhood of Queens, where Donald—one of five children—was born.

Trump's urge to build attention-capturing edifices manifested itself early. At the age of 8, Trump "borrowed" his brother Robert's toy blocks and glued them together to form a giant toy skyscraper. The blocks were never unglued and returned. (Any hard feelings seem to have passed; Robert is now a highly placed executive within the Trump Organization.)

Trump was deeply influenced by the minister at the family's church, the late Reverend Norman Vincent Peale. Peale became famous for espousing positive thinking, and his book, *The Power of Positive Thinking* (Prentice Hall, 1952), became an international best-seller. Trump was mesmerized by Peale's passion and enthusiasm. "You would leave church and say, 'Gee whiz, it's too bad that's over, I would love to hear some more,' " Trump recalled. For Trump, positive thinking has become a kind of mantra, something he claims has gotten him to the heights of success and helped him battle back from the depths of defeat: "You don't just say to yourself, 'I'm going to do it.' You never let the negative thoughts enter your mind."[8] Perhaps this Peale-influenced mode of thinking more than any other single element of Trump's personality has permitted him to remain a winner throughout three decades of professional life.

His father judged him something of a wild child (Trump's taste for sermons notwithstanding) and sent him packing to the New York Military Academy. The boy thrived there, becoming captain of the baseball team and head of a student regiment. In addition to nurturing fantasies of grandeur, Trump was also gaining valuable experience in something that would prove useful to him in both his rise and his comeback: the art of leadership.

Trump went on to study at New York's Fordham University and, eventually, gained a BA in economics from the prestigious Wharton School of Finance at the University of Pennsylvania. He graduated in 1968 at the head of his class. (Curiously, Trump seems to have little respect for whiz kids from top-ranked business schools, like Harvard and Wharton, preferring instead people with gritty, real-world experience.)

## Choosing Real Estate Because
## of "the Creativity Involved"

Upon graduating, Trump considered entering the oil business, but eventually decided to join up with his father in helping to run the Trump Organization. His job involved the refinancing of many of the company's apartment units; working together, he and his dad helped grow the Trump Organization's holdings significantly. "I learned a lot about real estate just through osmosis from my father," Trump has said, "but what really made it appeal to me as a career was the creativity involved."[9]

Trump began exercising that creativity on his own beginning in the early 1970s. His first major move was to secure options on several properties held by the Penn Central Railroad as it collapsed into bankruptcy. Trump not only got the chance to buy the failed company's railroad yards on the Upper West Side of Manhattan along the Hudson River, he also got a 60-year-old hotel called the Commodore that sat adjacent to Grand Central Station and was in a state of serious disrepair. Trump talked the city into giving him a 40-year, $120 million tax break on the property and the banks into giving him $70 million in finance capital. And he built the Grand Hyatt Hotel.

Trump's next big deal marked the beginning of a period that led to many of his troubles and may yet spell his greatest period of success. Starting in the mid-1970s, he began investing in land in Atlantic City, New Jersey, prior to the legalization of gambling in 1976. He bought the land quietly, a few parcels a time.[10] Trump says he would send a different employee to represent his interests based in part on the ethnicity of the seller. Thus, if the seller were Italian-American, "we sent an Italian."[11] Already, Trump had learned that making it in the world of business took more than a knowledge of numbers and balance sheets. He was beginning to appreciate the fact that business has a softer, less calculable side, one requiring a subtle grasp of psychology and interpersonal dynamics. For someone who says he's never even considered psychotherapy, Trump nonetheless has acquired a sophisticated understanding of how other people's minds work—especially in business and financial dealings. And he's used it to considerable advantage. By the early 1980s, the land he bought was worth over $20 million, and today, he has emerged as arguably the major player in developing and running casino properties in Atlantic City.

❀   ❀   ❀

Trump won his niche in the mogul hall of fame with a single deal in 1979. He had for several years been eyeing the lease on the Bonwit Teller department store on Manhattan's Fifth Avenue, at Fifty-seventh Street, but to no avail. Then, in 1979, a new chairman took the reins at Genesco, Bonwit's parent, and offered to sell the lease to Trump. Trump jumped at the chance to secure a property in such close proximity to the exclusive Tiffany & Company retailer, also nearby on Fifth Avenue. "If you go to Paris, if you go to Duluth," holds Trump, "the best location is called the 'Tiffany location.' That is a standard real estate phrase." Trump, it appeared, would get not only *a* Tiffany location but *the* Tiffany location. In so doing, he trusted his gut and his years of formal and informal exposure to the New York real estate market. Trump likes to say that it requires a very special kind of knowledge and toughness to make real estate deals in New York, a rarified something that can't be gained anywhere else in the world. Furthermore, Trump says that he learned at his "father's knee" the following truism about buying and selling property in Manhattan: "New York is a minefield, and if you don't know what you're doing, you will get screwed."

Trump envisioned a grand edifice on the Bonwit Teller site, housing prime retail and business space and luxury condominiums. He lined up as his partner the Equitable Life Assurance Society, which owned the land, and secured the necessary credit from the Chase Manhattan bank. Though the deal was progressing smoothly, Trump was about to encounter his first landmine. He applied for a residential tax abatement under Section 421-A of New York's real property law. But the city turned down Trump's request, arguing that the statute was intended to encourage low- and middle-income housing rather than the super-high-end pads Trump dreamed of erecting.

Trump knew that giving up was no way to make it in the fierce world of New York City real estate. So he hired notorious lawyer Roy Cohn as his advocate. After losing his case in the Supreme Court Appellate Division, Trump later was awarded a huge tax abatement (amounting to some $50 million) by the Court of Appeals. He was only 33 years old. In using the courts to achieve his ends, Trump was also defining a strategy that has served him well: Fight back. Always fight back until you win.

Three years later, his grand 68-story Trump Tower, at the time the tallest and most expensive reinforced concrete structure in New York City, opened to great fanfare. It has a six-floor atrium, an 80-foot waterfall, a host of top-notch retailers, and a lobby known for its luxurious pink marble. Trump Tower reportedly draws 100,000 visitors each day and has boasted such residents as Johnny Carson and Steven Spielberg.

But while the public face of Trump Tower suggests glitz and glamour, behind the pink marble and dazzling finery are solid numbers worked out by a person who knows how to make high-end real estate profitable. In 1988, by one estimate, Trump had made a cool $100 million on the Trump Tower deal, while his partner, Equitable Life Assurance, raked in slightly less, say, $90 million.

The possibility of profits did not stop there, however, because after most of the condominiums had been sold, Trump bought or retained ownership of much of the office and shopping space—not to mention his own three-floor apartment plus five floors of condos he could rent to tenants. Space for which Trump originally had paid $45 million was now paying him some $30 million annually. The Tower became one big glass-covered annuity for him personally.

Take the deal that resulted in his possession of 40 Wall Street. The 72-story building, one of the tallest in lower Manhattan, was built in 1929 and was, for a brief time, the tallest building in the world. The building's fortunes rose and fell with the Depression and the recovery of the U.S. economy; by the 1960s and 1970s, the skyscraper was fully occupied and doing well. "Sprawling law firms and big banks were its primary tenants," said Trump. "It was a hot property."[12]

So hot, in fact, that in the early 1980s it was purchased by the soon-to-be-besieged premier of the Philippines, Ferdinand Marcos (who was then busy acquiring New York real estate). Marcos's involvement complicated matters, however. "The problem was that when it came time to renew or extend [his] leases, it was virtually impossible—due to lack of management and the nagging legal question as to who, in fact, owned the building. Marcos claimed he owned it. But the people of the Philippines claimed Marcos had bought the building with money stolen from them, and therefore, it was owned by the Philippines," said Trump.[13]

What resulted was a bidding frenzy for the troubled but potentially lucrative property. Though the company Jack Resnick and Son seemed initially to be the winner, the property was eventually purchased by the Kinson Company, a Hong Kong outfit that was mainly in the apparel and footwear business. After the Kinson deal was settled, Trump approached the Hong Kong investors with idea of forging a partnership of some kind. Unfortunately, the Kinson people and Trump had different views as to what to do with the building. Trump felt the building could be left more or less alone, though spruced up externally and made more habitable. The Kinson people had other ideas. They wanted to gut the inside of the lobby and create a Trump Tower–like atrium, even though the location did not lend itself to such a plan and doing so would actually require moving several of the load-bearing steel columns that supported the building.

Trump then walked away from the table and left the Kinson folks to their own devices. Without much experience in New York real estate, Kinson began pouring millions of dollars into renovations and re-designs. Yet all of it seemed to amount to nothing more than pouring money into a vast, bottomless pit. The contractors and architects hired by Kinson were getting richer, but the building was coming no closer to being reborn. The Kinson people were also having trouble dealing with the Hinneberg family, which owned the land under 40 Wall Street. Basically, the Kinson group wanted out via as easy and quick a route as possible. So they approached Trump.

It was at this point that Trump struck a masterful deal. He realized he had the experience and expertise to revivify the 1.3-million-square-foot building and that the beleaguered Kinson people were simply seeking an exit strategy. So he offered them $1 million for the building. One million dollars. That was less than many of the individual condos in Trump Tower sold for. "They accepted my terms—without a complaint! I was stunned. They just wanted to go home. They'd lost their shirts—vast sums of money—battling in New York real estate," recalls Trump.[14]

Trump immediately worked out a new and favorable lease with the Hinnebergs, extending the term from just 63 years to over 200. He then settled all of the $4.5 million in liens and trade payables on the building, not to mention $400,000 worth of insurance claims. The closing took place on November 30, 1995, and Trump was the proud owner of 40 Wall Street. More importantly, he held a property, acquired for a song, that now had the potential to become a money-generating machine for him, not unlike Trump Tower. Trump says he expects to earn some $20 million annually from rentals at 40 Wall Street. "Not bad for a building that cost me less than $1 million." In characteristic style, Trump rechristened his property the Trump Building at 40 Wall Street, and placed bronze lettering atop a new granite facade to let the world know who was now in charge. In the new age of his comeback, Trump seems to have retained a knack for self-promotion and the moxie to make it happen.

## The Midas Touch Wears Off

How did Trump, with all of his business know-how, ever slip from the heights of greatness in the first place? The answer is a bad combination of a downturn in the U.S. economy, overly eager lending institutions, and, for Trump, a lack of self-control buttressed by a belief that anything he touched would turn to gold.

The first signs that Trump's boom period might be coming to an end began to make themselves manifest in 1989. Specifically, it was Trump's prize casino developments in Atlantic City that began to threaten his empire. Trump had acquired three casino-hotels in the New Jersey seaside locale, which has been described as decaying and poorly served by public transportation: the Trump Taj Mahal, the Trump Plaza, and the Trump Castle (later the Marina). Of the three, it was the Taj Mahal that began causing Trump his greatest woes.

Trump acquired the Taj Mahal somewhat inadvertently in 1987. That year, he bought $96 million worth of class B stock in an ailing hotel and casino company called Resorts International. Even though this represented only 12 percent of Resorts' equity, it endowed Trump with 90 percent of the company's voting power. Trump had intended to buy out the rest of the public stock at $22 per share and take the company private in a very 1980s-style buyout. However, "out of nowhere," according to Trump, former talk show host and would-be entrepreneur Merv Griffin came forward with a competing deal to offer Resorts shareholders $35 per share. Trump had no intention of besting Griffin's inflated offer, but was able to get him to negotiate. The deal that followed left Trump with $12 million in cash and an unfinished behemoth of a casino, the Taj Mahal, into which Resorts had poured some $500 million before selling it to Trump for $288 million.

Trump was now faced with an enormous casino that needed further construction and financing, an economy that was starting to slow down, and little cash on hand. In order to finance the construction of the Taj Mahal—which, at 120,000 square feet, was scheduled to be three-and-a-half times the size of its namesake in India—Trump formed a partnership (with himself as sole limited partner) and issued $675 million in junk bonds. Those bonds called for hefty interest payments semiannually, so it was essential to get the Taj Mahal up and running, throwing off plenty of cash to service Trump's large and growing debt load. But Trump was twice forced to delay the opening of the Taj Mahal; the casino was to open in December 1989, but was subsequently pushed to February and then to April 1990.

The other problem was that, even with the Taj opening, it was uncertain that the huge casino would solve all of Trump's problems. In fact, it threatened to create more. Although the casino, with its minarets and huge onion-shaped dome, would certainly draw its share of crowds, experts estimated that the Taj Mahal would have to generate revenues in excess of $1 million per day just to break even. Trouble was, this meant doing about 15 percent better business than the highest-grossing casino in Atlantic City (which happened to be the Trump Plaza). Overall, the Taj added 20 percent to the capacity of Atlantic City's gaming market, but industry experts predicted only a 7 percent increase in demand. "Those numbers just do not add up," said a casino industry executive at the time.[15] For its part, the Taj continued to consume money, about $1 billion, in order to become a viable entity. And even if the Taj Mahal, with its 211 gaming tables and 4,152 slot machines, did succeed beyond nearly everyone's expectations, it still threatened to cannibalize crowds away from Trump's other Atlantic City casino properties.

Trump then went on a spending spree, even though by the late 1980s his Atlantic City developments were beginning to weigh him down with debt. He bought the famous Plaza Hotel in Manhattan for $408 million (a price some observers said was too high) and the Eastern Airlines shuttle for $365 million. To make these and other acquisitions possible, he borrowed still more. Then, less than a year after its purchase, the Trump Shuttle lost $85 million, making it hard to unload. This was due in part to a 5 percent downturn in shuttle service passengers as the nation entered a recession. In addition, the Plaza Hotel was to lose $100 million in the two years following Trump's purchase and eventually failed to provide enough money to cover the full interest payments on its $430 million debt.

Trump had bet all along that the junk-bond market would hold up, permitting him to refinance his billions in bond debt at more favorable rates. However, just as Trump began to feel a serious need to do just that, the junk-bond market fell apart. He was busy shelling out millions to improve and refurbish his Atlantic City properties, but could not raise the liquidity to keep it all going. The result was that in 1990, he unexpectedly found himself unable to refinance junk bonds and bank loans for which he *personally* was liable—to the tune of some $2 billion.

By the middle of 1990, Trump was in trouble. He needed money to keep his complex of enterprises running, but his businesses weren't throwing off enough cash to do that; nor, as previously mentioned, were the capital markets working in his favor. In the second quarter of 1990, just as Trump was in his worst financial pinch, the Taj Mahal reported a pretax operating loss of $15 million—a figure that did not include some $75 million owed to contractors or the $30 million that still needed to be sunk into the place to finish it. In addition, though the Taj was attracting hordes of gamblers, it was not doing break-even business. Accordingly, Trump let on that he might, for the first time in his professional life, miss a debt-service payment. "This announcement reverberated around the world," recalls Trump with characteristic hyperbole.

## Trump's Bankers Wake Up—And Stop Lending Him Money

So Trump turned back to the banks that had lent him much of his money in the first place and asked for more. Specifically, he needed $65 million to meet bond payments that were looming large and close. The banks agreed and gave him an immediate injection of $20 million to meet his payments. In return, Trump had to begin selling off assets— notably his 282-foot yacht, the *Trump Princess,* which he had acquired from beleaguered Saudi businessman Adnan Khashoggi. Perhaps more humiliating was the fact that Trump now was forced to live on a paltry allowance of $450,000 per month—not bad by most people's standards, but meager rations for the 1980s poster boy.

However, if Trump were partly to blame for erecting a huge mountain of debt that was often disorganized or spread among myriad lenders, his bankers were perhaps equally to blame for his financial woes in 1990. In many cases, the banks had made *undersecured* loans to Trump, meaning that they had demanded less collateral than they should have, given the amount of money they were lending him. They were, it seems, in Trump's thrall and figured he could do no wrong. "The bankers got mesmerized. They thought it was almost an honor to lend to Donny," explained a fellow New York developer. "Based on his track record, the banks opened their wallets to Trump, seemingly without undertaking the normal financial analysis." An attorney who worked with Trump said: "Donald Trump could have walked into any bank and said, 'I want $25 million,' and nobody would ask for a financial statement. They'd say, 'Donald Trump, $25 million? Done!' "[16]

To be fair, some of Trump's key lenders, Citibank chief among them, felt that they had been adequately prudent in lending to Trump and began speaking out publicly to defend their banking practices. "While we can't speak for the other banks, we believe our loans were not imprudent," held Frank Creamer, head of real estate lending at Citibank. "They were consistent with our underwriting standards and based upon the value of the specific assets, giving effect to Trump's proven ability to take existing assets and add substantial value through capital improvements and improved marketing efforts. . . . We believe that over time, the long-term values of Trump's assets will be realized, proving us to have made the right decision."[17]

In effect, money center banks like Citibank had to stand by Trump, because if they pulled the rug out from under him they themselves stood to tumble. Like the Chrysler corporation of the late 1970s, Trump had grown almost "too big to fail." And acting as his own Lee Iacocca, he argued that point persuasively. "Listen fellows," Trump recalls saying, "if I have a problem, then *you* have a problem. We have to find a way out or it's going to be a difficult time for both of us."

If the banks moved to foreclose on Trump's properties, they might find the values of those properties seriously diminished without Trump's name attached to them. In the case of his casinos, any prospective owner would have to go through the costly and time-consuming process of reapplying for gambling licenses from the state of New Jersey. So when push came to shove, the banks—though Trump still owed them millions—were forced to stand by him and to live with the decisions they had made. They not only helped Trump restructure his loans and reduce his personal debt from over $900 million to a little over $100 million, they gave him five years to turn his operations around.

## Buried under Debt

Time is exactly what Trump needed. By November 1990, he was in default on $345 million in bank loans on two of his casinos and the Trump Shuttle. At about the same time, the Taj Mahal reported a net operating loss of $11 million, despite record revenues for the quarter ended October 31, 1990. In addition, Trump Castle casino had a loss of $7 million for the quarter, compared with a profit of $7 million a year earlier. The Trump Plaza casino's profits dropped by almost 70 percent from $16 million to $5 million.

Certainly, Trump may have had himself to blame for making some imprudent business decisions. But his near-demise was also precipitated by forces beyond his control. Trump regards the economy of the early 1990s—the one that almost drove him into personal bankruptcy—as staggeringly bad, even in retrospect, even beyond what most people thought at the time. "I personally witnessed the end of the real estate market and the beginning of what I term the Great Depression of 1990. That's right: I use the word *depression*. It was not a recession. It was, in fact, a depression, more severe than anything that had taken place since the early 1930s," said Trump.[18]

Whatever one wishes to call it—recession, depression, or cyclical downturn—the truth is that it continued to ravage Trump throughout 1990 and 1991, with his debt later reported to have been a whopping $8 billion. In mid-1991, about a year after his first life-saving, $65 million deal with his bankers, Trump sought and was given a new pact to help ease his troubles. The new accord forced Trump to sell more assets, such as the Trump Shuttle airline (which eventually went to

USAir Group), plus a number of other properties. The deal also forced some of Trump's casino bondholders to accept a greatly reduced interest rate on their securities in return for 50 percent of the casino's equity. He was also forced to work out new terms for the Plaza Hotel, the crown jewel of his empire. The trouble with the Plaza was that it had lost $100 million between 1989 and 1991 and was failing to pay full interest on its $430 million debt. In 1990, "cash from operations fell short of covering interest expense by about $20 million."[19] The banks, which had initially supplied Trump with the $400 million plus he needed to buy the Plaza from the Robert M. Bass Group of Texas, agreed to defer some $7 million in interest payments. (Citicorp now owns 49 percent of the beautifully restored and majestic old hotel.) Still, going into the Plaza, at the price he did, proved one of Trump's least-shrewd moves. Knowing what the cash flow from the property was likely to be, Trump agreed to terms that necessitated a higher income stream than he was ever likely to see.

By late 1991, things began looking up, if only slightly. The bonds on his Atlantic City casinos soared from their 1990 lows. Taj Mahal bonds doubled in price; Trump Castle's bonds shot up 81 percent, and Trump Plaza's debentures went up by 66 percent. And in the fourth quarter of 1991, operating profits at the Taj rose 70 percent, to $22 million. Trump Castle earned $4.6 million, versus a $600,000 loss in the last quarter of 1990; and profits at the Trump Plaza were up sevenfold, to $7.8 million.

Even so, Trump was far from being out of the woods. The total debts on his Atlantic City casinos still outweighed their market value. The Taj Mahal, with a total debt of $746 million, was valued by analysts at $475 million; the Trump Castle carried a debt burden of $380 million, compared to its market value of around $200 million; and the Trump Plaza, arguably the healthiest of the lot, carried $272 million of debt, versus its market value of about $250 million. In December 1990, Trump suffered perhaps the ultimate humiliation. His father bought $3 million worth of chips at one of Trump's casinos and left the chips in the cage so that Trump would not fall short of an impending bond payment on Trump's Castle.

Trump's fate was anything but sure as the early months of 1992 rolled on. "The name is a punchline now, associated with the worst of 1980s extravagance, egomania, and greed. Once, the world marveled at the scope and mastery of Trump's megabuck deals. Today, he's widely regarded as a washed-up real estate mogul who has been stripped of his once lustrous possessions."[20] In March 1992, Trump completed the final portions of his debt restructuring. The complex maneuverings permitted him to reduce his debt by a third (all but ensuring that cash flows from his operations would cover his interest expenses), stay out of bankruptcy court, and reduce his personal debt—that which was backed only by his word and signature—by a significant sum.

Still, Trump's finances were open to question. In early 1992, *BusinessWeek* estimated Trump's net worth to be a negative $1.4 billion. The ever-plucky and optimistic Trump, on the other hand, claimed to be worth a positive $1.5 billion. The trouble with assessing Trump's net worth is and always has been the fact that his Trump Organization is a privately held patchwork of complex ownership patterns and joint ventures. Trying to fish the truth out of Trump's financials is like trying to find Waldo in a sea of faces.

## Changing His Management Team and Reinventing Himself

Throughout all this, Trump was changing, recasting himself from brash investor to rational manager. This was in part a result of the emergency restructuring. The banks, as one of their restructuring demands, insisted that Trump hire a chief financial officer. Trump wisely selected Stephen Bollenbach, CFO for Holiday Corporation, whom he had spotted on a magazine cover. Bollenbach was a good businessperson, a tough negotiator, and had the kind of mind that could master the myriad details of Trump's complex restructuring deals, making sure they all made sense and worked out favorably in the end. "Steve could say no with the coldest steel in his eyes, and nobody would get mad at him. That's what I wanted." Trump said.[21] It was Bollenbach who engineered the beginning of Trump's comeback by advising him to send the $800,000-per-quarter insurance premiums for his *Trump Princess* yacht to the mortgage holder, the Bank of Boston, the idea being that if the boat sank uninsured, the mortgager would be left with no collateral. The ploy worked, and demonstrated to the financial world that if Trump were to come back it would be as much on his own terms as possible. Bollenbach was helping Trump to realize that bankers who were barking at his back could be turned into allies; he helped Trump to see that the way out was by talking the banks into working *with* him rather than against him. "Bollenbach's key insight was that Trump's bankers and investors were handcuffed to the legend they had helped create."[22]

Bollenbach did such a good job, in fact, that he later was tapped by the financially troubled Marriott Corporation hotel chain to serve as its chief of finance in 1991. He currently is president and CEO of Hilton. In addition to helping Trump clean up his finances and stay afloat, though, Bollenbach's presence seems to have instilled in Trump a new sense of discipline and rigor. He appears to have helped Trump recognize the need to streamline and rationalize operations. This had been a major shortcoming of Trump's in the years leading up to his financial crises:

> Calling his enterprise the Trump Organization is oxymoronic—one former employee calls it the Trump Disorganization. In truth it is little more than one man's investment portfolio. Over 15 years Trump's expanding collection of businesses has become a queer jumble of free-standing operations badly in need of coherent management. The next phase in Trump's career will be a public test of his ability as a manager.23

As the U.S. economy slowly began to recover from its moribund state, so too did Trump. In 1993, Trump announced that he'd be coming to the market with two new junk-bond offerings. Underwritten by Merrill Lynch, these offerings would give investors a shot at $375 million in new notes, some of which were rated below the debt they currently held. Of the total, $315 million were 8-year mortgage notes and $60 million were 10-year payment-in-kind (PIK) notes (so called because they pay out further securities, not cash). The mortgage notes yielded about 11.5 percent, while the PIK notes yielded over 13 percent. The point is that Trump was back. He had successfully come to market with new junk-bond securities based on assets in his portfolio. The wave of disgust and distrust that had characterized the attitude of both the public and the financial world for the past few years was beginning to subside.

With his usual acuity at estimating public opinion, Trump decided to lose no time in reinventing himself—from poster child of the recession to poster child of the 1990s comeback (even as the rock band Aerosmith was angling for this very distinction). Late in 1993, things began to look even cheerier. "Donald Trump is close to agreements with his bankers and bondholders that may allow him to recapture full ownership of his casinos, take his gambling empire public, then retire the roughly $200 million in personal debt left over from his massive 1991 bailout," reported the *Wall Street Journal*.[24] In addition, bondholders of the Taj Mahal agreed to a swap, exchanging $750 million in existing debt for $692 million in new, higher-yielding bonds that came with cash interest payments, plus about $75 million in cash. It seemed certain that Trump, by focusing on his core money-making businesses in Atlantic City, ceding power to talented, professional managers like Bollenbach (and, later Nick Ribis, whom Trump appointed president of his casinos), and looking to the future rather than being mired in the past, would emerge once again a winner. Looking back at the personal transition that accompanied his financial machinations, Trump wrote, "I learned a lot about myself during these hard times; I learned about handling pressure. I was able to home in, buckle down, get back to basics, and make things work."[25]

His period of torment, Trump says, also taught him much about loyalty—a quality he prizes every bit as highly as any mob boss. "There were people that I would have guaranteed would have stuck by me who didn't, and, on other hand, people who I had *made* who, when it came time to help me, didn't lift a finger," said Trump. Trump singles out fellow New York real estate developer Sam LeFrak as someone who was warm and fuzzy when things were good but backstabbing when the walls began to close in. According to Trump, LeFrak was "openly happy" about the dismal state of his affairs in the early 1990s. When things began to turn around, LeFrak suddenly evinced a new interest in his friendship, calling up, according to Trump, "for anything, breakfast, lunch, dinner—just any kind of association." Rather than grant LeFrak audience, though, Trump replied with his usual swagger and pugnacity. He sent the elderly LeFrak a copy of an article in which LeFrak had "slightly derided" him in Trump's estimation. "On top of the article I wrote just two words: 'Fuck You,' " recounts Trump.[26]

Trump has never been afraid to play hardball, and seems willing to go to practically any length to right a perceived wrong or deliver his own version of divine retribution. Turning the other cheek just isn't his style. It can be argued that this trait has caused him to burn bridges, to put ego ahead of business. But it also makes him able to put up a self-confident persona to the world, a persona on which he can trade. Being hard, fighting back, and erecting a tough exterior are more than psychological qualities. For Trump, they are essential business tools that have played a key role in his success and his comeback.

Consider Trump's attitude toward Kinson, the Hong Kong company that failed miserably at rehabilitating 40 Wall Street and eventually sold it to him for a mere $1 million. "You've got to negotiate tough, and you cannot, at any time, let anyone take advantage of you, the way people had taken advantage of the Kinson execs. Suddenly, word gets out on the street that you're a pushover—or worse—and whoosh! You're history."[27] These aren't merely words to Trump, for if they were, he'd have been down and out many years ago. For better or for worse, they are an ideology, a marching strategy that keeps him going—even if it means sending an obscene note to an old man from time to time.

## The Art of the Comeback

By 1994, Trump was poised to snatch New York's most famous landmark—the Empire State Building. Health was returning to the American economy and to Manhattan's in particular. Yet this time Trump—made wiser by the heavy price he'd paid for his 1980s acquisition spree—defrayed his risk, and stalked his prey with partners. They included French-born investment banker Jean Paul Renoir, Renoir's wife, and her father, an 81-year-old Tokyo real estate magnate named Hideki Yokoi, among others. Trump created Trump Empire State Partners as an owning agent, though the financial details of the transaction are unclear.

An even greater illustration of Trump's comeback, however, is his ongoing development of the West Side rail yards, a 76-acre plot of land stretching from Fifty-ninth Street to Seventy-second Street in Manhattan along the Hudson River. Trump acquired the rights to the yards back in the 1970s, bought the land, sold it, and then repurchased it in the early 1980s from Argentine businessman Francesco Macri. Trump envisions it as the largest commercial/residential development in New York since Battery Park City, a project that, unlike Trump's, relied on significant public funding. When complete, the West Side development will contain 5,700 apartments, 1.8 million square feet of commercial space, parking areas for 3,500 cars, and a 25-acre park. Noted architect Philip Johnson is playing a major role in the land development.

Here again, Trump has chosen to defray his risk. Rather than go it alone, as he once did with his Atlantic City properties, he is using partners—this time from Asia—and is proceeding with them in a joint venture. He is working with a group called Polylinks, a consortium representing the interests of six of the wealthiest families in Hong Kong. Trump will retain roughly a 40 percent stake in the development and will not have to shell out an additional penny on the project. Trump has also learned a degree of very uncharacteristic humility. He has deferred to his Asian peers on several important design issues. In fact, the project will built according to the principles of *feng shui,* the Eastern principle of balancing elements to strike a delicate harmony between people and their built environment. Some suggest that the deal has forced Trump to open his mind, to pay attention, to cede the position of expert to others, when necessary. "People say you can't talk to Donald, that he's closed-minded, but that's not true. He learns very quickly and has an innate sense about whom to listen to," according to Susan Cara, a New York real estate agent who was central in orchestrating the Polylinks deal. For his part, Trump is ecstatic about the new project, which he calls "The Really Big One."[28] "This is the biggest fucking deal in the history of New York real estate. And it's the best deal I've ever made,"[29] says Trump, demonstrating that he's still got a goodly dollop of the swagger, self-confidence, and occasional coarseness that characterized him at his height during the 1980s.

Trump was also able to bring another of his greatest assets to the West Side project—a deep knowledge of how to navigate the red tape and political details of financing a complex undertaking in New York City, the minefield of potential hurdles for the would-be developer. Many years before, he had stepped in and taken over the construction of the Wollman skating rink in New York City's Central Park. After local government had dithered with the project for seven years—spending some $20 million—Trump got skaters happily shooshing along the ice again in just four months' time. Total cost: $2 million. Recently, when community opposition threatened to derail his West Side project, Trump skillfully managed all the power players of city government—no mean feat—and eventually, after making some concessions, saw his plans approved by a New York City Council vote of 42 to 8. He has shown himself ready and able to address the needs of constituencies outside of his own hungry id.

In 1995, Trump added another new set of constituents to his list: public shareholders. That year, he floated $150 million in common stock for his Trump Plaza casino in Atlantic City. He also sold $140 million in bonds (10-year senior notes). Though stock is something relatively new to the Trump mix, it forces him to play by the rules of business that other chiefs of publicly held enterprises must also follow: developing a clear and logical business plan, keeping expenses and debts down, and recognizing that the livelihoods of many others depend on his business decisions. These are lessons that the gimme-gimme Trump of the 1980s might have been loathe to accept. Trump used the money from the stock offerings to pay off his $115-million personal debt load and pare down some of the Trump Plaza's heavy financial burdens, as well. Six months after its issue, the casino stock had risen over 50 percent in value. Trump eventually merged his Taj Mahal and Castle (now called the Trump Marina) into the Plaza company that had issued the stock, permitting a streamlining of operations and a greater capital base. Trump's three Atlantic City resort casinos have received four stars from the *Mobile Travel Guide* and four diamonds from AAA. Trump's casino company also owns a floating casino in Buffington Harbor, Indiana, near Chicago, suggesting that Trump may one day be a major national, rather than regional, player in the development of gaming properties.

## "I Got a Little Too Complacent"

By 1996, Trump was breathing a sigh of relief, if not actually dancing for joy. His empire was beginning to emerge from its maelstrom of debt and obligations. His heavily leveraged casino properties were helping him ring up more money than a bank of slot machines at the hands of 100 superstitious gamblers.

Only five years after suffering what critics and rivals had hoped would be a fatal fall, Trump had staged a stunning upset, thanks largely to the rebound of Atlantic City gambling. By the late 1990s, the once-dumpy seaside resort was taking in some $3.7 billion a year from gaming—20 percent more than the Vegas strip. Of those fat winnings, some

30 percent—an estimated $1.2 billion a year—went straight to Trump. The value of his shares in Trump Hotels & Casino Resorts appreciated to $375 million, and suddenly such would-be competitors as Mirage, Circus Circus, and ITT were pounding on the Boardwalk to get in. On top of his Atlantic City properties, Trump had other trophies, including Manhattan's Grand Hyatt. Not only had he climbed out of his $900 million black hole, but he now was worth at least $700 million.

It didn't hurt that the U.S. economy was picking up steam, heading into perhaps its strongest period of robust health since the 1950s. Despite this, Trump was learning not to count his chickens and to evince a new humility (if, in Trump's case, one can call it that). "I got a little too complacent. I definitely blame myself for it. I came out of Wharton and it was, like, boom! Fifteen years of unbroken success. One thing after another. And I got to thinking, this is easy. I just didn't work like I used to," Trump said.[30] He may also have been chastened by the collapse of his second marriage, to actress and model Marla Maples, which was also announced in 1997.

All of which is not to say that Trump is totally in the clear. While net revenues of his Trump Hotels & Casino Resorts, Inc., were up slightly for the nine months ended September 30, 1999, to $1.1 billion, net income fell precipitously, from negative $23.3 million to negative $99.3 million. The company's stock, of which Trump owns a little under 16 million shares (some 40 percent of the equity), is presently languishing in the $2- to $3-dollar range. Standard & Poor's, the debt-rating agency, downgraded his debt from a rating of B– to CCC+. And Trump has a long way to go to pay off Trump Hotels' $1.8 billion in debts and obligations. "No one is ever going to lend him another dime," the *New York Post* quotes a source as saying.[31] Trump was also slammed for rejecting a buyout bid from a Los Angeles–based investment firm that would have given ailing stockholders between $12 and $15 for their shares. If Trump wants to see his casino company recover fully, he'll have to watch spending, keep good management in place, and hope the economy stays healthy. Meantime, he seems to have an inexhaustible supply of 20-something girlfriends to keep his spirits up.

Donald Trump made the ultimate transition. From cultural icon to . . . well, just another highly leveraged rich guy trying to make a go of it in the tough world of American commerce. Hopefully, he has learned his lessons and learned them well. If he wants to stay on the comeback trail, he knows—or should know—what he needs to do. No more capricious spending to acquire assets that he has no business owning and that bring with them more potentially ruinous debt; a careful selection of which deals to do and which deals to stay out of, no matter what his generous ego demands; and an increased emphasis on the tough task of being the rational manager of a large business empire. If he wants history to remember him as the comeback kid—and it's almost certain that Trump wants history to remember him somehow—he may have to get used to being something he never was during his heyday: a businessperson who has to play by the rules just like everyone else.

Don King

✦ ☷◈☷ ✦

# Don King

*Founder of Don King Productions*

*"I totally eradicated the word* failure *from my vocabulary."*

I MAGINE YOU ENTER the ballroom of a hotel. The room is filled with prominent male executives dressed in similarly styled tuxedos. All stand 6 feet, 4 inches, weigh over 250 pounds, and are approaching 70 years of age. For all intents and purposes, these captains of industry are indistinguishable from one another—all the same height, same weight, and same hulky build. But as you scan the crowd, a curious feature of one man arouses your interest: the *hair.* The thick head of hair seems to be standing straight on end, as though the strands had been coated with an electrically charged hair cream and the room's ceiling concealed a powerful electromagnet.

By now the man has realized that your gaze rests squarely on him. He pushes his way through the throng and heads in your direction. As he moves closer, you notice that the top of his gravity-defying hair displays what appears to be a powdered white ring, and for a moment you wonder if it's a halo. When he's a few feet away, you recognize he is the famously infamous boxing promoter, Don King—and therefore it could not be a halo, because no one has ever used the terms *angelic* or *saintly* to describe this controversial businessperson. Still, the white markings cry out for characterization, and you struggle for an instant, trying to find the right word. As he approaches, a wide affable smile sweeps his face, and he says, "Hi, I'm Don King." You realize that the white ring sits on his head like wisps of a royal crown.

King and his crown of hair have once again succeeded in pushing through the crowded clutter of other people. You do not have to bother with the other executives in attendance but you can't ignore this man, because King has done what he has always done best—he has won your undivided attention. The large mitt of a friendly hand—covered in fancy jewelry—pumps yours, and now perhaps you'd like to move on, but King places a paternal arm around your shoulder in a bear hug and begins talking. The conversation is part evangelical sermon, part literary quotations from Shaw and Shakespeare, and also part street-patter hustle. It's an impromptu spiel because King has something he wants to sell you: that he's a very successful businessman and, together, the two of you can find a deal to make money.

It is important at the outset to state that King is an African American, and although race is important to his story, it is also incidental. The rise and fall and rise of King to become the preeminent boxing promoter of the last half of the twentieth century is not filled with the any of the racial ground-shattering impact or high moral purpose of Jackie Robinson's breakthrough into professional baseball or Arthur Ashe's entry into tennis. Yet it does mark the first time in America that an African American boxing promoter has reaped the riches and fame that for decades had been the purview of whites. King's critics—who are vocal and numerous—would say that racial equality in the sport of boxing should not be proclaimed because a black man instead of a white man generated millions of dollars of blood-stained purse money from his stable of black and white fighters.

King instinctively follows the age-old adage that if you don't vote for yourself, don't expect others to vote for you. He has crowed about his achievements: "Every day of my life is history. I've broken every record known to man in promotion: I've had the first $1,000,000 fight sold on TV, the first billion-people audience for one of my spectaculars, I've done more than 200 world-title fights, and no one has touched that from Tex Richard to P. T. Barnum."[1]

Larry Holmes, former world heavyweight champion, and a boxer who made money with Don King and later sued, said, "Don looks black, lives white, and thinks green." Seth Abraham, who was associated with King for many years until they had a falling out, said, "Don King is the most brilliant mind I have ever encountered. Don King is formidable in his sleep."

It is essential to remember that King promoted and named two of the greatest heavyweight title fights of this century—the third Muhammad Ali–Joe Frazier fight, called the "Thriller in Manila," and the Ali–George Foreman "Rumble in the Jungle" in Zaire. Even his harshest critics generously admit that without King, one or both of these events might not have occurred. Others, of favorable opinion, might say the King made these bouts happen by dint of his vision, his hard work, and business savvy. With Don King, there is always disagreement about what is true and what is not, a sort of they said versus he said. The one point of agreement among critics and fans is that King has always made money for himself: lots of money.

What makes King different from other self-made American millionaires—black or white—is that he had to overcome the stigma of a long jail sentence. Not the penal judgment that comes from white-collar crimes such as embezzlement, racketeering, or stock fraud, where the time served is at one of the "country club" Federal prisons. No, Don King did almost four years in an Ohio jail for manslaughter, and that death marked the second time in his life that he had killed another man.

After being released from prison in 1971 at age 40, King rose from obscurity to become one of the most successful businesspeople in the United States. By 1973, a scant two years after finishing his sentence, he was a millionaire. Like the boxer who is dealt a bone-crushing blow and falls to the canvas for what everyone is sure is a knock out, King rose at the count of nine and came back for the battle of his life. King would break through the anonymity that had historically cloaked African American businesspeople and become the only African American executive recognized in both black and white America. "My life is an incongruity and a contradiction to what America thinks is success. I started not at zero, but subzero. As a black man, I'm one of those who've been dispossessed, disenfranchised, left out somehow."

"No one can judge me by my accomplishments but by how far I have come. I had to crawl from below the ground just to get to the starting line."

## Early Years: Selling Peanuts, Then Running Numbers

Donald King was born in 1931 in an all-black neighborhood of Cleveland, Ohio, the fifth of seven children of Hattie and Clarence King. His father died in a freak accident at a steel mill, and the family survived for a few years on the insurance payments ("tragedy money," as King called it). But when the settlement money ran out, the entire family started to pitch in to earn extra income. His mother and sister baked pies and roasted peanuts, which the brothers would bag and sell in the neighborhood.

But the brothers found an inventive way to sell more bags more quickly than anyone else. They would put a scrap of paper with a number penciled on it inside each bag and hawk these "lucky" bags at the policy house where locals congregated to play the numbers. King says, "I was very organized. I'd write down where I sold my bags and what the numbers were, and if one of my customers won on them, I'd track him down and get a tip."[2]

King credits his mother with providing him much of his courage and grit. "My mother always told me that life might be unfair, but that I always had to be fair. She also told me the importance of being appraised by people. It's not what I think of myself, it's how the world— particularly those doing business with me—look at me that counts."

King was accepted at Kent State University and in order to raise the $600 freshman year tuition, he took over his brother's number-running collection route, picking up the neighborhood bets. He forgot to turn in one bet that, unfortunately, hit the winning number. The bookie demanded that King use $580 of the saved tuition to honor the debt. The bookies refused to provide him with a loan for college tuition.

With no money for college, King took up the life on the street, working the only business he knew, running numbers. In a year, he had succeeded in taking over the number-running business, and the bookie worked for him. Then, he attended college at Case Western in Cleveland, where he aspired to become a lawyer, but after a year he returned to the street: "I made the irrational realization that you go to school in order to get educated, you get educated so you can make some money, but I already was making money, so why should I go to school."[3]

During his twenties in Cleveland, King became successful at the policy game, as number running was called. He kept good accounts and always paid off the winners. Over time, he was acknowledged as the premier numbers banker in Cleveland. This early King has been described as a "street Machiavelli, a ghetto Einstein." King's ability was always to think a few moves ahead of anyone else—competitors, the mob, or the police. By 1966, it was reputed he was grossing $15,000 every day. King was a very good businessperson, even though the business was illegal.

King owned a house in the tony suburb of Shaker Heights, drove a big Cadillac, and carried large sums of money in his pocket. But the joy of his life was owning the New Corner Tavern Supper Club, which

featured black entertainers playing on what was called the Chitlin'
Route. King expanded the seating to 600, built a revolving stage, and
offered cuisine cooked by gourmet chefs. Into the club came the
crème de la crème of African American entertainers—B. B. King,
Esther Phillips, Muddy Waters, Oscar Peterson, Lou Rawls, and
Lloyd Price. And into the club came white people to hear the music.
And King was at center stage, welcoming black and white guests, par-
tying with the musicians.

The years operating the supper club would stand King in good stead
later in life:

> I realized that when you're dealing with entertainers, you have to
> understand where they're coming from. You have to listen to their life
> stories because they put their stories into their music and songs. Every
> good story has a beginning, middle, or end. When I read Shakespeare
> or Edmund Rostand (the author of *Cyrano*), I could tell how important
> the story was to their writing. That's why many of my fights would be
> more than just boxing matches, they would be stories larger than life.

In 1966, Sam Garrett was a low-level runner in King's employ who
misrecorded a bet and owed King $600. When Garrett refused to pay, he
and King came to blows, and the fight spilled out in the street. In the
melee, Garrett died from the beating, and King was indicted for second-
degree murder. A jury found him guilty, punishable by life in prison. In
private chambers, the judge in the case reduced the charge to manslaughter, for a term of 1 to 20 years.

## Jail Time

At age 36, at the top of his game and in the prime of life, King, a husband and father, was sent to prison in the Marion, Ohio, Correctional
Institute to serve a sentence of indeterminate length. When the cell
door closed, the outside world could regard King as just another street-
wise policy-number highflyer whose anger had exploded once too often.
For some, he was a hustler who had skirted the legal system and finally
got was coming to him. For King, the slam of the cell door was the real
beginning of a second chance.

King went to prison as a middle-aged man who had enjoyed the good
life. In one sense, the memory of this life allowed him to focus on two

goals: He would be a model prisoner to reduce the length of his sentence, and he would improve his mind:

> I really didn't serve the time, I made the time serve me. I escaped through books; I read thousands of books. My first day, someone handed me *The Meditations of Marcus Aurelius* and I just went deep into the book. I tried to escape by reading other people's ideas and putting my ideas with theirs and developing a sense of discipline.[4]

While in jail, in addition to the continual life-saving book reading, King took university correspondence courses and got good grades in economics, business law, and political science. He has often told reporters that he received a scholarship offer from the Harvard Business School. On face value, there seems to be no truth in this statement. But the question becomes what prisoner—particularly, one doing time for manslaughter—would even dream of making this admission (what chutzpah!) or have the confidence to believe that he ever would have been accepted had he applied? And maybe he would have.

King also credits the life and words of former slave Frederick Douglass, the black abolitionist who overcame racism to become U.S. minister to Haiti in 1889. King, finding some part of himself in the Douglass legacy, says: "I read his words and the ones that impressed me were, 'Those who fight for their country have the right to claim the country for their own. And they deserve to have that right respected.' I am a proud flag-waving citizen of the United States and agreeable to take the bitter with the sweet."

The one economic lesson that King learned while in prison was the importance of money: "I understood that freedom was a very cherished and precious thing, but in all cases, there remained one factor; economic independence." Years later would amend the statement by saying, "Money is the by-product of the deal. And my deals are based on selling what I call an *attraction*. If the attraction is successful, then the deal works and everyone makes money. I married the attraction to the money."

He served 3 years and 11 months before he was paroled in 1971. When asked how prison had changed him, he replied, "The Don King who went in was armed with a peashooter; the one who came out was armed with an atomic bomb of knowledge and understanding. I was thinking universally and in terms of society as a whole. I changed considerably."[5]

"I came out armed and dangerous. Armed and dangerous with wisdom and knowledge."[6]

## Getting Started in Boxing: An Accidental Entrepreneur

Budd Schulberg said, "Boxing is just show business with blood." Maybe that's why it has produced as many colorful types—boxers, managers, and promoters—as Hollywood. Certainly, it's one of the reasons why it would ultimately attract King.

The rise of professional sport today, with its million-dollar salaries, promotional monies for endorsement, and hero worship, began with the storied career of one American heavyweight boxer, Jack Dempsey. Dempsey, more than Babe Ruth or Red Grange or Bobby Jones, exemplified the new hero-millionaire athlete that emerged in the 1920s, the heyday of sport's Golden Age. When Dempsey beat Jess Willard in 1919, the fight drew fewer than 20,000 fans, and Dempsey's purse was $27,500. Nine years later, when Dempsey fought Gene Tunney, the crowd totaled close to 105,000 in Chicago's Soldier Field, and the gross receipts reached $2,700,000. The two fighters in the famous "long count" title match shared $1,540,000. Thanks to Dempsey and his astute manager Doc Kearns, big-time sports had entered onto the American scene.

Boxing personified Willy Sutton's insightful response when he was asked why he robbed banks: "Because," he replied, "that's where the money is." Boxing would become the bank that fight promoters, managers, and anyone else with an angle would always try to exploit for easy cash.

King did not find boxing; boxing found him, through the suggestion of an old-time friend from the New Corner Tavern Supper Club, singer Lloyd Price. Price recognized King's intelligence, his skills as a businessperson, and his innate showmanship with his larger-than-life personality. Price's message to King was simple: Because the sport of boxing featured mostly black fighters while the promoters were white, didn't this represent an opportunity for a black promoter?

During the years of his prison sentence, King had been slightly aware of the growing groundswell of black pride and rising black consciousness throughout America. The 1968 Olympics in Mexico City had witnessed the power salute gesture of medal-winning sprinters John Carlos and Tommy Smith, whose raised fists on the victory stand sent a powerful and revolutionary message back to white America. But one black athlete most personified emerging black pride and the break from the white-dominated past—the boxer Muhammad Ali.

Later, while King was performing community service, he learned that Cleveland's Forest City Hospital, the only black hospital in the city, desperately needed funds to stay open. It then occurred to him that a fund-raising charity boxing match might generate the monies to keep the hospital going. And then King experienced a spark of genius that would ignite his career: He would ask Lloyd Price to use his connections to contact Muhammad Ali.

In 1972, Ali, who had lost the title to Joe Frazier earlier that year, was beseiged with solicitors interested in using his talents. At first, Ali told Price that had no interest in a fund-raising exhibition in Cleveland, but then King took the phone. King's magical tongue, his powers of persuasion, his idealism, his brother-help-a-brother chatter, and whatever else was needed to make the sale flowered in the course of the conversation. Ali acquiesced and agreed to come.

With Ali on the card, fighting a 10-round exhibition against four different opponents, as a draw, King, with Price's help, lined up other African American performers for the Cleveland concert. Marvin Gaye, Johnny Nash, Wilson Pickett, and Low Rawls all donated their talents. The event was a fantastic success, a promotional feather in King's cap, grossing $82,500, which was more money than any other fight in the city's history. King was back in business.

King had also spoken to Ron Elbaum, the most prominent white boxing promoter in Cleveland. Here was a smart move—learning the business from an expert and forming a loose and informal partnership with someone who knew the sport. For a few years they worked together, with Elbaum the matchmaker, making fights among local Ohio boys, and King the showman, creating excitement with hype and style. Elbaum remembered a teary conversation with his new partner. King told him: "I want to become legitimate, I want to do something in my life for my family, I don't want to be known as a numbers man anymore. I want boxing."

Jack Newfield wrote King's biography, *Only in America: The Life and Crimes of Don King* (William Morrow, 1995), and offered this reason for King's success. "[In 1971] Boxing was ready for, and in fact needed, a black entrepreneur. Don King would prove to be the wrong man at the right time. In all that follows, it should not be overlooked that Don King was a trailblazer—the first successful black boxing promoter in boxing history."[7]

## Learning the Ropes

The success of the Ali exhibition convinced King that boxing was the business he wanted to pursue. The time in Cleveland had given him an insight into how the sport was promoted and also a certain legitimacy among the boxing crowd, which regarded Elbaum as a square guy. In fact, it was Elbaum who introduced King to Hank Schwartz, the president of Video Techniques, a company that was involved with satellites and closed-circuit technology. Elbaum was enthusiastic, telling Schwartz, "Boxing needs a black promoter. He's going to be able to control fighters because he's black, and all the good fighters are black."[8]

In January 1973, King, a wannabe boxing promoter, arrived in Kingston, Jamaica, as a spectator and hanger-on for the Joe Frazier–George Foreman title fight. Frazier had won the title from Ali and was a heavy favorite to keep the crown from the bulky, boyish Foreman, best remembered for waving the American flag after his 1968 Olympic boxing victory. King had met Frazier through his manager, Yank Durham. But this story is best told in King's own words:

> I still had celebrity status from the other side of the street. Meanwhile, Ali shows up in Kingston; and he's selling my virtues about what I'd done staging the hospital benefit. I stared playing golf most every day with Durham, and afterwards, I'd go over and watch Joe work out.[9]

King also visited Foreman's camp and introduced himself to the challenger. King maintains he told Foreman that he was going to knock Frazier out and shock the world. Assuming this is the truth, King's confidence must have inspired the young boxer, and he must have never once bothered to wonder whether King was playing both ends against the middle, placing psychological bets on both fighters.

King rode to the title event as part of Frazier's entourage and paraded down to ringside with the champ, sitting in a front-row seat behind Frazier's corner. But in round 1, Foreman charged out like a roaring bull and pummeled the stunned Frazier to the canvas. King's instincts told him that Frazier was on his way to a crushing loss, and he rose from his seat and sidled around the ring to Foreman's side. In round 2, Foreman slammed Frazier with a haymaker that lifted the champ into the air. The fight was stopped, and Foreman was declared the winner. King dashed into the ring to congratulate Foreman. For all the world to see at ringside and on television, King, a face few recognized, was hugging and being hugged by the new heavyweight champion. Who was this guy?

If there is one sentence that sums up King's adoption of Willy Sutton's philosophy, it's this one, regarding the Frazier–Foreman title bout: Often, and repeatedly, King has boasted, "I came with the champion and left with the champion." The winners would come and go or become losers. The important fact was that King would make out fine regardless of which fighter won.

Sportswriters would use this incident in Jamaica to castigate King for his short-term loyalty (to Frazier) and to grouse about his flagrant opportunism (with Foreman). But beauty and betrayal are really in the eye of the beholder. King had done what businesspeople in all industries always do: Replace a losing product with a winning one. Where is the loyalty of television networks when a once high-rated show drops to the bottom of the Nielson ratings? King was smart enough to realize that his future rested with George Foreman. It was nothing personal against Joe Frazier; it was just business—good business.

Remembering the image of King congratulating Foreman at the Kingston fight, Hank Schwartz hired King because of his sudden "apparent influence" with Foreman. Schwartz's company wanted to line up a Ken Norton–Foreman fight, and it used King's friendship with Foreman to make the deal. In his first assignment for an establishment business, King had proved how helpful he could be. More important, this experience confirmed what Elbaum had trumpeted: African American boxers reacted positively to an African American promoter, and the only African American promoter in America who understood the boxing business was King.

## Building the Stable

After the Foreman–Norton fight, King was eager to go off on his own and rightly assumed that he needed fighters who reported directly to him. He headed off to Ali's training camp in Pennsylvania, soliciting advice on how to get started. Ali provided advice, encouragement, and a sparring partner named Ray Anderson, who signed to let King promote a fight in Cleveland. Anderson also suggested that King manage another fighter named Ernie Shavers, who also signed up to let King manage his next bout. King felt doubly fortunate; he had a lightweight in Anderson and a good punching heavyweight in Shavers. The road to promotional riches beckoned

King's first foray would be back in his hometown of Cleveland, and to ensure its success, he allowed Anderson to handpick any opponent that he was confident he could beat. Anderson chose an airline baggage handler from Dallas named Cookie Wallace. King booked the Music Hall downtown, and everyone in Cleveland came out to watch, especially the black community. Wallace won easily, and the crowd wondered about King's ability to judge boxing talent.

Next, King lined up a fight for Shavers with Jerry Quarry in New York's Madison Square Garden. Quarry knocked out Shavers in the first round. King could have thrown in the towel on his fledgling promoting career, but the next day he got a phone call from Ali, who said, "Don, I know you're disgusted and you probably want to get out of boxing, but don't. Send your Shavers to my camp and I'll teach him how to box."

The affiliation between Ali and King has been much analyzed over the years. Many people believe that King's relationship with Ali was one of a series of father–son or mentor–acolyte relationships that he would establish with young African American fighters, starting with Ernie Shavers in the 1970s and continuing with Mike Tyson in the 1990s. It is clear that at the start of King's eager attempt to make a name for himself in boxing, Ali proved helpful at each turn. There is little doubt that at the outset Ali wanted to help another black man in an historically all-white business.

Remember, when Johnny Carson asked Ali, "Why did heavyweight title fights attract so many people?" he responded, "Because white people will pay big money to watch two black men beat their brains in." Carson cracked up, as did everyone who watched the *Tonight Show* that evening, but the remark had more than a kernel of truth in it. Ali was deadly serious.

## Landing the Big Fight: Ali versus Foreman

In January 1974, Ali defeated Frazier in their second rematch at Madison Square Garden. Everyone in America with even the slightest knowledge of boxing wondered when George Foreman would defend his title against Ali, the most serious challenger. Every boxing promoter and everyone who yearned to be a promoter desperately wanted to sign these boxers for the match. Someone who could keep an eye on the prize was going to make a bundle of cash.

Hank Schwartz promoted King to vice president and gave him carte blanche to pursue Ali and Foreman to secure the television rights. This challenge would require all of King's multifaceted powers of persuasion, cajoling, pleading, conning, and, most important, business skills. He sensed that if he could bring this fight to his television team, he would vault over all other boxing promoters and be recognized as the number-one promoter in America:

> This was the opportunity of a lifetime for Don King. He put every-thing into it—all his will, all his energy, all his showmanship, all his mastery of numbers, all his skill at preaching an evangelical paradise in the future to black brothers. He would compete against boxing's incumbent power brokers in marathon negotiations, with the most bizarre cast of characters in history, to stage the richest prizefight in history.[10]

The geometry for making the fight happen was simple, even two-dimensional. First, draw a square with Ali and Foreman on opposite diagonals; next, connect the sides to a promotional group; and finally, draw a line to a venue where the fight would be held. Crisscross the lines so that every point on the square meets every other point, and all points will be connected. The more experienced promoters, like Bob Arum, Ali's lawyer, or Teddy Brenner, from Madison Square Garden, realized that there was a third dimension to the shape of the negotiations—big money for the purse.

But King intuitively sensed that negotiations would be four-dimensional, the square becoming a hypercube with *time* the added component. Muhammad Ali, then age 33, feared that Foreman would stall in offering him a chance to regain the title, and months would tick away. King also realized that Foreman had once idolized Ali—he called him "the people's champion"—but now Foreman was jealous that the fans adored Ali more than they adored him.

King cornered Foreman in a parking lot in Oakland, California, where he hinted that if Foreman didn't commit to the bout soon, Ali would back away. King said to Foreman, "This is a victory you must achieve. Otherwise people will never accept your greatness. But you must move *now!* Ali may not want this fight for long."[11] And Foreman signed for the fight.

King had been the sole go-between in the two boxers' negotiations, and then, after receiving written agreements for the rematch, he faced two more daunting tasks: raising $10 million to pay the shared purse and finding a place outside the United States for the fight. Foreman was tied up with lawsuits and a divorce and could not fight in the States. Legitimate businesspeople around the globe and con artists everywhere knew that the search was on for a stadium somewhere that would host this fabled bout.

Hank Schwartz of Video Techniques had looked at London and other locations, which were all rejected. Enter Joseph Mobuto, president of Zaire, with a proposition: Stage the fight in his country. Mobutu perceived that his country was like Rodney Dangerfield; it got no respect. A heavyweight match would force the world's population to find it on a map of Africa. For one evening, all the world's media would be turned to Zaire. When the $10-million letter of credit (each fighter was promised $5 million) from Barclay's Bank passed through Schwartz's hands, the deal was done. George Foreman would fight Muhammad Ali in Kinshasa, Zaire, for the heavyweight championship of the world.

King had done what no one else could do: He had connected all the lines, and he had obtained signed contracts from all parties for a heavyweight title fight.

The press conference in Caracas, Venezuela, to announce the finalization of negotiations for the Ali–Foreman title bout should have been one of the highlights of King's life. But it wasn't. The press release had relegated his contribution to an insignificant place way down on the fifteenth line. King stormed out, and screamed at Schwartz. Even Schwartz's later attempt to credit him for arranging the bout did not mollify King. For many African Americans, the slight was reminiscent of NBC's egregious error in dropping off a bottle of scotch as a birthday gift to Redd Foxx when Sanford and Son was near the top of the Nielson television ratings. Whites did not understand the emerging black business pride of accomplishment. The people in the boxing world would underestimate King's talents for the last time.

## Negotiating Skills and the Ability to Build a Boxing "Brand"

The "Rumble in the Jungle" is history, best remembered for Ali's rope-a-dope punch-taking brilliance and knocking out Foreman in the eighth round. Few knew that the fight was in serious jeopardy after Foreman injured his eye in training. The resulting wait and postponement caused anxiety in both camps. Into the maelstrom jumped King, using all his consummate skills, quieting officials, meeting frequently with reporters, assuaging government fears, and, generally acting as the one voice of calm and reason.

Hank Schwartz said, "There is no doubt Don saved the fight. He held the deal together. He knew how to talk to Foreman. He stopped Foreman from bolting. He was magnificent."[12] Ali and his manager, Herbert Muhammad, also were impressed with King's skills.

Norman Mailer described meeting King in Zaire: "King had the ability to take all his true love (which given his substantial Black presence was not necessarily small) plus all of his false love, and pour them out together through his eyes, his lambent eyes."[13] And Mailer also penned a picturesque account of King's attire: "King wore diamonds and pleated shirts, dashikis with gold pendants, powder-blue tuxedos and suits of lipstick-red; the cummerbunds of a sultan were about the waist, and the pearls of the Orient in the cloth he wore." And of course, Mailer praised one of King's greatest attributes: "How he could talk. He was the kunta of full dialogue, and no verbal situation could be foreign to him."[14]

King walked away from the fight with only a 4⅓ percent share of the profits, hardly a significant piece of the pie. But King had also walked way with the most valuable future moneymaking elements—the trust and loyalty of Ali and Foreman. The promoters had the lion's share of the money, but King would soon own the rights to the attraction.

Boxing's inner circle—with the help of some sportswriters—would accuse King of robbing the crown jewels while their backs were turned (counting the receipts), but this was a case of sour grapes. It was King who had demonstrated that he would go the extra mile in Zaire to guarantee that the fight took place, and it was to him that fealty was owed. The powers-that-be in boxing would become the powers-that-had-been, because King emerged from the fight with the promoter's crown.

Back in the States, King used his newfound persona to persuade Ali and Foreman to sign with Don King Productions for the rematch. His detractors cried "Racism!" when they learned that he had spoken of black pride and black power to both the Ali and Foreman camps. No one among the white power structure wanted to credit the fact that King used his version of the old boys network—the traditional method of personal relationships—to make the deal. No one then wanted to admit that it made both financial and racial sense for African American fighters to make a deal with this new African American promoter.

King would disagree that having fighters who lost was not a money-making prospect: "Once you learn the modus operandi of how the business like boxing worked, then it didn't matter if your boxer won or lost because you'd be promoting the fight from the beginning of the deal." But more important would be King's clever ability to give each fight a name so that the media and the public could talk of the pending fight as though it were an established name brand.

## New Ventures, New Problems

King's next venture was to promote Ali's easy victory over Chuck Wepner, a journeyman heavyweight whom Ali described as a "white with no hope." (Wepner had lost to 40-year-old Sonny Liston.) Wepner was a colorful New Jersey brawler who lived above a disco and became the model for Sylvester Stallone's *Rocky*. The movie rags-to-riches story was not lost on the boxing community; only in Hollywood could a white heavyweight triumph over a black champion. King would continue to find white heavyweight hopefuls, knowing that white audiences in the United States still hungered for a white champion. His list would include Peter McNeely, Wepner, and Gerry Coetzee.

Ali allowed King to copromote his third battle with Joe Frazier, known as the "Thriller in Manila." It would be the apogee of Ali's career—his age, and the terrible beating that Frazier inflicted in a losing cause, would start the slow spiral of losses yet to come. King overplayed his hand with Ali by trying unsuccessfully to drive a wedge between the champ and Herbert Muhammad. Ali remained loyal to his advisor and to his faith.

By 1976, King was without a fighter and rued the loss of Ali. He could have gone back to the heavyweight ranks and looked for another challenger. But he had a greater and more timely vision than scheduling just one fight: He would promote a multiweight elimination tournament to match many of America's best young boxers. The Olympic boxing victories that year of Sugar Ray Leonard and the Spinks Brothers had convinced King that the country was eager to see more of these gold-medal winners.

King took the idea to ABC executives, who realized that the popularity of boxing was on the upswing in America (thanks in some part to Stallone's *Rocky*). The television network agreed to bankroll the tournament. The first two bouts would be held on the deck of the battleship USS *Lexington* and then at the U.S. Naval Academy. The third would be held at the Marion Correctional Institute in Ohio. King was taking a fight to what he humorously referred to as "my alma mater."

What looked like a brilliant stroke of promotional genius turned into a quagmire of deceit and falsehood. The records of some of the boxers' fights turned out to be inaccurate. Some boxers' records listed phantom bouts that had never taken place. When the boxing cognoscenti researched the fighters' real records, all hell broke loose. The boxing media accused King and his associates of misrepresentation, of fabricating fights of imagination.

ABC, with its reputation at stake, hired well-known Manhattan lawyer Michael Armstrong (formerly of the Knapp Commission, which conducted the investigation into police corruption in New York City that inspired the movie *Serpico*) to look into the charges. The Armstrong Report found that ABC could not be faulted, nor could King. King, for his part, blamed associates.

If the boxing establishment and the press hoped that the ABC scandal would damage King's reputation, they were wrong in that assumption. King was still the power in the sport; and HBO, Las Vegas and Atlantic City hotel-casinos, and even ABC would continue to use him for promotion.

## Don King in Every Boxing Corner

King's brilliance as a boxing promoter was in controlling as much of the heavyweight inventory as possible. The better boxers would rise to the top of their weight classes, so it was unimportant to King who won, as long as he had the monopoly on all the fighters. Using the analogy of consumer packaged goods, if you view this in terms of maximizing shelf space with as much product as possible, then the plan reflected standard business practices.

By 1978, Don King's heavyweight list read as follows:

- Larry Holmes, heavyweight champion
- Ken Norton, first contender
- Jimmy Young, second contender
- Ernie Shavers, third contender
- Leon Spinks, fourth contender
- Alfredo Evangelista, sixth contender

And so forth down the line. Mike Katz, the sports journalist for the *New York Times*, wrote, "In this corner a Don King fighter. In that corner a Don King fighter."

King convinced Ali to fight one last title bout against Holmes, in a fight that King famously entitled "The Last Hurrah." Again, the event was part boxing, part storytelling. Holmes destroyed the popular but aging Ali, who had even dyed his gray hair black. Many in the boxing game were outraged that King had made big money from such a sad debacle. But Ali made millions from the fight and had eagerly looked forward to the big paycheck. And millions of fans hoped beyond hope that The Greatest might recoup a fourth heavyweight title. All King did was give the fighters and the public what they wanted.

King continued to be highly successful in promoting epic-making heavyweight fights. In 1982, he scheduled the Holmes–Gerry Cooney bout, which he named "The Pride and Glory," and which grossed a then-record $45 million. Next came "The Crown Affair," at the Dunes Hotel and Casino in Las Vegas. This was the first-ever heavyweight champion double header; it featured Holmes defeating Tim Witherspoon for the World Boxing Council Title and Michael Doakes beating Mike Weaver for the World Boxing Association title.

Over the next years, King would dominate the heavyweight division until Mike Tyson lost to Buster Douglas in 1990. But even after Tyson lost to Evander Holyfield in 1996, King had the rights to promote Holyfield's future bouts. His memorable old line, "I came with the champion, and left with the champion," was still being played out more than 20 years after the Frazier–Foreman match in Jamaica.

King would make millions of dollars through promoting boxing events. And with the profits came the lawsuits—over 100, many from boxers in his stable who believed they had been cheated out of their fair share of the purse money. Most suits were dropped and some were settled out of court, which led King to be characterized as the "Teflon Don."

## "Go Get Some Money"

King's boxing business flourished in the 1980s. He established the Don King Sports Entertainment Network, a cable system similar to HBO. And he started the D.K. Chemical Company. His corporate empire is reputed to be worth more than $50 million. He owns a 400-acre estate and family compound in Ohio, where he and his wife raise Black Angus cattle.

Today, King lives in Deerfield Beach, Florida, and conducts a thriving business that promotes 100 boxers. King, ever the visionary, has purchased the old West Palm Beach jai alai fronton and will convert it into a 10,000-seat arena for basketball and concerts and as a showcase for the black circus. He is also considering using the site to stage and televise fights. He will conduct a promotional search to let the locals choose the name for the arena.

King is also in an ongoing promotional partnership with Park Place Entertainment, which owns Caesar's Palace, the Las Vegas and Flamingo Hiltons, and hotels in Paris and Australia. King reaps the rewards of having wedded boxing to the casino world. King credits "relationships, results, and respect for people" as the cornerstone of his ability to continue to make lucrative deals for all parties in pay-per-view television.

King also is considering an Internet business that, although amorphous today, will reach millions of viewers online. His experience tells him that it would be easy to have an audience of a billion people or more sign on to view a championship fight through the World Wide Web. As he says, "The Internet is all content and I own 30 years of providing content."

Over time, King has become interested in other black-owned businesses, and now owns the *Cleveland Call and Post*, the largest minority-owned newspaper in Ohio. With the ownership comes six other small black-oriented newspapers. King hopes the newspapers will provide more uplifting news about African American successes.

In September 1996, King was a featured speaker at the Harvard Business School, where he offered the students advice that "Money is the answer to all things, so go get some money." It was reported that the students listened attentively.

In June 1999, the city of Mount Vernon, New York, honored the promoter with the first Don King Day. Local African American leaders in the community believed that honoring King was long overdue, referring to him as a "Our black hero, our black economic hero." Never finding an audience he could not charm, King said, "My magic lies in my people ties. I walks with the masses, not the classes."[15]

King has surpassed the limiting description of "black economic hero" to become an American hero, recognized by everyone for his achievements. "I'm a winner not a whiner" is his motto. Once asked why his hairstyle evolved into the now-famous comb, King replied, "I want the people to see my hair in all its crowning glory." And they do.

Bruton Smith

# Bruton Smith

## Cofounder of the Charlotte Motor Speedway

*"Negativity? That's not the way to make any money."*

NOT ONLY IS BRUTON SMITH'S a story of romance, it's romance in the classic mold: *Boy meets girl; boy loses girl; boy gets girl.* There, in just nine words, you have the whole Smith saga. But though the plot is easy, its casting takes considerable imagination: For the "boy," of course, you've got Smith himself. But for the "girl," no human actress can suffice. Since 1959, the object of Smith's love has been an inanimate (if lively) property: the Charlotte Motor Speedway—among the most costly and outrageous sports venues in the world. It's to other racetracks what Disneyland is to country fairs. And on its building and beautification Smith has lavished more than $200 million and four decades of his life.

As in many a romance, the couple's courtship was rocky at first. For a time, fate thrust the two entirely apart. But Bruton remained faithful, trusting that he and his Speedway were fated to be mated. And eventually they were. Theirs is a story of discovery, loss, and redemption.

### "A Heritage of Hard Work"

Though Smith, by *Forbes'* most recent estimate, is worth upwards of $1.2 billion, he started with the clothes on his back, a full stomach, and not much else. Born in 1927 in Oakboro, North Carolina (20 miles east of where the Motor Speedway is today), he grew up a cotton farmer's son, youngest of nine children. Early on, he says, he concluded that farming was not the life for him: "We always had plenty to eat. And plenty of clean clothes—such as they were. But that was it." They had no money; they didn't have things. "And everybody," he says, "wants *something.*"

In his case, it was a racing car. He'd seen his first stock car race when he was only 6. "I was hooked. Seeing those cars rooster-tail in the dirt and hearing their engines roar was the most awesome thing." Meantime, though, he had to contend with matters more prosaic. A particular incident turned him against farming: "I was eight or nine years old, and an older sister and I had been told to go out on a Sunday morning, early, to pick some beans. We had a lot of company coming over, and we had to pick all these beans. I remember thinking to myself, 'This is so ridiculous. I hate this.' " He turned to his sister and said, "As soon as I graduate from high school, I'm gone!"

His classmates voted him "most athletic, most popular, and most conceited." Most lazy? Definitely not. The single best part about his upbringing, he believes, is that it equipped him with "a heritage of hard work." At age 12, while still in school, he was working in a sawmill, and later, at 16, in a cotton mill. By 17 he'd bought his first race car—a white-and-red Ford for $700.

He didn't go college. Instead, he kept working in the local mills. He sold cars on the side and organized races. He easily might have become a professional racer himself, he says, were it not for the opposition of his Baptist mother. She'd pleaded with him for years not to race, but he'd resisted. Then a day finally came when (in Bruton's words) she started "fighting dirty": she started *praying* that he'd stop. After that, he says, "I wasn't just going against Mom. I was going against God." He quit. There was another reason for his decision: As a young man with an eye for the main chance, he saw there was more money to be made in promoting races than in competing in them, more in selling cars than in driving them.

## The Racetrack Was His Dream

In 1955 he had bought his first track—a half-mile dirt oval in Concord, North Carolina—for $20,000. Just four years later, he announced plans to build what eventually would become the Charlotte Motor Speedway. There was one problem: Curtis Turner, a race driver and Charlotte businessman, had the same idea—plus better backing. Because Charlotte could support but one track, the two rivals eventually agreed to collaborate, with Smith offering to sell 100,000 shares of the 300,000 they needed to sell to help finance the project. (Turner subsequently died in an aircraft accident.)

Today, the fruit of their collaboration looms large: It's a complex that, seen from a distance, looks as big as any major metropolitan airport. The speedway employs 9,000 and comfortably seats 167,000 fans, not counting another 30,000 to 40,000 who can watch races from the track's infield, some from the comfort of parked motor homes. The 1.5-mile oval could contain seven Giants Stadiums. Strung around it, like jewels set in an asphalt necklace, are amenities of every sort, calculated to appeal to race fans of every taste and income level. There's outdoor seating, indoor seating, and luxury skyboxes. For the very highest rollers, there's a private club serving five-star food. And most amazing of all, perhaps, there are trackside condominiums, whose owners literally are at home with the racing action, having paid a minimum of $90,000 for the privilege of seeing rubber burn right outside their parlor windows.

Racing aficionados—especially big-name drivers living in the Charlotte area—consider the speedway their second home, and the track the unofficial centerpiece of the prestigious National Association for Stock Car Auto Racing (NASCAR) circuit. As such, the speedway has become the number-one beneficiary of the country's fastest growing professional sport. Says speedway race director Harvey Walters, who's worked the track for 30 years, "We took an old, country-type deal and really built it into something."

Taking in the size and scope of the speedway, it's hard to remember that back when Smith was starting out, the "deal" was completely different. Racing was looked down on as a pastime fit only for moonshiners and scofflaws. Indeed, the sport's roots go back to a time in the South when freelance distillers souped up their cars in an effort to outrun revenuers (or, as Walter Brennan would have called them, "guvamint men"). Rivalries over who had the fastest car were settled in the woods, around oval tracks cut into the dirt. Back in the 1950s, mommas (nice ones, anyway) didn't want their boys to grow up to be racers. Says H. A. "Humpy" Wheeler, Smith's longtime friend and the speedway's chief executive, "Stock car racing was just a hair above the carnival business—or maybe a hair below. It's not something polite Southerners wanted their children to do. Our mothers and fathers had spent years trying to get away from hillbillies and moonshiners and stock cars and log houses. They'd just gotten out of log houses themselves."

Nor were even the most legitimate tracks, back then, any too sophisticated. At the time Smith started promoting races, there wasn't a single asphalt track in the whole state. "In that era—the 1950s—they were dirt," he says. "They were old fairground tracks, where you'd had horses racing." Staging a race on one of these, says Wheeler (who, like Smith, grew up on farm and started out promoting races), "was a bit *like* farming. You had to deal with the elements and learn how to operate without any money." Smith remembers watching some of his own races—ones that he'd produced—and realizing that because of forces beyond his control (weather, especially) they were costing him money. At a time when he barely had two nickels to rub together, he remembers thinking, "It's costing me $4,400 just to see this race. That's an expensive ticket!" He was all by himself—just a lone operator without a company or any organization behind him.

What kept him going? Two things: His fighting spirit, and his vision that racing could be something bigger, better—his belief that the sport's potential audience was huge. That conviction sprang from Smith's own insight into human nature. Racing's appeal, he believed, was rooted deep in the soul—the male one, at least. "I think that it's hereditary," he says. "When you were just a kid and had your first tricycle, you went racing with your buddy. You can put a couple of kids on the floor that can't even walk yet—little kids, still in diapers—and pretty soon they're racing with each other. It's just an inherent trait of most humans." He felt certain that if the sport were promoted aggressively and given a more upscale venue—one with plenty of fan amenities—its popularity would skyrocket.

## Problem 1: Raising Money by Selling "Stock" out of a Car Trunk

First, however, he had to raise $2 million. That was the amount he and Curtis Turner figured they would need to build the speedway. Initially, no bank would lend them anywhere near that much, since neither Smith nor Tuner had enough collateral. "At that time," explains Smith, "speedways were not a favorite subject with bankers or lending institutions." Bankers, in fact, tended to belong to the very class of people that regarded racing with disdain. So Smith and Turner raised money in what Smith calls "some legal but strange ways."

Smith hit the road, selling interests in the speedway out of the back of his car to anyone who'd buy them, at $1 a pop. It wasn't exactly stock he was selling, he explains, because he hadn't registered with the SEC. It was a "preincorporate subscription." "I don't know whether anybody ever does that today or not. You have a simple piece of paper that shows that you, as the potential shareholder, have written a check to the bank as escrow agent. Your funds go directly to the bank." When and if the subscription promoter ever "has something"—in other words, if the promoter caries through and opens up the business—"then you're a shareholder." Asked how much money he raised this way, Smith replies without a moment's hesitation, as if the number still were dancing right before his eyes: "$406,000."

A few of his original investors are still with him. "Some of those people think I hung the moon," he says, "because they ultimately made a lot of money. Some of them for a $2 investment got $750. So you can imagine they today might be some of my very best and dearest friends." When he says this, his eyes twinkle with a kind of rascally amusement.

He and Turner still didn't have enough money, so Smith set out to sell more subscriptions. "I got disgusted," he says. I took the telephone directory and I thought: 'I'll just call everybody in the phone book.' I started with the As. So every day, I figured if I could make 100 phone calls, I'd eventually get through that phone book. I was selling, selling, selling." And he got more subscribers. "Then I got another idea, which was a little edgy." *Edgy?* Edgier than selling stock out of the trunk of your car? "I didn't have any funds to buy advertising, so I went to one of the radio stations here and got an agreement with them that, uh, I could run a commercial in exchange for my giving them a subscription. I was very proud of myself for selling them, because they were a very sophisticated entity. It was the CBS station. I wrote the commercial, stood up, and completed it on the second take. Gee whiz. In my next life, maybe I'll do advertisements. I got people's attention to such a degree that they literally lined up at the bank. The line came out even on the sidewalk. I was pleasantly pleased." Where did he learn to sell? "I didn't. I picked it up. It's called 'out of necessity.' All I had was the desire. I was determined to build that speedway."

## Problem 2: Building the Speedway—on Solid Rock

Late in 1959, construction started northeast of Charlotte on land described by Humpy Wheeler as "the worst piece of ground he could have found. Bruton couldn't afford anything better." What made the ground especially miserable wasn't just the rocks beneath the soil but the size of them. *Groundbreaking* here took on new meaning. "I saw it out there, in the early '60s, when it was still under construction," says Wheeler. "It was a truly a monstrous undertaking. There were all these trucks. And blasting. It was just one giant earthmoving job. They had huge front-end problems with it." Builders piled heaps of excavated rock onto what later would become the infield—so much, in fact, that a minimountain rose.

As the mountain rose, so did construction costs, and Smith realized that he still was badly undercapitalized. So he decided to to explore the possibility of filing with the SEC. "I had some young lawyers," he says. "They dressed well. They meant well. But they gave me poor advice. I got poor investment advice. I got poor legal advice. I don't think it could have *been* any worse. The road . . . got rather bumpy." Specifically, the lawyer handling the filing had never done one before. Says Smith, "There just wasn't a lot of stuff filed in this part of the country with the SEC. It took us, like, six months to get that darned thing right." When the filing finally was finished, Smith was then able to raise $600,000.

That still was not enough. This didn't worry him, though, because he still had a secret weapon. "I had a wealthy brother-in-law who'd been smart enough to see, early on, that somewhere down the road I'd probably need his help desperately. So he'd told me, 'I'll be there for you.' " The man had more than implied that if Bruton ever got hard up against it, he'd bail him out. That day had now arrived. "When we were about 65 percent completed with the speedway, he died suddenly, of a stroke. That was devastating to me. He was like a big brother to me, a second father. To lose him at that time . . ." Smith's voice trails off, and his eyes get a faraway look. "He was my absolute ace in the hole."

A series of Job-like troubles descended on him, starting in March 1960. "For three Wednesdays in a row, it snowed. I'd have the guys out there with the 'dozers. We'd move the snow; it would melt, and we'd have mud. Then we'd remove all the mud. And afterwards it would snow again. We were on a tight construction schedule, working two shifts, 20 hours a day. The weather put us three weeks behind."

Smith's plan had been to stage the track's grand opening for Memorial Day weekend, but the weather forced him to postpone that to June 19. By then, the weather had changed again—but not for the better.

"It was hot," he says. "Like about 104 degrees." The track's asphalt turned green from the heat, a sure sign it hadn't cured properly. "You literally could go out there and take your thumb and press your thumb real hard, right down into it like it was a pie. You could stand on one of the banks and your heels would sink down into it." What would happen, he wondered, when cars began racing on it? "I knew the track was going to get torn up, so I called the Asphalt Institute to find out what we could do. They didn't know of anything." The race started. The track began to come apart—so much so, that one of the cars suffered a punctured gas tank from the flying asphalt. Not that fans could see this drama: The mountain of rock left over from construction still remained on the infield, making it impossible for spectators on one side of the track to see what was happening on the other.

Despite all this—the rocks, the heat, the flying asphalt—Smith persisted, and the speedway's first race was run. The hours leading up to it had been especially tough ones for Smith, and he hadn't slept, he says, for two whole days. "Once the race began, I stayed awake until the halfway point. Then, sitting on a stool up in the control tower, I went to sleep." The attendance—about 78,000—wasn't bad, but it was smaller than it might have been, had the weather not intervened.

The disappointing gate meant Smith was unable to pay bills:

By the time I'd run that first race, I had creditors that had not been paid, and I needed another $600,000. I'd been all over New York City. I'd been to Boston, to Miami, to Philadelphia. You name it— I'd been there. Chicago. I'd been everywhere hunting for investors. I was trying to get some type of a mortgage. They asked me intelligent questions, such as: "Do you have a five-year operating statement?" At the time, that question hurt my feelings, but now I understand it: Nobody in their right mind ever makes a loan without a five year statement. We found we could not borrow any funds—nowhere, no way. We had the equity, but we had no history of success.

As a person who'd survived flying asphalt, Smith wasn't about to knuckle under easily. "I went home one night and said to myself: I'm going to stay here until I can figure out some way to do this." He came up with an idea for a "participation mortgage." "I went to a good lawyer the next morning and said: 'I want to work out a mortgage where people can participate—where they can buy a piece of a mortgage.' He said: 'You can't do that.' I said: 'Well, there's got to be a way. Draw it up so I can do it, and I'll sell pieces of that mortgage.' So he drew up an instrument, and I put some people together for a dinner party at my house one night—about 40 people. I also asked my banker to be there. He was somebody who always enjoyed a good steak, and he came. That evening I raised about $150,000. We gave the checks over to the bank." The dinner went so well he hosted more of them, eventually raising $450,000.

He still didn't have enough to pay off all his bills, though, because he owed creditors in excess of $500,000. "It was like hanging onto the side of a cliff with your fingernails." Finally, a grading contractor named Flowe got fed up and forced the speedway into bankruptcy court. As Smith later described the crisis to the *Charlotte Observer*, "There was no question that we owed Mr. Flowe $90,000. But we had a slight problem—we didn't have the money."[1]

## Fending Off Bankruptcy

Smith was worried, but lawyer friends of his up in New York had reassured him he had nothing to be concerned about—he still had lots of equity and was "a natural" to file for a corporate reorganization. "What's that?" Smith says he asked them. "I'd never heard of it. When I came back to Charlotte and talked to my lawyers, they hadn't heard of it, either. In 1961, there had never been a filing here. Isn't that amazing? There had never been a corporate reorganization, a Chapter 11. Nobody knew anything about it. I said, 'You've *got* the damn law books—go in there and see if you can't figure out what to do.' They came back a few days later and said: 'You petition the court to allow you to do this.' And I said: 'That sounds right; I believe you're there now.' So that's what we did."

Or almost. A small glitch arose:

Bless their hearts, instead of filing for a corporate reorganization—a Chapter 11—they made a mistake. They filed Chapter 10. Chapter 10 puts a trustee in control. That adds greatly to your expenses: Now you've got a trustee to pay. And the trustee hires more lawyers, so you've got to pay them.

The trustee, after finding not just $500,000 in debts but evidence of what he considered to be financial improprieties, fired Smith, who nonetheless stuck around to help keep the track afloat, since he had 40,000 shares of his own at stake. In Smith's telling of this part of the story, he says he and the trustee "became friends. I worked for him for months, behind the scenes, because I knew what to do to make sure this corporation got saved. We just waltzed on down the road."

The music stopped abruptly in 1964, when the speedway emerged from the court's protection—the first corporation in North Carolina business history ever to do so. At a stockholders meeting in 1965, Smith sought a seat on the board but was repudiated by his fellow shareholders, who, according to the *Observer*, booed him.[2] He was 38, and out of a job. In the language of romance, he and the speedway now were officially *pffft*.

"It hurt. It hurt." is all he says today about that moment, shaking his head from side to side. The pain hit him not only in the heart, but in the wallet: As an unsecured creditor, he says, he was shorted $100,000. To friends and associates at the time, he kept up a brave front. Says Wheeler: "I'm sure it had to have seared his soul, but you'd never have known it. He grew up during the Depression, and people of his generation just cover up bad news. There *is* no bad news to Bruton." Larry Walters, manager of speedway maintenance at the time Smith got the axe, describes him as somebody always able to maintain a classy demeanor, no matter what: "He's the kind of guy who, if he was hungry and had only 25 cents to buy a hotdog, would spend it on a shoeshine."

As for the bitterness he most certainly felt, Smith says: "I had a private conversation with myself. I said: 'This has got to stop. There's no percentage in it. I have to get over this.' " What was guiding him out of his dark period, he says, was "just an impulse in me." He's not religious, he's just naturally well grounded, practical, imbued with a sense of what does and doesn't fly, in terms of mental health. He attributes his ability to cope to simply "knowing right from wrong."

## A New Beginning: Selling Cars Instead of Racing Them

The upside to his being estranged from the speedway was that he now was free to pour his energies into another of his ambitions: making

money in the car business. In 1966, he signed on as a salesman with Bill
Beck Ford in Charlotte. After just three months, he became manager.
The next year, he left Charlotte to manage a Ford dealership in Col-
orado. And in 1969, he was able to buy his first Ford dealership, in
Rockford, Illinois.

Over the next decade, Smith enjoyed the not inconsiderable conso-
lation of becoming rich, acquiring 10 car dealerships and two insurance
companies in Texas, Arizona, and Illinois. In 1975, he told a reporter
that his net worth was $8 million, and that he owned his own jet.[3] All the
while, however, the speedway was never far from Smith's thoughts, and
he held out hope that he would someday win it back. In 1971, he began
buying stock in it aggressively, as blocks occasionally came on the market.

Why did he do it? What forces fueled a fidelity more lasting than that
found in most marriages?

The answer, says, Smith, was threefold. First, the speedway was
unfinished business for him. "It was like my having given birth, and then
having had the baby taken away." Second, he still believed in the vision
that had inspired him to build the speedway in the first place: The
potential of the sport was huge, its appeal universal. And last (but by no
means least), R. J. Reynolds had jumped into auto racing with both
tobacco-scented feet.

Reynolds—like other big cigarette companies—had had a wad of
advertising dollars burning a hole in its pocket, ever since the federal
government prohibited advertising cigarettes on television. In 1970, the
company had decided to explore the marketing possibilities of having its
Winston brand sponsor NASCAR's premier racing circuit, which was
soon renamed the Winston Cup.

When this happened, Smith's eyes lit up. As he later explained, "This
big old fat company making a billion dollars a year [was] going to come
in" and take care of track-owners' own advertising for them. Henceforth, owners wouldn't have to spend a dime promoting races in the
Winston Cup. "I thought, this has got to be a wonderful business."[4] It
soon became one. Today, sitting in his office, Smith makes a gesture
with his hand in explanation of why his ardor for racing, after 1971, blos-
somed all anew. "Up to then," he says, putting his index finger and
thumb so close together that just a pinch of light shows through,
"there'd been only *minute* growth. But Reynolds brought marketing to

the sport." Since then, stock car racing has grown more corporate and more mainstream. McDonald's, Du Pont, Home Depot, Procter & Gamble, and a host of other household-name companies now sponsor teams. Stock car racing has become the fastest-growing of all professional sports.

## Regaining Control of the Speedway

However, not everyone in the early 1970s foresaw this future with the same clarity as Smith, and he had little trouble buying up more speedway stock. "Over a series of months, I'd acquired several hundred thousand shares of it. Then I got a call from one of the directors. I'd heard rumbles that there had been a falling out. He was angry. He wanted to sell his stock, and wanted to know if I would buy it. 'Yes sir, I will.' Would I buy his friends' stock, too? I said I would. I didn't have mathematical control just yet, but I was close." In another few weeks, Smith had his majority.

He hopped a plane (his own) to Charlotte, with a briefcase full of stock certificates, and asked to see the speedway's transfer agent. "The agent, at that time, was the secretary-treasurer of the company." Smith handed him the briefcase. "I could see the blood draining from his face, because he knew then it was over. I didn't particularly like him. He probably didn't like me, either."

The year was 1974. Smith had worked and waited 13 years for this very moment. How did it feel, being reunited with his speedway? "It felt pretty good. Some of these people had made up their minds that I would never be back. And all of a sudden . . . *He's back!* I kept on buying stock, and finally I ended up with 82 percent. After that, I decided to take the company private. Ultimately, I bought all the stock." Says Larry Walters, "I like to say that Bruton left here in a Chrysler 300 with his clothes in the back. And he flew back here in a jet plane—his own—and bought the place."

Understandably, relations between the new owner and the track's past administration were strained. "Sometimes I'd walk into a room," says Smith, "and you could cut the atmosphere with a knife. Very, very icy." He solved that problem, he says, by firing people. "Either you were for me, or against me. I had a strong attitude about that." In the end, he kept only one holdover employee: Walters. Walters himself isn't sure why, except to say that "There were a lot of people here at that time with a bad attitude," and he wasn't one of them. "I was just trying to make a living."

Firings weren't the limit of the unpleasantness that followed Smith's return. Smith himself later was the object of a suit brought by a group of minority stockholders who asserted that he'd tried to squeeze them out by offering them an unfairly low price. Not until 1985 was this suit settled, with Smith agreeing to pay them 150 percent over his initial offer. This was but one in a series of legal and regulatory dustups that have hounded him, and he's acquired his share of critics over the years (including *Forbes* itself, which once termed Smith's financial dealings "questionable"[5]). Still, only a single judgment ever has been lodged against him. That was in 1962, when the IRS fined him $4,000 for late payment of his taxes.

In 1976, Smith hired as CEO his friend H. A. "Humpy" Wheeler, a former Firestone press agent who, like Smith, originally had been a dirt-track operator. The two proceeded to remake racing in their own image, eventually investing some $200 million in speedway improvements. Under the previous administration, the speedway had done "just fair," says Smith, making by his estimate only 10 to 15 percent of what it could make if it were run right. "There was no expansion, no nothing," he says. "It was just hanging on." Fans were offered few amenities, yet they still kept coming back. How much better might the business fare if fans were treated right? Asked in 1999 why he had returned to the scene of his failure, Smith said: "All of us who were in this business tried to kill it, but it would not die. So I figured it must be a hell of a sport." With Wheeler's help, he embarked on a series of innovations and improvements.

First, they got rid of all that rock on the infield. They cleared the minimountain so that spectators, for the first time, could follow the action all the way around the track. They landscaped the speedway, adding flowers. They expanded the number of women's rest rooms, assuming (correctly, as it turned out) that if more women came to the races, they would bring along their men. Female attendance then zoomed, from 10 percent of the gate to about 40 percent today. Overall seating capacity was increased by 10,000 seats.

Smith and Wheeler also added $1.7 million in new lighting, which allowed them to use the track at night for the first time. This meant that races—especially the heavily promoted Winston Cup events—now could be televised live and still reach prime-time audiences in Western states. Also, Hollywood was able to use the speedway as a venue for movie making, and a number of films, including *Days of Thunder* and *Stoker Ace,* were filmed there.

Smith added services for fans of every income level. No more was this a sport fit only for rednecks. He added 700 skyboxes, of the sort found in football stadiums. When *Sports Illustrated* visited the speedway, it reported finding rich folks "devouring caviar, champagne and single-malt whiskey, Häagen-Dazs and Dove Bars."[6] Smith also added an exclusive trackside Speedway Club, where members could watch races while they dined on five-star food served on china. Though skeptics laughed, Smith sold several thousand club memberships, at $8,500 each. Later, when he and Wheeler expanded their empire to include other racetracks, he added other clubs with fatter fees. Memberships at the Texas Motor Speedway, for example, go for $15,000. Smith's club in Atlanta has a health facility and racquetball courts.

Wheeler was put in charge of mounting prerace shows—bread-and-circus-type extravaganzas—that became drawing cards in and of themselves. They ranged from the surprisingly classy (Van Cliburn performing the national anthem on a specially made piano), to fireworks displays and reenactments of military battles. Wheeler's staging of the invasion of Grenada, for example, required 6,000 soldiers (with helicopters). For a simulation of Operation Desert Storm, the life-sized turrets of a battleship, erected on the race track's third turn, swiveled their guns toward the first turn, where a mockup of Saddam's bunker had been built. *Blamo!* Saddam's bunker exploded in a cloud of wreckage. Fans loved it.

Wheeler became a Ziegfeld of race promotion. His shows featured parachuting dogs, Elvis impersonators, stealth bomber flyovers, school bus jumps, and a race between New York City taxicabs. One of the very few ideas he ever nixed as too far-fetched was interspecies combat to be held in a huge, water-filled Plexiglas tank. Its title would have been "Man versus Shark: One Must Die."

While the entertainments always were amusing, they also showed a shrewd awareness on Smith and Wheeler's part that their bread-and-butter customers remained the guys on Slim Jim–and–Snickers budgets. For every millionaire up in the Speedway Club hefting silver service and bursting tiny fish eggs against the palate of his or her mouth, tens of thousands more were drinking soda pop and eating wieners. "They want action, they like noise," says Wheeler of these fans. He gives it to them.

When in 1984 Smith announced he was going to build a cluster of pricey condominiums on the speedway's first turn, doubters thought he'd finally lost it. Even Wheeler rejected the idea as too preposterous. So close to the action were these units that, had they not been perched on stilts, their owners would have had to worry about race cars coming through their living room windows. Plus, they were expensive. Prices ranged from $90,000 to $125,000. David Letterman (a NASCAR fan) made fun of them for the better part of a week on his television show. But seven months after they were put up for sale, every single unit had been sold, and Smith was the one smiling. The condos' resale values have since appreciated as much as threefold. Smith, emboldened, went on to build far fancier condos at his Atlanta and Texas properties, pricing them at $550,000 and $650,000, respectively. In his mind, the units are a logical extension of tailgating. Instead of picnicking on cheese and crackers from their parked cars, fans can eat home-cooked meals on their own couches.

Nor is Smith done innovating. At Charlotte, he is spending $640 million to add more than 91,000 seats, plus an industrial complex, a hotel, and a golf course. Operationally, he remains ever vigilant for ways to heighten fan excitement, experimenting with races featuring cars whose tops have been removed, so that spectators can see drivers fighting not just each other but to keep control of their own cars. On the financial front, Smith has begun selling naming rights to his properties. In February 1999, the Charlotte Motor Speedway became Lowe's Motor Speedway, in exchange for $35 million from Lowe's Home Improvement Warehouse. In 1995, Smith became the first person ever to take a racing company public, listing Speedway Motorsports, Inc., on the New York Stock Exchange. The stock opened at $9 on a split-adjusted basis and, at this writing, was trading at $20 to $22. Revenues for 1999 were $318 million, profits $41.4 million. Smith, as chairman, owns 70 percent.

Smith's empire today includes his beloved speedway, plus four healthy offspring in Georgia, Texas, Tennessee, and California. Of these, his Texas property, built in 1995 on 1,600 acres bought from Ross Perot, Jr., is the largest and most costly ($250 million), boasting 200 luxury suites set in a double-deck configuration spanning almost a mile. On opening day, its grandstands—with over 150,000 seats—were the largest of any sports facility in the United States. There are 900 acres of parking lots, infield parking for 1,300 motor homes and campers, and, for high rollers, nine helipads. Cost to build: in excess of $250 million. Smith also owns 60 percent of Sonic Automotive, a public company worth over $600 million, which controls 159 car dealerships, including Town & Country Ford in Charlotte (where Smith keeps his office).

## "All Great Rebounders Have Got to Have Vision"

Smith's friend Wheeler says about him: "I think there's some genetics at work, here. Some people are just *made* to come back. Maybe they've got high seratonin levels or something else that keeps them optimistic. It's a primeval thing, probably going back to the cave. Probably there's some kind of comeback *gene*."

Smith definitely does seem to have something good going for him genetically. At 73, he looks 53 and acts 33. Wheeler compares the challenge of keeping up with him to trying to keep up with an overactive toddler. Wheeler calls Smith "the Energizer Bunny," and there's no reason to quibble with that description. He's compact, robust, sturdy, smooth-skinned, bald (with a fringe of close-cropped hair)—looking like a fiftyish Mickey Rooney, well turned out in navy slacks, a salt and pepper sport coat, a white dress shirt with lapis cufflinks, and the kind of tie—wild—no one would find out of place in a car dealership.

In conversation, he's self-effacing about some aspects of his career—including how he staged his comeback. Talking about how he coped with the frustration he felt when he lost the speedway, he says: "If I'd had any money back then—if I'd been living in a place like, I don't know, *Hollywood*—I'd probably have gone to see a psychiatrist." As it was, he didn't and he wasn't. Instead, his survival was instinctual: "It's like getting knocked down: You've got to get up. You've got to fight 'em. You want to win, not lose. Negativity? That's not the way to make any money."

Wheeler ascribes Smith's ability to roll with the punches to his having grown up around farming, a business he calls "perilous at best. It's a series of battles—some you win, some you lose. Sometimes it rains, sometimes it doesn't." For whatever reason, Smith's equanimity seems so bulletproof as to be at times comical. Asked by a reporter in 1990 if he felt bad that he'd lost $5 million in a savings and loan that regulators had declared insolvent, Smith replied, "No siree. No more than I do if I have an old suit that's wearing out." He likes taking chances. Friends say his predilection comes from having grown up poor. Opines one, "Bruton didn't have anything to start with, and therefore he has been quite willing to put everything he has on the line, year after year."

When challenges arise today, he isn't passive. Nor has the man once voted "most conceited" allowed himself to become a prima donna. Says Larry Walters, "He doesn't mind getting personally involved." Walters remembers a rock concert at the speedway in 1973 that drew a crowd of 200,000 that left the track choked with litter and debris. "Who do you think ran the cleanup operation? Bruton. I've seen him personally park cars." More recently, after the Texas Motor Speedway opened, problems developed with its track. Water seeped up from underneath the asphalt, cracking it. After the inaugural race was marred by spinouts and crashes, drivers deemed the roadway ill-designed. By the race's halfway mark, 26 of 43 cars had been involved in accidents. Said driver Rusty Wallace, "I really believe they are going to have to go to a total reconstruction to get it right."[7] And "they"—meaning Smith—did. He supervised the job himself, working 12-hour days for nearly a week.

Another trait has served Smith well, thinks Wheeler: He's a visionary.

> All great rebounders have got to have vision. IQ alone won't do it. They do things ahead of their time. And not surprisingly, it often doesn't work. So they have to come back. When a person loses everything, grief follows and depression. It's very difficult to see the future, and what you do see is black. But if you have the gift of vision, it makes life so much better. If you can't see the rainbow, you can't see the end of it. "I Can See Clearly Now" should be the theme song for comebackers.

Another friend of Smith's compares him to "an old mountain man"—always looking over the horizon for the next thing. "He gets bored real fast," says Wheeler. "He always has to have something new on the table." Now, at the same time that he's happily adding a whole new block of bleachers to the speedway, he's also launching a new online auction Web site—SoldUSA—designed to auction off cars, sports collectibles, and NASCAR merchandise.

"He's the epitome of a workaholic," says Wheeler—a description Smith quickly seconds. His focus on his business is total. Divorced, he lives alone. He doesn't play golf, doesn't belong to a church, doesn't go in for social climbing. Instead, he works. Says Wheeler, "Generals like wars; kings like to govern; Bruton likes to build things." Nor does he need to fritter any of his time away looking for love: He's found it. "I *love* business," he says. "It's my golf, my tennis. It's like a good meal to me. It's fun." He doesn't mean just any business, of course. He means the speedway. And ever since that happy day when he returned to Charlotte with a briefcase full of stock certificates, he and it have been inseparable.

Earl Stafford

# Earl Stafford

*Founder of Universal Systems & Technology (UNITECH),*
*a Leader in Net-Based Training Systems*

*"Bloody, but unbowed."*

I‍T WOULD BE EASY to get the wrong idea about Earl Stafford.

One might, for instance, draw the wrong conclusions from the way he handled the worst Christmas of his life. That was in 1990, when his fortunes were at their lowest ebb; when just about everything that could go wrong in a person's business life had gone wrong in his; when he'd lost all his customers and laid off all his employees; when his kids had had to go without presents because Earl could not afford to buy them any; when bill collectors called and called and called the Stafford home, badgering the family until, mercifully, the phone itself was turned off for nonpayment and the lights went dark and the Staffords, for a time, were compelled to live by candlelight. At that juncture, a reasonable person might have reached out for help.

Help certainly was available. Stafford has 11 siblings. He has many friends from church and from his neighborhood. They could have banded together and, in a dénouement worthy of Frank Capra, sent Earl's troubles packing. Imbued with the holiday spirit, everybody could have pulled together and pitched in to save their best pal Earl. It really would have made a lovely and inspiring sight, with even the crabby old bald guy breaking down and tossing his gold watch into the collection plate. There'd have been caroling and punch drinking and somewhere, in the distance, very faintly, a sound of tinkling bells.

But there wasn't. It didn't happen that way.

Stafford's relatives and friends didn't help him out, because they didn't get the chance: He never told them of his troubles. He kept his crisis secret. His attitude—most definitely un-Capraesque—could best be summed up as: *If I have to tunnel my way out of hell with a teaspoon, I'll do it; and I'll do it on my own, thank you very much, without any help from you.* The more you get to know Stafford, in fact, the more certain you are that if any of his friends had dared to show up, he'd have said to them (in the nicest way, of course), "Get lost."

Asked if during this dark time he ever considered taking charity—his friends', his relatives' or anybody else's—an expression of utter disbelief passes over his smiling face, as if the question must have been intended for some other Earl Stafford. "Oh, no, no, no," he laughs, finding the idea ridiculous, "I have too much pride for that. I have this . . . *pride.*"

He sure does. And from his having so great a superabundance of it, what might you conclude? That he's a prima donna? A martinet? A jerk? Or perhaps that he's just a bit too stiff-necked and bull-headed for his own (and his family's) good? You'd be wrong on all these counts, but not unreasonable in your assumptions. Because pride, more often than not, hinders a struggling person. It becomes a fatal disability. No less an authority than the Bible imagines it as such when Scripture says, "Pride goeth before a fall.' It blinds people, preventing them from taking the hard, distasteful steps most necessary to their own survival. Proud people, typically, are too fastidious to shoulder the hard work of saving their own skins. And make no mistake—pride radiates off Stafford.

You feel pride in his handshake, you see it in his eyes. It's apparent in the way he dresses, in his choice of words, and in his manner. He's a formal person, disliking strangers who immediately assume the false familiarity of calling him by his first name. He belongs to a private club. He wears Canali suits tailored for him in Sausalito. Hearing him talk about his likes and dislikes, one is somehow not surprised to learn that his favorite poem—the one from which he says he's drawn the greatest inspiration—is *Invictus*, whose last lines are: "I am the Master of My Fate; I am the Captain of my Soul."

Yet in Stafford's case, pride proved not to be an impediment. Since Christmas 1990, he has rebounded strongly from near insolvency, going on to build a $40-million company that employs some 300 people. He's rich, his family thriving. Gone are the days when the Staffords had to worry about the telephone being turned off. Today, if they choose to dine by candlelight, it's an aesthetic choice, not one forced on them by poverty. How did Stafford accomplish this?

## An Early Entrepreneur—and a Hard Worker

Stafford's attitudes toward work and money were established early on by his father, a Baptist preacher. Young Earl and his 11 siblings ("I was one of the younger ones") grew up in Holly Park, New Jersey, a town he describes as having been "one of those 'George Washington Slept Here' kind of places." His childhood? He remembers it as "wonderful." Though a preacher's salary didn't go far with so many mouths to feed, Stafford doesn't recall ever having felt the least bit poor. "We were never allowed to think that we were poor," he says, referring to the tone set by his father. "*Poor* deals with your head. *Broke* denotes your wallet." There was no shame in not having money. Nor was there any mystery about what to do to make it: "If you wanted something and you could not afford it, you just went out and found something to do to make the money. I cut grass. I picked up empty soda bottles, at two cents each. I shoveled snow." In that respect, he wasn't proud—and his willingness to do whatever came to hand served him well. What did he do with his earnings? "Oh, I spent them on sneakers—on the same kind of unwise things kids spend their money on today." He laughs.

By age 8, he was already well along toward being an entrepreneur: "My mother decided I was to sell hot dogs and sodas on Saturday mornings. I think, now, that that was the beginning of my enthusiasm for business. Little did I know, when I was sorting out my change, that I was learning finance."

Soon after graduating from high school in 1966, he joined the military. "That was an easy decision," he says: The Vietnam war was raging. Stafford didn't want to get drafted—which would have meant a sacrifice of his control over his own destiny—so he enlisted in the Air Force, where he was trained to be an air traffic controller.

Around the same time, on his own initiative, he began studying Swahili and pursuing an interest in black history. (He's African American.) He was attracted to the Black Panthers, though he never joined the movement. "I was more curious than anything else," he says. "I liked some of what they had to say—'*stand up and be a man*'—that sort of thing." He liked the Panthers' emphasis on pride. Some of what they preached he'd never heard before. "They brought up issues that were interesting to me. It wasn't so much antiestablishment as it was pro-cultural." He read books they recommended, including Lerone Bennett's history, *Before the Mayflower* (Johnson, 1969). Speaking of such firebrands as Eldridge Cleaver (whom Stafford refers to "the tall black guy with the beard"), he says, "These were guys thought to be radical, even in the black community. 'Why can't they behave?' is what people asked. But they brought up issues to me that were interesting. They brought up questions that heretofore hadn't been addressed."

He also found time, while in the military, to fall in love with and marry Amanda, who's still his wife today. Though he'd planned to leave the Air Force right after his first hitch was up (so he could go straight into business), he suddenly found himself about to be a father. With his first child on the way, the Air Force made him an attractive offer: If he stayed in, they'd pay him to complete his education. So he re-upped as a commissioned officer, eventually earning his BS in finance at the University of Massachusetts and, later, a masters' in business administration from South Illinois University.

Today he looks back on his years in the Air Force as time well spent. He had his share of adventures: There'd been the time, for instance, when he'd heard a lost pilot's plea for help on his control tower radio. Stafford never for a moment lost his cool. Calmly, for over an hour, he guided the plane to safety. It's an accomplishment he still recalls with satisfaction. "The training I got in the military was probably the best I ever received, as far as leadership is concerned," he says. "It's helped me even more than my MBA. That can-do attitude, that esprit de corps, the idea that you lead by example, by getting out in front of your troops and refusing to retreat—all those things apply in business, even more than the ratios and analyses I learned in business school."

## Chasing the Entrepreneurial Dream

In 1987, with his most recent hitch complete, Captain Stafford decided his moment of truth finally had arrived: He would close the door on his 20-year Air Force career and start chasing the dream he'd dreamed since childhood—of someday owning his own business. He retired. Then, in order to gain private-sector experience, he went to work for RVA, a contractor that supplied personnel and aviation services to the Federal Aviation Administration (FAA)—for example, air traffic controllers for control towers. As a former air traffic controller with an MBA, he fit perfectly into RVA's management.

After only four months at RVA, Stafford got restless, though, and decided he would "step out on faith" to pursue starting his own company. Not everybody thought this was such a great idea. "When I told family and friends I was going into business, I got some laughs," he admits. "There were those who said, 'You're crazy'. But I took that almost as encouragement." How so? Their skepticism egged him on. "After they'd said those things to me, I just could not see myself failing. I didn't want anybody ever to be able to say to me, 'I told you so.' "

Nor was Stafford deterred by the fact he had few financial resources. "When I started out," he says, "I had no capital. On top of that, I was in debt." How had that happened? "Well . . . by my spending more than I made, I guess," he laughs. He goes on to explain that toward the end of his tenure in the military he was forced to support two households. The Air Force assigned him temporarily to posts in Missouri and Illinois, while his wife and children stayed at the family's home in Alexandria. "My son was in high school. It didn't make sense to uproot my kids or have my wife leave her job, so we had two households to maintain." Though the military picked up the cost of one, the other was Stafford's own responsibility. He charged some of the bills to his credit card, and, before he knew it, he was in the hole and going deeper.

Mike Gottlieb, UNITECH's CFO, sums up Stafford's situation this way: "You take somebody who's had a career in the military. He gets this job with RVA, so now he's got his pension plus he's working at a good, stable job. What could be better? Wouldn't you love to be doing what you're doing plus you still have this steady income from 20 years in the military? Then . . . he then takes this huge risk." Gottlieb says he can't imagine doing the same thing himself. "It's one thing to take that kind of flyer when you're 23. Then it's safe. If you screw up, if you fail—what have you really missed? But when you're 40, and you're married and you've got grown children and you say, 'You know what, guys? I'm quitting and I'm going to start my own company. I'm rolling the dice. I'm gambling everything we have that I know what I'm doing and can make a go of this. . . .' That takes fire. I personally wouldn't have the guts. That's why I'm in finance!"

When Stafford told RVA early in 1988 that he was quitting to start his own company, they replied the way he'd hoped they would: "They said, 'You can't do that; we need you.'" He stayed on, but not as an employee. Instead he became a subcontractor to RVA, which assigned him some of the very same air traffic support contract on which he'd previously been working. Not only was he now in business for himself, he'd landed his first contract.

That contract called for a team of air traffic controllers under his direction to operate radar scopes at a combat aircraft testing range in Maryland. Their responsibility was to make sure the area was clear of friendly aircraft before combat air maneuvers commenced. ("You'd hate to hit something," says Gottlieb.) The contract wasn't big. "But," says Gottlieb, "when you're just starting out, like Earl was, and somebody gives you a $20,000 or $25,000 contract, you think you've hit the lottery."

Stafford, needing a name for his new company, called it Universal Systems & Technology, Inc. (UNITECH). Why that? "Earl wanted a name that sounded cool," explains Gottlieb, "a name that sounded like it really *was* something. Twelve or thirteen years ago, every company had 'systems' in its name—it was 'systems' this and 'systems' that. Systems was what 'dot-com' is today." How about the "Universal" part? "That just sounded good."

## Early Obstacles: Not a Lot of Cash and a Contract Disaster

There was at least one major difference, however, between Stafford's start-up and today's red-hot dot-coms: Nobody came running to throw money at it. "There was no instant infusion of dollars," says Gottlieb. Instead, UNITECH was strictly a one-step-at-a-time proposition. "Earl was managing to pay his staff, but not himself. He struggled mightily."

Stafford shrugs off his early travails as no big deal. Referring to his having given up the emoluments of a military life—subsidized housing, health coverage, three square meals a day, and the glories of the post exchange—he says simply:

> Those are choices that I made. I'm a big cheerleader, a drum major for entrepreneurship. I love to hear people say, "Yeah, I've been safe and secure, but I have this talent—this ability—and it's marketable; I'm stepping out. I might not have all the resources . . . all the wisdom. And

I really don't have a solid business plan; but I'm going to do it." Man I love to hear that.

Business plan or no, he began bidding for more contracts. And he soon landed a beaut, through the auspices of NYMA—a company which, like RVA, specialized in supplying personnel and services to the government. In this case, NYMA was assisting the National Aeronautics and Space Administration (NASA), which was preparing to launch its $2 billion Hubble Space Telescope. Stafford signed on to be a subcontractor to NYMA. "We were part of the prelaunch testing phase," he says. "They needed some lower-end type of help for a team of scientists—runners, help-desk staff, receptionists, administrative people, computer operators—things of that nature."

Then or now, what makes any neat and tidy description of UNITECH all but impossible is that the company stands ready to provide anything and everything its clients need—professional services, staff, even hardware. It's a problem solver, a need filler. Since its inception, the company has been, at various times, a reconciler of bills, a monitor of radar screens, a provider of receptionists, and a designer and fabricator of weapons training systems. UNITECH's specialty might fairly be called providing "the works"—from high tech to low.

There was nothing high-tech about UNITECH's contribution, but the mere association with a project as large, sophisticated, and prestigious as the Hubble telescope lent luster to the little firm. Not only would Hubble be the most advanced telescope ever sent to space—where it would see 10 times more clearly than any terrestrial scope—it would (in the words of the *Washington Post*), "reconfirm American supremacy in science and innovation," peering into distant galaxies and opening up "a new chapter in human understanding of the universe." *Popular Science* anticipated it would be the greatest leap forward in astronomy "since Galileo."

Even before it went up into space, Hubble was paying off like a slot machine (if one may be so crass) for its legion of contractors and subcontractors. Stafford alone was getting $300,000 for UNITECH's small role. Between this contract and the radar contract he still had with RVA, Stafford now employed some 20 people. Finally, he was making enough money that he could rent and furnish a small office. He could even, for the first time, start paying himself a salary. "I signed a lease over in Greenbelt, Maryland, for office space, and everything looked positive.

Things looked like, 'Wow—they're going to take off for us.' We were happy, working hard, doing a great job. Everything looked rosy."

The Hubble bubble burst abruptly for Stafford—as for many other NASA contractors—in the spring of 1990, after the telescope, having ridden into space with great fanfare aboard a space shuttle, failed to measure up to expectations. The recognition that Hubble was in trouble dawned on controllers at the Goddard Space Flight Center over the weekend of June 23 and 24, when they tried and failed to achieve a perfect focus. What they eventually discovered was an optical defect in the Hubble lens, which caused images to be distorted by a ring of hazy light around each star. Hubble could see; it just couldn't see $2 billion better than an earthbound instrument—at least not at first. NASA, red-faced, sought to put the blame on its subcontractors, especially those responsible for having made the mirror.

The flub occasioned a national orgy of self-doubt and self-recrimination. "Can the U.S. Get Things Right Anymore?" asked the *Washington Post*, in a story calling the telescope a "great techno-fiasco."[1] A group monitoring U.S. technological competence called the Hubble experience "humbling." NASA was subjected to a swift and merciless drubbing in the press for having sent the thing aloft without first testing it thoroughly on Earth. Popular ridicule reached its zenith when the 1990 comedy *Naked Gun 2½* made the Hubble the butt of many of its jokes.

NASA immediately cut back on Hubble staffing until the problems could be fixed (as they ultimately were). Recalls Stafford, "After things went sour, they immediately started laying off contractors, and we were one of them." The bad news didn't stop there, however: During the same week he lost the Hubble contract, Stafford learned that RVA had pulled the plug on his radar contract. "I got a call saying they didn't need me any longer and that my efforts were terminated immediately." Unitech's revenues fell from six figures down to one—zero—forcing Stafford to lay off all his employees. In a matter of a few days, Unitech had gone from being a flourishing business with two contracts to a lifeless entity that existed just on paper. The only assets it had left were its fancy name and Stafford. "That was a pretty tough time," he says. "I'd have jumped, but the windows wouldn't open." Though he immediately started calling around town to see what other contracts he could find, none were immediately forthcoming.

## In Debt—with No New Contracts

By fall, Stafford's family was having trouble paying its bills. The Air Force pension was only large enough to make the mortgage payments on the their suburban Alexandria home. For living expenses, they were dependant on Amanda, whose government job offered decent benefits but didn't pay a lot. Not only did they have three kids to provide for—a son, age 18, and two daughters, 15 and 9—but they still had Stafford's credit card debts, left over from the military. Financially, theirs was not a pretty picture.

"It definitely was a strain," says Amanda Stafford. "We were overextended. My check could take care of only so much, and Earl's could cover just the mortgage." Didn't she find the calls from creditors nerve wracking? "Yes, it was all those things—difficult and nerve wracking. My son was in college at the time, so not only did we have all the other bills, but there were his college expenses to be taken care of."

Meantime, Stafford kept trying and failing to land new contracts. The contrast between where he was now, in November, and where he'd been as recently as June weighed heavily on him. With Christmas approaching and the year drawing to a close, he felt pressure of a kind he hadn't known before. Asked what previous defeats he'd suffered in his life, he says: "I don't know if I'd really had had any. I'd had disappointments, yes, but no real knock-'em-down-get-out-of-the-mud situations." He recalls two incidents, both relatively minor: "I'd been disappointed in life by things I didn't get. There was a school in the military I'd wanted to be selected for, and wasn't. Getting in would have been an honor, and I was disappointed. But I prayed and told myself, 'Life is more than this.' " He got over it. The other incident dated back to high school: He'd been cut from his freshman basketball team. "I still remember how hard it was for me to go home and tell my dad. But all he said to me about it was, 'Well, son, they missed a good player.' "

Compared to what he and Amanda were facing now, these troubles seemed like nothing. The parents tried not let their worries affect their kids. "We tried to keep them busy," says Stafford. "Kids are much more resilient than adults. We kept them busy in the church. But, sure, there were things every now and then they couldn't participate in that the kids with money could." There were, for instance, travel and admissions costs for children's outings organized by Jack & Jill of America, a group to which the Staffords then belonged. "We had to give that up," explains Amanda. "Most of those activities cost money. They have trips to museums or to conferences. It's a family organization that promotes culture." From time to time, there would be things the kids would want to buy. When that happened, says Amanda, "We would tell them, 'We'd like to buy it for you but we can't. We can't afford it.'" When the phone or lights were turned off for nonpayment, the parents sometimes made up stories. "You might tell the kids, 'They're fixing it,' or something like that. And sometimes the kids were at school when those things happened."

How long did all this go on? "I would imagine about a year," says Stafford. "That doesn't mean the lights were turned off for a year. But for about a year we had real tough times." Amanda eventually asked him why he didn't go out and get a regular job—at least something part-time. "I did say that," she allows, "not thinking, at the time, that what he really needed was to hold out a little longer. That happens, if you don't understand all that's entailed in getting a business going. I said, 'Maybe you could get something part-time.' Even in the military he'd had part-time jobs, when we were newly married."

Increasingly, husband and wife found they were communicating on two different wavelengths. "Instead of coming together," says Amanda, "we seemed further apart."

"I'm a risk-taker," explains Stafford. "And if I have a dream, if I believe in it, I'm going after it. My wife doesn't always share that. So, you know, she wanted the security. The whole family was under pressure—the phone calls and all. And then the phone was turned off. 'Why not get a job and get a steady income?' 'Let's live like other people.' We were trying to look respectable." Was he tempted to go get a regular job? "Oh, it crossed my mind. You know the feeling: When people are calling you, knocking on your door; there's steady stress and you're working 18 hours, 20 hours and there's no appreciation. You say: I could go out and get a decent job, at least get a paycheck."

## "I Was Overwhelmed"

The low point came just before Christmas 1990. Stafford had continued to prospect for contracts but hadn't yet landed any. "After a while, you know," he says, "you just can get worn down—with the stress and everything." The full weight of his troubles hit him suddenly one evening as he was driving home. "I was coming from Greenbelt. I knew I really didn't have anything for the kids. It was going to be real tough. Probably the toughest Christmas we had." Up until that moment, he'd done his best "to keep a stiff upper lip and to stay strong in front of my wife and the kids." But here, alone in his car, with no one to see, there was no need to keep up a brave front. "I just pulled over to the side of the road, Exit 15, near Central Avenue. I pulled over, and the tears rolled down. No dramatic epiphany or anything, just . . . I was overwhelmed. It was a culmination of things, of tough stuff. Sometimes you just need to have an emotional release."

It's here, at this nadir in Stafford's story, that a Frank Capra ending would be so satisfying: Stafford, eyes still moist, arriving home to find the house filled with merry friends, discovering the collection taken in his honor, phoning the electric company (if the phone were working) to tell them their account would be paid in full and that they henceforth could stuff their bill up their Yuletide goose. As we already know, though, he'd ruled out taking help from friends. In fact, he'd ruled out even telling them he was in trouble. "We didn't want anyone to know, so we just finagled as best we could," he says. "We talked to our creditors, we restructured debt, we did different things." They endured from day to day.

What had kept the Staffords going during these worst of times? Did Earl's religious upbringing help? Did he, perhaps, remember something inspirational he'd once heard or read?

Well, as you know, I'd come from a religious family. My father was a Baptist preacher and we were raised in the church. So we had that faith in Christ—that belief you should hold out and continue to endure, if you know you're doing the right thing. That was inbred in me. It was almost innate. But you're right, you do remember things you read, and even today I still quote to myself a poem by William Henley—*Invictus*. I quote that even still. . . . I drew strength from that, and from the writer's own story: He was an invalid, and he overcame things. Part of what he wrote says, "My head is bloody, but unbowed." I don't bow my head for anybody, only to the Lord. It's those sorts of things that inspire you, that motivate you.

As for how Amanda hung on, she says:

Both Earl and I, when we took our vows to be married, knew it would be through good times and bad times. And I think, even when you're fed up, something in the back of your mind says: You can stick it out one more day. Or one more month.

She attributes her family's survival in large part to her husband's sheer determination:

Earl is a person who, if he sets his mind to something, he's going to do whatever it takes to get that done. He's got a very strong constitution. I mean, he's going to keep his family together no matter what: what he believes in, what his aspirations are. He's going to do whatever he can to get it done, to meet his goals. Sometimes I'd be discouraged and I'd say, "Well, I don't think," and he'd say, "Amanda, look. Don't worry about it. We're going to do it." My husband is my soul mate. Even though we would go through things, he was going to bring us out of it.

And he did. But it took three years.

## Willing to Do Anything

Their first big break came from a call Stafford placed to NYMA, the same outfit through which he'd landed his Hubble job. When he phoned one day, prospecting for work, NYMA told him they'd just gotten a big new piece of business and could use some help. "They said, 'There's this new agency—the Resolution Trust Corporation [RTC]—and we just picked up a contract to do some support. We have a position open. Would you like it?' And I said, 'Sure I would!' " UNITECH was back in business.

It hardly mattered what the RTC needed done, because, at this point, Stafford was willing to do anything. The same can-do attitude and flexibility he'd shown at age 8 as a kid entrepreneur served him well again, now, as an adult. In a sense, he was ready at age 42 to pick up soda bottles and cut lawns all over again. In the end, it's that attitude that saw him through—a saving humility.

Just as with the Hubble job, this arrangement required UNITECH to supply a wide mix of services, ranging from the managerial to the menial. In the mornings, Stafford-the-MBA worked as part of an RTC systems integration team. Dressed in his business suit, he attended meetings, working with a group of 30 or 40 other professionals who evaluated contracts and proposals that had been submitted to the agency. By the time five o'clock rolled around, the team's offices were strewn with papers and debris. One part of UNITECH's responsibility was janitorial—seeing that the rooms were cleaned and straightened, the sensitive documents safely put away. "They had to be secured," explains Stafford, referring to the confidential documents. "Unitech had to do that work. Or rather, I had to, because I *was* the company." The RTC may have thought it was getting a staff of people when it hired Unitech, but in reality it had gotten only Stafford.

"When the other guys on the team left for the day," Stafford explains, "I'd lag behind." He'd change into work clothes, and then as Stafford-the-custodian, would begin straightening the place up, cleaning, lugging boxes of documents to storage. For months he worked long into the night as the world's only officer-grade, MBA-trained janitor. "I tried to keep it discreet at first," he says, "but eventually the news got out that I was picking up the boxes, packing up the material, moving the boxes, and cleaning the rooms—all that kind of thing." The RTC, rather than disapprove of Stafford's dual role, was impressed. "I think they were impressed by the diligence," he says. "I was working my butt off. Supposedly, I was president of UNITECH—but it was just me, you know? Afterwards, they gave me another opportunity—thank God for that."

Specifically, the RTC awarded UNITECH a three-year, $2.5 million contract to provide systems integration support. "I didn't know there was that much money in the world!" laughs Stafford. CFO Mike Gottlieb, who joined UNITECH in 1994, says this contract marked a turning point in the company's fortunes for two reasons. First, it ensured UNITECH's short-term survival:

When you're contracting professional services to the government, there's no room for overhead. It's very lean. You need at least a couple of million dollars coming in before you can pay yourself a decent salary. Earl probably did something like a half a million dollars worth of business in 1991. In 1992, it was $2.5 million; and by '93 it was $5 million.

The RTC contract also allowed UNITECH to begin expanding its range of competencies. Explains Gottlieb:

> First, you get your foot in the door one way; then you start to grow your business. If you're hired to do systems engineering and integration—as we were—you market your customer by finding out what else he needs. It's evolutionary. One thing leads to another, and all of sudden you find yourself with expertise in an area that, three steps ago, you never planned on being in.

The company's activities have since expanded across a wide spectrum, with growth in revenue topping 400 percent. Stafford prides himself on UNITECH's ability to supply clients with what he calls "a total solution." "Sometimes that means people, sometimes it might mean hardware." The company stands ready to do *anything* a customer needs done, from reviewing and reconciling telecommunications bills for the FAA, to designing military training simulators, to equipping and operating a computer training school in the former Soviet republic of Belarus, to running network control centers for the U.S. Customs Service.

Looking back, Stafford says: "You know when you're first starting out, you're praying to make the payroll, to just make the rent. All these costs are hitting you, and you'll do anything. I'd have washed your car. I'd have painted your house. You're a generalist. Your first priority is to resolve financial issues—to generate revenue and abate some of the costs. Then, as those issues are taken care of, other issues come up. And one of them is: Wait a minute . . . what business do we want to be in, and why?" He likens the process to "stepping backwards into a master plan," and admits it wasn't until about a year ago that he and UNITECH's senior managers began to get clear on what lines of businesses they most wanted to be in. In fact, he says, they're still "crystallizing that vision."

## Growing the Business in New Directions

Work UNITECH undertook for military agencies in the early 1990s has led it into two new areas Stafford now considers his company's main focus for the future—training and simulation. One of the first opportunities arose when the Naval Surface Warfare Center in Maryland (for which UNITECH already had supplied systems engineering and integration services) said it needed help devising a simulated M-16 rifle. The idea was that soldiers could gain experience on the simulator safely and without wasting live ammunition. Later, they could graduate to shooting the real thing. The navy supplied the guns, then UNITECH's engineers removed the firing pins, put lasers in the barrels, and linked the guns with targets by computer. "When you aim and hit the trigger," says Gottlieb, "the laser shoots out at the target, and the result is recorded on the computer, so that a supervisor can monitor the accuracy of the firing and give the soldiers feedback." The whole thing isn't unlike one of those arcade games where you see a kid shooting at a screen. But this is a real weapon. The soldier gets the feel of the real weight, the real trigger.

Since completing the M-16 project, UNITECH has been asked to develop other training and simulation tools for the military, including a precision gunnery training system that teaches Marines how to fire mortars. "That was even cooler," says Gottlieb, "because not only did you have the real weapon, but when the soldier looked in the sight he would see, by video, a computer-generated image of enemies and objects moving around on the ground. He'd have to go through all the same steps as sighting and firing the real mortar." The advantage of such systems, he thinks, is obvious: "You take somebody who's never shot a particular weapon before, and it's expensive for them to keep firing off rounds until they finally learn how to operate the equipment. With this, you can learn how to operate expensive, dangerous equipment in a safe manner, so that when you finally put the real McCoy in somebody's hands, it's not the first time they're touching it. They're less likely to hurt themselves or somebody else, or to just fire aimlessly."

UNITECH has gone on to craft all sorts of other training products for the military, including interactive CDs that teach recruits everything from how to read a map to how to service a Humvee. But probably the biggest and most impressive example of its training expertise is a tank warfare simulator in use at Quantico. There, in a motor pool bay, sits a full-scale tanklike vehicle called the Light Armored Vehicle—Full Crew Interactive Simulation Trainer (LAV-FIST). Wires and computer monitors protrude from every port and window. Not only is the trainer versatile, allowing tank crews to practice some 400 different combat scenarios, it's realistic—so much so that even though the unit doesn't move, trainees regularly are overcome by motion sickness. LAV-FIST came into being when Marine Corps reservists—who typically aren't available for more than one or two days a month—complained they were not getting enough live-fire experience. LAV-FIST not only simulates live fire, but reservists trained on it outperform those who've been exposed only to the real thing. Plus, it does it at less cost and at less risk of injury. The only safety consideration with LAV-FIST, jokes a supervising officer, is climbing in and out of it.

These and other high-tech programs developed for the military have brought UNITECH tens of millions of dollars in revenue. But how much more might the same technology generate if it were adapted to the private sector's needs? It's a question that excites Stafford and causes not only him, but also potential investors, to view UNITECH's future with considerable optimism. "We still do a lot of systems integration stuff; we still do work for the FAA; and we're still active in telecommunications services," he says, reviewing the major lines of business that have brought the company to where it is today. "But on the other side of the house, we're producing interactive courseware—what we call intelligent learning solutions—all these advanced training and simulation efforts. We're transitioning to that more and more. We're investing in that."

There's no reason, really, that the same CD-driven technology that now teaches a soldier how to read a map can't be modified to serve corporate needs. Mike Gottlieb regards corporate human resources departments, in particular, as being potentially big customers. "That's where we see the market," he explains. "The technology is interactive—that's its most attractive feature. Until recently, if a company wanted to do some form of training, it did it by using videotapes. You'd watch the video, and it would be like watching PBS." (It's clear from his tone of voice what he means: dull.) "But the beauty of CDs is . . ." He stops, searching for the right illustration. "Have you ever played the CD game Doom? It's not a linear experience. You don't have to move from A to B to C. Let's say what you need to learn about is your employer's 401(k) program. With a teaching video, you'd have to sit through the policy on sick leave and vacations and all the rest of it to get to the 401(k) part. But with a CD, you can skip to it directly—or to any other thing that interests you. That's the joy of interactivity. Imagine a training room with 20 people and an instructor. They can all be working on the same CD, but each of them can be going at their own pace and in their own direction. That's why we think this has such good potential in the commercial area. And there's a testing feature built right in, for the supervisor's benefit." For employees who can't physically be present, the same content can be accessed through the Internet. So-called distance learning, thinks Stafford, holds enormous promise, as does a public-sector experiment that the company now has underway in Iowa.

The Drug Intervention Office of the State of Iowa recently asked UNITECH to help it develop a CD-based game that could teach kids the dangers of using illegal drugs—methamphetamines, especially. The teaching program that emerged, called "Meth or Life," allows kids in grades 4 through 8 to explore safely, in a classroom setting, the real-life consequences of decisions they make regarding drugs. What happens, for example, if you buy drugs and get caught? In this game "Go to Jail" takes on new meaning. Now antidrug agencies in other states—including those in Maryland, Virginia, and the District of Columbia—have expressed interest in having UNITECH develop programs for them, too. And the socially beneficial applications of UNITECH's technology need not stop there. Stafford foresees the day when similar teaching technology might be used to rehabilitate inner-city kids, mothers on public assistance, and prisoners. "I'm very big on social responsibility," he says. He's proud that technology he developed may someday "help people make the right decisions."

## "If This Is Really What You Want to Do . . . Don't Quit!"

Until the day that Stafford and his engineers devise some special piece of software to help persons facing comebacks make the right decisions, he offers the following low-tech advice:

- *Find your own deep source of inspiration and tap into it.* "If you don't feel strongly about that which you're doing, you shouldn't be doing it," he says. "You need a spiritual base. You'll find in life that you will always be overwhelmed with the concerns of the world. But you have to have something that's supernatural in your life to overcome them. Some spiritual foundation. And mine is my faith in Jesus Christ.

- *Be determined.* "If this is really what you want to do, and you've researched it—don't quit! If you're running a 100-yard dash, no one gets a medal for quitting after 90 yards. You have to cross the finish line. I really believe in that." Amanda Stafford seconds this: "Just don't give up. When you're in a storm, it seems like, *boy,* this will never end. But two days later the sun comes out and you forget that storm ever happened. No matter how bad things seem to you, remember that somebody else has gone through a lot worse than you and still managed to keep the faith. I tell friends, 'If we could make it, anyone can make it.' "

- *Never forget: The world needs you and what you're offering.* "When I look at what's driving America's economic engine today, it's entrepreneurship—guys who have something that's marketable, and who say 'I'm going out there and introduce it to the marketplace.' People are becoming aware of that—they're saying 'Wait a minute, the reason these large corporations are keeping me around is because I have something of value.' " Amanda Stafford agrees. All the sacrifices she and Earl made for UNITECH's survival were, she feels, ultimately worth it. "Never lose faith in yourself," she says. "Sometimes trials come into your life associated with the blessings that will later be forthcoming. But if you wallow in them [the trials] or retreat or lose your self esteem or faith, you may never receive those blessings." She offers this advice: No matter how bad things get, "remain grateful for the things that still are good. Think of the glass as half full. Through all that happened with us we still had our health, we had three loving children that never gave us any problem. We really had just one bad thing: the finances."

- *Keep cool.*   One of Stafford's greatest assets, thinks Mike Gott-lieb, is his ability to "keep rolling along," no matter how bad things get. "The worse the news, the calmer Earl gets. That's when calm counts. If you panic when your team is 14 points down, that's bad. You're never coming back. Maybe you can yell and scream when you're only a point down, but not 14." The same stiff-upper-lip attitude that saw Earl and his family through their bleak Christmas continues to inspire UNITECH today. "We've had some setbacks since Hubble," says Gottlieb. "Last year, for instance, we didn't win a contract we really thought we could have won and should have. It was a huge disappointment. Earl, though, took it in stride. All he said was, 'Okay, let's pull up our pants and move forward and win the next one.' He didn't cut off anybody's head for it. He didn't blame anybody privately or publicly. He went right on to the next thing." Then adds Gottlieb, laughing, "But just put a scratch in the conference table, though, and there's hell to pay! Don't print that!"

- *Be flexible.*  "Or maybe 'innovative' is the better word. Be improvisational. Use whatever comes to hand, and don't be too hung up on any one particular solution." Stafford might well have said the same thing another way: Don't let your own pride stand between you and your goal. If what you need to do is pick up soda bottles, pick 'em up! Move boxes. Have enough humility to do whatever victory demands.

Jim Stovall

# CHAPTER 11

✦ ≍✦≍ ✦

# Jim Stovall

## Cocreator of the Narrative Television Network

*"I was more scared than I'd ever been in my life."*

THE TELEVISION ROOM in Jim Stovall's Tulsa, Oklahoma, home was the sort of sanctuary that many a tired businessperson only wishes that he or she had—tranquil, comfy, and stocked with tapes of favorite films and television shows. It was just the kind of place, in fact, to which a person might want to retreat after a tough day. And Stovall—an entrepreneur and onetime stockbroker—had indeed retreated there. The problem was, he hadn't retreated to it for an hour, or an evening, or even a long weekend. At the age of only 29, he had retreated permanently. The room that once had been his respite from the world now *was* his world.

Stovall and the room made an unlikely pair: He was big—6 feet, 4 inches, 240 pounds. The room was puny—scarcely 9 by 12 feet. Since youth, Stovall had been strong and powerful. He'd been a national champion weight lifter and had worked summers in construction jobs, carrying loads of concrete. If anyone had tried to restrain him physically or to block his egress from the room, Stovall could have muscled his way out. If anyone had tried to lock Stovall in, he easily could have broken down the door. But there was no human jailer; the door remained unlocked. Still, Stovall sat there, hour after hour, week after week, chafing at his self-imposed confinement. Even the videotapes he used to watch, which previously had brought him pleasure, now only frustrated him. He found once-familiar storylines and plots impossible to follow.

His problem with the tapes could not ascribed to wandering attention. Stovall was concentrating on them hard. His intelligence was as acute and disciplined as when he'd graduated from college summa cum laude. Nor was he suffering some kind of psychosis. His mental health was fine; he was socially well adjusted and happily married. And behind him lay a string of successful accomplishments in both business and athletics.

Stovall's problem was simple: He'd gone blind.

## Ignoring His Problem Instead of Dealing With It

Stovall had been going blind, by small degrees, since the age of 7. Yet so gradual had been the deterioration of his sight that he'd always managed to convince his family and friends (and most of all, himself) that nothing especially bad was happening. "I bought into the popular notion," he now explains, "that a problem ignored is a problem dealt with." As he got older and his vision worsened, he simply got better at making normalizing compensations.

On his sixteenth birthday, he insisted that—like every other kid his age—he ought to get his driver's license and begin driving. He opted against taking driver's education, because he figured an instructor might notice his impairment. Instead, he went straight to the Department of Motor Vehicles and took the physical and written tests. When the moment came for him to read the eye chart, he listened carefully to the answers given by the man ahead of him in line. Then, when his own turn came, he repeated them verbatim, and passed. Against his parents' wishes, he spent an entire summer's wages buying his first car. And finally, late one hot Tulsa night, after his folks had gone out to an evening function, Stovall hopped into his car and motored off. He drove to the end of his block, turned left, and before he had gone a quarter of a mile, drove into the back of a parked car. Not just any car. A parked police car. The incident marked the beginning of the end of his career behind the wheel.

His sight remained fairly good in daylight, so such embarrassments were few. He managed to excel in football (night games excepted). It was while he was applying for a football scholarship to college—one requiring him to take an eye exam—that doctors first found and diagnosed his problem. Stovall had macular degeneration—a disease common in older people, but rare in kids. "Jim," said the specialist examining him, "We're not sure when, but we know that someday you're going to be totally blind. And there's nothing we can do about it."

In response, says Stovall, he redoubled his efforts to "escape reality." Was football out? Then there still were lots of other sports in which he could compete. He switched to weight lifting, where his size and strength mattered more than visual acuity. He trained hard, working his way up to becoming National Weightlifting Champion and a favored contender for the 1980 Olympic Games. (He never got a chance to compete in them, however, because the United States withdrew from the Moscow games in protest of the Soviet invasion of Afghanistan.)

Earlier in his weight training, Stovall's response to a setback proved prophetic: Two weeks before he was to compete in a crucial qualifying event, he broke three fingers of one hand in a practice lift. Not only did he still compete (with three fingers bandaged), he won a gold medal. Clearly, this was one determined guy.

He embarked on college with equal determination and, eventually, despite a few missteps, graduated with honors, thanks to the aid of volunteers who read his textbooks to him. One of these readers—a pretty young woman named Crystal—he asked to marry him. She assented, and by 1988 the Stovalls had settled down in Tulsa, with Jim earning a comfortable living as an investment broker and entrepreneur. He had a wife, a career, a house. And he still had a small measure of his eyesight. Life, he felt, could be a lot worse.

Then one morning, suddenly it was: Stovall woke up, opened his eyes, and saw absolutely nothing—only blackness. What his doctors had predicted had finally come true. He was completely blind. There was no refuting it now, no compensating for appearances' sake. This was it. "I realized my worst fear," he says. "The thoughts and doubts that came over me that morning would be almost impossible to describe." He groped his way into the bathroom, where he put his face close against a light bulb. "Up to that moment, I'd had at least some sense of light—a sense of shadow and of forms. Now everything was dark." *It's happened, it's happened,* he remembers saying to himself. He'd never even met a blind person. He had no idea what they did. He'd always considered himself sighted. "I was 29 years old and had no contingency plan for the rest of my life."

## More Denial: Retreating from the World

It was then that Stovall retired to his television room. After his first panic had subsided came a more lasting, deeply rooted fear: "I was scared to think about going outside my front door. I'm not too proud to admit that. I was more scared than I'd ever been in my life. My overriding thought was that I was never going to leave my house again." To venture out, he reasoned, was to invite further hurt—or worse, embarrassment. Stovall imagined himself awkwardly tripping over all the things he could no longer see: garden hoses, kids' bicycles, curbs. His overwhelming desire became "to insulate myself from anything else bad happening." Having done well in his brokerage business, he could afford to insulate himself for years, if he wanted.

In the television room, everything was comfortable, warm, and familiar. All the resources he might ever need were organized close at hand. "I thought: This is it for me, this is the rest of my life right here, with my little radio and my telephone and my tape recorder; and I'll never leave this room again." This room would be his fortress, his redoubt, his bastion against further upsets. "This was my whole world, and I really fully intended never to walk out of that room again." To while away his time, he started playing his collection of videotapes. And then, as day followed day, his exasperation grew.

He'd pop in a tape—something he'd watched many times before. But even with familiar films, the audio track seldom if ever supplied enough information for him to keep up with the action on the screen. His supreme moment of frustration came courtesy of Humphrey Bogart: "It was an old Bogart film entitled *The Big Sleep*. I had seen it enough times that through the sounds alone—and my memory—I was able to follow along fairly well until, in the middle of it, somebody shot a gun, and someone else screamed, and a car sped away, and I forgot the plot of the movie."

Stovall then uttered seven words he'd later come to see as golden: "Somebody ought to do something about that!"

"The only thing you have to do have a great business idea," he says today, "is to go about your daily life and wait for something bad to happen. When it does, you ask yourself: How could I help other people to avoid that?" Voila! An idea for a potentially great business: Somebody needed to provide a service that would make tapes "watchable" by blind people, by adding narration that would explain what was happening onscreen.

To take action on that idea, though—or to do anything else—Stovall first would have to leave his room. And he was having none of that. He didn't feel he could suffer any more disappointments or embarrassments. There would be no tripping, no walking into walls. He was better off where life was safe, predictable, and free of unpleasantness. His fear held him prisoner.

As days turned into weeks, he sometimes grappled with it, but the fear always won. Meanwhile, friends and well-wishers tried hard to help him—none more so than his wife. Yet Stovall steadfastly refused to be coaxed out. "I'd decided," he says, "to insulate myself permanently. I literally believed I'd never leave that room again."

Looking back on this awful period, he ascribes his own intransigence to what he calls the spider-monkey syndrome. "Spider monkeys," he explains, "are very small, approximately four to six inches tall, and look very much like humans. They live in the tallest trees in the most dense jungle in the Amazon basin." For years, he says, outside people tried without success to capture them—until a native showed them the proper method:

> To capture a spider monkey, you simply put one peanut inside of a small glass bottle, which you leave at the base of a tree. While you leave, the spider monkey will climb down the tree, put his hand inside the bottle, and grab the peanut, making his fist too large to get out of the bottle. You have now captured a spider monkey. You can return and put a whole bag of peanuts right next to the spider monkey, and he will not let go of the one peanut he's holding onto that he can't eat and maybe didn't especially want in the first place. You can take away his freedom, but he will not let go of that one peanut.

Ignoring, for a moment, the question of *why* the monkey won't let go (stupidity, pride, and sheer frustration seem to be top contenders for the reason), he's helpless to achieve a better situation for himself until he lets go—literally—of the present one. "Failure and success," muses Stovall, "cannot occupy the same space. You must let go of one to begin enjoying the other." In Stovall's own case, he eventually was *forced* to let go.

"I hit bottom," Stovall says, finally sinking to a depth of despair so low it grabbed him by the lapels. And in that moment came a kind of epiphany: "It was true that nothing bad had happened to me while I stayed there in the room. But where nothing bad happens, nothing *good* does, either." It became a question which was the worse hell: remaining a prisoner of his own fear or risking the knocks he might suffer if he were to venture out. Stovall remembers saying to himself: *"This isn't living. This is only existing. I'm not going to lose any more of my sight; but if I continue to sit here, I'm going to lose my life. Blindness has happened. Deal with it."*

He decided he would risk the knocks.

## Building a New Life—and a New Business

"The process of getting myself out of that room was not easy or swift. It happened a little at a time. But it all began with that decision." The first day, he walked 52 feet to his mailbox, then returned indoors. From that humble start, he says, his whole life began to change. "I got a new vision of who I could become." All at once, it seemed, he was launched on a new path.

Daily, progressing by small increments, he gained confidence:

> The first time I stepped out of my house and walked to the mailbox, I was tentative—scared stiff might be the better description. But the 500th time, I was anything but that. I could just as easily have stumbled on the 500th trip as on the first. A neighbor could have left a tricycle in my path, or a tree limb might have blown into my driveway. But by the time I'd made 500 trips, I knew that if I tripped over something, I could get back up. Nothing about the driveway or the potential hazards had changed. I had changed.

His confidence had strengthened. "And in that," he says, "lies all the difference in the world."

He ventured even further out and began attending a support group for the blind and visually impaired. There, he met Kathy Harper, a partially sighted legal assistant, who, like Stovall, was attending the group for the first time. They hit it off, and Stovall shared with her his Humphrey Bogart frustration. The two began discussing various business services that could supply audio-enhanced movies and other programming to the blind.

Their idea, originally, was to produce videotapes with the voice of a narrator inserted during lulls in preexisting dialog—tapes that would let people "hear what they couldn't see." If, for example, the existing sound track offered only a thud followed by a squeal of brakes, the added narration might say something like, "The crooks try and fail to run down Philip Marlow with their car."

A little preliminary research showed that the audience for such a service was potentially vast. There were some 13 million blind or partially sighted consumers in the United States alone. Neither Stovall or Harper knew anything about the business of movies or television, nor about the technicalities of recording. But they didn't let that faze them. Instead, they felt spurred on by a shared sense of excitement and by an optimism born of total inexperience. Because they didn't know what they couldn't do, they moved forward experimentally, by fits and starts. "If you look back at any great success," says Stovall, "You'll see it hardly ever begins with some supremely self-confident guy who says 'I know I'm going to make it.' More often than not, it begins with a bit of fear and trembling and some such statement as, 'Well, I'm willing to try and try, until I get there.' " Alluding to the fact that Harper herself is only partly sighted, he jokes that the two of them represented, "in more ways than one, a case of the blind leading the blind."

## Their First Office: the Basement and the Broom Closet

They established the Narrative Television Network (NTN), with Stovall as president and Harper as minority partner. (Today she serves as vice president for strategic planning.) They then sought and got permission from producers and syndicators of such hit shows as *Matlock* and *The Big Valley* to insert NTN's added narration.

Working from their own makeshift recording studio, the pair began trying to produce an example of the kind of tape they thought their audience would want. "Actually," says Stovall, "I'd use the term *studio* a bit loosely. We were working out of the basement of a condominium, here in downtown Tulsa, which, as you may know, is not the entertainment capital of the world. There was a broom closet underneath the basement stairs, and we took the brooms out of it and hung up some boat cushions to help soundproof the space. *That* was our first studio." They got their electronic equipment by cold-calling manufacturers and explaining they were working on a new idea—television for the blind. After a few such calls, Stovall says, "I realized that one of our first obstacles was going to be getting ourselves taken seriously."

At last they found one manufacturer who offered to loan them what they needed for free. As Stovall explains it, "The guy said, 'Obviously I'd like to sell you a whole lot of expensive equipment, because that's how we make our living. But we feel it would be embarrassing to us to have a blind guy buy all this stuff and then find out his idea doesn't work. So we'll loan it to you. As soon as you find out your idea doesn't work, you call us, and we'll come pick it up." Good enough.

In their studio beneath the stairs, Stovall and Harper got to work. Harper, sitting at a card table, ran the recording equipment. Stovall handled the narration—or tried to. First, Harper would read him the lines that he was supposed to speak; then, he would run into the room with the boat cushions on the wall and talk into the microphone. He'd then run back out, so Harper could read him his next line. It wasn't what you'd call a smooth arrangement. "Then one morning," he says, "Kathy told me that, as chief recording engineer, she had come up with a breakthrough that would improve our efficiency tremendously." Harper had removed the handle from one of the brooms that previously had been stored in the closet. She told Stovall that under the new arrangement, he was to sit still in the closet and wait for her cue. "When the moment came for me to talk," he says, "she stabbed me in the back with the broomstick. Then I'd know it was time for me to deliver my next line." Sitting there, waiting to be poked with a stick, he remembers thinking, "I wonder if Ted Turner got started this way?" (Turner now serves as a member of NTN's advisory board.)

## Creating a Product and Getting It on Television

By such haphazard means the two eventually managed to tape new narration for seven programs. They then sought the services of a professional broadcast studio, which, they hoped, could help them merge their new narration with the original sound tracks.

Stovall contacted the manager of what he believed to be the best recording facility in the area, and asked if NTN could have a meeting with its chief engineer. He explained that he and Harper needed an engineer who was "truly an expert," because the idea that NTN was pioneering had never been tried before. "Sure," said the manager, "come on over." So Harper and Stovall arrived, with the contents of their own "studio"— tapes, wires, and recording machine—in a large box. They explained their idea to the manager and his engineer. A long pause followed.

"Jim," said the engineer, "I've been in this business 21 years. I have seen everything and done everything, and I can absolutely tell you, beyond a shadow of a doubt, that what you want to do won't work." The engineer wasn't even interested in taking the lid off NTN's box.

Stovall, disappointed, refused to let things end there. Keeping his composure, he turned to the studio head and said: "I need to apologize to you. I know I asked if we could meet with your best expert—and apparently this is he, right here. But do you have anybody we can talk to who's maybe a little *less* expert?"

The less-expert expert was a college kid who told them that he was working at the studio just to earn a few extra bucks. "But if you want," he said, "we can wire 'er up and see what happens." Confided Stovall to Harper, "I think this is the expert we've been looking for."

Frame by frame and word by word, the two soundtracks melded together seamlessly—just as NTN's proud parents had hoped they would. And six months later, Harper and Stovall were presented with an Emmy for having "expanded the scope of television" by the Academy of Television Arts and Sciences. Not only did NTN's cofounders come away with a prestigious award, they gained a reluctance to take no for an answer from experts ever again.

Their conviction was only underscored by a experience they had shortly afterward with a man described to them as being "the gorilla of cable television"—a guy with the ability to get *any* kind of programming on television.

Stovall and Harper understood that NTN could reach only so many viewers by providing its tapes directly to consumers. But if they could somehow get the same tapes played on television, they could reach a much wider audience. Toward that end—and before their meeting with the gorilla—Stovall approached his local cable operator, Tulsa Cable Television, to see if it would be interested in carrying NTN's wares. Stovall and Harper lugged their studio-in-a-box over to Tulsa Cable's office, and again did their stuff. *Presto!* They were on television. Said the program director, "That's the most amazing thing I've ever seen!"

The following week, they had their meeting with the gorilla—who turned out to be a smallish, rather unprepossessing man. He listened to them for two hours, then announced politely that he was sorry, but NTN didn't have a prayer of getting on cable. "Not even onto one station?" Stovall asked provocatively. No, said the gorilla, shaking his head sagely, not even one. "Well," said Stovall, "we may never get onto *more* than one station, but we got on one last Friday."

Their final problem was coming up with enough product. In order to persuade stations to carry NTN, Stovall found that he usually had to commit to delivering solid 2-hour blocks of programming. That's what stations wanted. But the running time for NTN's movies averaged just 1½ hours. How to fill the 30-minute gap? Stovall decided, pretty much on the spot, to produce and host a talk show, which would run for 15 minutes before and after every 90-minute feature. He figured he could interview some of the old stars featured in the films, plus television celebrities and other luminaries.

But how was NTN to get these stars? Stovall and Harper went to the Tulsa Public Library, where they found a reference book called *Addresses of the Stars*. They jotted down the addresses of Katharine Hepburn, Jimmy Stewart, and Jack Lemmon, among others, then started banging out letters requesting interviews. The letters explained that the stars—for no money—should agree to appear on NTN for an "incredible career opportunity": the chance to be interviewed by the blind host of an as-yet-mythical talk show on an as-yet-nonexistent cable network. And, oh yes, asked the letters—could the stars please *hurry along* their acceptances? The interviews had to be taped in the next few weeks.

"Less than two weeks later," says Stovall, "the first response came back. The return address said 'Katharine Hepburn, New York City.'" The note inside read, "Dear Jim: If you will call this number, we can discuss the interview," and it was signed *Katharine Hepburn*. Stovall phoned, and Hepburn herself picked up. When he told her he was surprised that she answered her own phone, the great lady replied (in those inimitably patrician tones): "But Jim, don't you answer your own phone? I've always felt that when one's phone rings, one should answer it."

The Hepburn interview became only one of more than 80 that now are played before and after every feature. Photos of the guest celebrities line the walls of NTN's Tulsa headquarters, as do NTN's many awards, which include an Emmy, the Evan Kemp Entrepreneurship Award from the President's Committee on Employment of People with Disabilities, and a Blue Chip Enterprise Initiative award (bestowed by the U.S. Chamber of Commerce and MassMutual on entrepreneurs who have surmounted great adversities).

## Finally, a Profit

Today, NTN is thriving. Its programming, carried on 1,300 cable systems and other outlets throughout North America, reaches an estimated 35 million homes. (It can also be found in 11 foreign countries.) Amazingly, 60 percent of NTN's audience consists of fully sighted people who simply like having extra narration. The company is profitable, debt free, and enjoys annual revenues of around $6 million. Says Stovall:

> I'm very proud of the fact that we're a for-profit business. "A lot of people, I know, spend their time doing charitable, nonprofit work. But I feel that in our business, it's really one and the same. I don't know of

many charities that do as good work as we do. I'm especially proud, as blind person, to have been able to create a company that makes a profit and pays taxes, since that only legitimizes the commercial power of our audience, in my view. It shows that these are people who spend money, who buy things; that they're worth advertisers' dollars.

The company's growth potential, Stovall maintains, is limitless. NTN has begun carrying new kinds of programming, including Broadway shows, and has just finished work on its first big-screen project: narration for an IMAX film on the life of writer Ernest Hemingway, which should be in theaters sometime in 2000.

NTN has branched out to the Internet. "We have a partnership with Broadcast.com/Yahoo!," says Stovall. "You can go to our Web site—narrativetv.com—24 hours a day, seven days a week, and watch narrated movies on demand, for free. They start when you want them to start. You can pause them, back them up. It's almost like instant home video delivery. The Internet gives us a global audience, access to all visually impaired people around the world." For the fully sighted, he notes, video delivery on the Web is premature, "because although the audio is perfect, the video is bad. That's why Broadcast.com was interested in us— we have a huge audience of people for whom good video is not critical."

Research, Stovall says, shows that visually impaired people actually own and operate computers at a rate higher than that of the general population. The blind are able to navigate the Web fairly easily, thanks to software that reads text aloud. "So, we feel that, long term, that's the delivery system for our audience. We're not giving up our broadcast or cable or satellite delivery, but with this we can be an around-the-clock source for movies and television."

There's one other promising development: The FCC, according to Stovall, is poised to *require* broadcasters to offer the kind of narration that only NTN and public television currently provide. "From a business perspective, that's a wonderful thing. It's like being an automaker and waking up one day to find the government is about to mandate universal car ownership." NTN, he thinks, is going to have to get much bigger soon, to meet increased demand for narration.

## A New Direction: Motivating Others to Achieve Their Dreams

Running NTN is but one facet of Stovall's burgeoning career. He's an author, writing a weekly newspaper column called "Winners' Wisdom," which appears in a number of papers nationwide. He's also written books, including: *The Way I See the World* (GSN, 1999), *You Don't Have to Be Blind to See* (Thomas Nelson, 1996), *Success Secrets of Super Achievers* (GSN, 1997; a compilation of his on-air celebrity interviews), and a novel, *The Ultimate Gift* (Executive Books, 1999). "It's a very creative working environment," he says of NTN's offices. "We have our core television business, of course. But we also have a personal development business. We provide content for people, whether it's TV programming or positive messages for people who read my books or columns, or audiences who come to hear me speak."

He's much in demand as an inspirational speaker, addressing upwards of 500,000 people a year at business meetings, sports events, and conventions. He has even addressed a meeting of optometrists. As keynote speaker, he's shared the podium with the likes of General Colin Powell, Tony Robbins, Robert Schuller, Paul Harvey, Christopher Reeve, and Barbara Bush.

Many who see Stovall onstage would never guess that he was blind, if he didn't tell them himself. Explains friend and fellow inspirational speaker Dr. Denis Waitley:

> I was spellbound the first time I saw Jim speak. After he was introduced, he walked to the podium confidently and with a strong stride, took the microphone from its stand, and proceeded to walk about the stage unassisted, occasionally coming right to the edge of the platform to peer into the faces of those who sat before him. Then he walked down the steps from the stage to speak directly to the people in the first few rows. He remembered not only what each person said, but also where each person sat, so that he might continue to have a dialogue with several of the audience.

There's no trick involved here. Everything that Stovall does is the result of his having arrived hours before an event to pace the stage, get the feel of it, and practice every move. In his mind, he visualizes his whole performance—a discipline taught to him by Waitley. Stovall's years as an on-camera interviewer have imbued him with all the grace and self-assurance of a fully sighted speaker. "Working in television has helped me a lot," he says, "because I have to look at the people I'm talking to and look as normal as I can, so people around me will feel comfortable."

He closes speeches by giving people two things: his personal phone number and a showstopping offer.

When you are willing to make a commitment to your destiny, I will be your partner in success. Any time you're depressed, discouraged, or any time you're not sure your dreams are going to come true, you pick up the nearest telephone and call that number. We have people who answer the phone 24 hours a day, seven days a week, and they know there's always one kind of call I'll always return.

The number is (918) 627-1000.

Having surmounted his own blindness, and having rubbed elbows as a professional speaker with some of today's best-known uplifters, Stovall has become something of a connoisseur of popular self-help advice. Much of it he finds lacking.

You know, I do three speeches a month now that usually get billed as inspirational, and I find myself sharing the same arenas with a lot of motivational speakers. I've learned to tell the difference between the ones giving out useful advice and the ones dispensing only theory.

What kinds of advice does Stovall automatically dismiss?

I've heard many motivational speakers say, with a bit of a strain in their voice, "You've got to pay the price for success." I don't necessarily believe in that. I believe when you follow your passion, you will enjoy the price of your success. If you don't follow your passion, you will pay the price for failure. In the final analysis, what you pursue is more important than how you pursue it.

Stovall also dismisses any advice that discounts "the seriousness or size of obstacles that struggling people have to face. Those personal obstacles are real. They're intimidating."

Stovall has also come to accept the fact that people seldom heed advice, good *or* bad. He makes an analogy to the in-flight safety instructions read regularly to passengers by flight attendants. "I fly two or three times a week, and they give this speech about the oxygen masks dropping down," he says. "No one ever pays attention. It's just a voice, talking." The only time you wish you'd listened, he says, is when your plane is crashing. "I think it takes a while for us to realize that self-help information really does apply to *us*." Absent some catalytic crisis, most people are content to sit buckled in their seats, eating salted nuts, leading lives that are at best mediocre.

## Choosing the Life You Want to Live

*"Bad,"* Stovall says, "is often not the enemy of good, so much as *mediocre* is. If something is bad enough in life, we will change it or deal with it. But when it's okay or just good enough, we often will suffer with conditions far below those to which our destiny could lead us."

As someone who once allowed himself to sit for weeks in a 9- by 12-foot room, Stovall understands that setbacks have the power to vitiate life and stop it in its tracks. But he also has little patience with people— disabled or otherwise—who allow their setbacks to hold permanent dominion over them. "You and I only have one right in this world," he says, "and that is the right to choose. We can't always choose what happens to us, but we can always choose what we are going to do about it. You are where you are in every area of your life because of the choices you have made in the past."

In his public speaking career, Stovall travels the world telling many thousands of people each year that they are where they are in their lives— both personally and professionally—because of their own past decisions:

> A lot of people don't like to hear that, because we have become a society of people that loves to blame someone else for our condition. So when I show up and tell them they are where they are because that's what they chose, they tell me things like: *"I know my life's messed up, but if you knew my spouse, you would know why I'm in the shape I'm in."* Or they will tell me things like: *"My boss is an idiot"*; *"The weather's too hot"*; *"The taxes are too high"*; *"I'm a middle child"*; or whatever the current excuse is that they use to justify their life of mediocrity.

Only when we accept the fact that we are where we are because of choices we've made in the past can we live every day of the rest of our lives in the certain knowledge that we can do anything we want to do if we simply make the right choices.

When Stovall addressed one of the largest organizations of the blind in America a few years ago, what he said to them was blunt: *"If many of you miraculously received your sight again today, you would have to come up with another excuse for the lousy way you live your lives."* ("I doubt," he says, "if I'll be invited back to speak to that group anytime soon!")

The most severe disability of all, he insists, is having low (or *no*) expectations of one's self. "We always live up to the expectations that we have of ourselves, or that we allow others to place upon us." For this reason, well-intentioned efforts by friends and well-wishers often exacerbate the problem faced by someone struggling to surmount a setback and forge a new life. Your friends' interest usually is in helping you get back to where you *were,* before misfortune struck. "What they do, by trying to protect you, is confirm your tendency to stay inside your comfort zone, to live with your existing limitations, rather than to challenge them and move on. They want to help you stay in your 'little room.' " The biggest mistake a person can make, thinks Stovall, is trying to get back to where he or she was.

"Once you come face to face with whatever it is—blindness, alcoholism, bankruptcy, whatever—your immediate thought is to get back to normality, to ground zero." Instead, Stovall says, you must force yourself—alone and without friends' support, if necessary—to risk further pain, uncertainty, and embarrassment. "Otherwise, you will sit at your house waiting for all the lights to be green before you start." And that, quite simply, never happens. Start now, no matter how awful the sensation. Stovall himself thinks he was blessed to have been blasted from his television room by the crisis of despair he suffered. If not for it, he might still be there. It forced him, for the first time in his life, to realistically confront himself. "Many people never have to do that. They roll through life without ever giving too much thought to what they can and cannot do. I knew I had to make some choices."

## "Ask Yourself 'What Really Matters to Me?' "

True recovery from a setback, Stovall thinks, has to start with rigorous and unsparing self-appraisal: Who are you? *Where* are you, in comparison to where you want to be? "As a blind person," Stovall says, "I am always intrigued with the way that sighted people get—or fail to get—from point A to point B. It is fascinating to me that people who can see perfectly spend a great deal of their time being lost." The reason they do, he argues, is that they too often have only the haziest idea of the point from which they're starting. "The single most vital piece of information necessary in order to get where you want to go," he insists, "is knowing where you are." There are millions of people who want to have a certain bank balance, weigh a certain amount, or achieve any other business or personal goal, he says, and most are happy to fantasize for hours about where they hope someday to be. But how many of them take the elementary and necessary step of seeing where they really are? The Chinese proverb that "A journey of a thousand miles begins with a single step" indeed is true; but if the pilgrim wants to reach a specific destination, he or she must be sure that step is pointed in right direction. "Think about all the things you want in the personal and professional areas of your life," says Stovall. "Then take account of where you are today. You may find that you're closer than you think. But, in any event, you will have taken the first step in the right direction, and you will have reduced an ethereal dream into a practical goal."

If he could presume to modify the Ten Commandments, Stovall says, he'd add Stovall's Eleventh Commandment: "Thou shalt not kid thyself." It's a rule that applies with special force to people coming back from failure. "We always live up to the expectations that we have for our own lives," he explains, so it's important for us not only to set goals high, but to make sure they're *really ours*—not some friend's or well-wisher's. "If we're not careful, we can find ourselves winning someone else's battle while we lose our own war." Having the courage to follow one's own goals carries with it an excitement, strength, and passion that are lacking when one tries to follow someone else's.

Stovall tells a story by way of illustration:

> There were two warring tribes in the Andes, one that lived in the lowlands and the other high in the mountains. The mountain people invaded the lowlanders one day, and as part of their plundering of the people, they kidnapped a baby and took the infant with them back up into the mountains.
>
> Although the lowlanders didn't know how to climb the mountain, they sent out their best party of fighting men to bring the baby home. They first tried one method of climbing and then another. They tried one trail and then another. After climbing only a few hundred feet after several days of effort, the lowlander men decided that the cause was lost, and they prepared to return to their village below.
>
> As they were packing their gear for the descent, they saw the baby's mother—with the baby strapped to her back—coming down the mountain that they had been unable to climb. One man greeted her and said, "How did you climb this treacherous mountain when we, the strongest and most able men in the village, couldn't do it?"
>
> She shrugged her shoulders and said, "It wasn't your baby."

Stovall recommends that goal seekers regularly review their objectives, weighing the passion that they feel for each one. "Take everything you want to do in your life and either do it now, put it on your calendar for a specific point in the future, or write it off as something you are never going to do." The single most important question seekers can ask themselves, he says, is "Does this really matter?" Before wasting time, effort, and energy on a host of exigencies, first ask yourself: "What really matters to me? Which of these demands, if met, will transform me into who I want to become?" "Great people down through the ages have demonstrated one consistent trait: That is the ability to focus all energy and their entire being on the elements of their life that they deem to be important." When we do this, Stovall says, we live our lives "on purpose" instead of at random, no longer distracted by whim or circumstance.

To achieve his own comeback, Stovall had to acquire what amounts to a second kind of sight—one he now considers superior to the ocular kind he lost when he was 29. He uses mental visualization not just for preparing speeches but for every other aspect of his life. He has used it to draw for himself, figuratively speaking, a mental map that he can consult regularly to see where he is in relation to his goals. Says his friend Waitley, who has written extensively about visualization, "Jim may not have his eyesight, but he's never lost his vision."

Anyone, Stovall believes, can acquire this same facility if they define, very simply and clearly, their core objectives. "You have to reduce your life's goals to what I call an 'elevator speech.' If you can't explain it to a total stranger in 20 seconds, then you really have not defined it in your own mind." Formulating a personal mission statement helps. Stovall's own? He says his grandmother once expressed it as well as he ever could himself: "My grandson helps blind people see television, and he travels all around the world telling people they can have good things in their lives."

## "Failure Is Not Defeat. It Is Merely a Stepping Stone to Your Destiny"

What messages would Stovall want to convey directly to readers of this book? He gave five:

- *The fear never leaves.* Even today, after all he has accomplished since being a depressed blind guy trapped in a 9- by 12-foot room, Stovall still suffers episodes of the kind of doubt and fear that originally immobilized him. The persistence of fear in the lives of people who have successfully staged comebacks, he says, is a fact glossed over by most self-help books. "I think that there's this myth around that once you get to a certain level in your life, it's all downhill and shady. That's not been my experience." He recommends people read Richard Nixon's book *In the Arena: A Story of Victory, Defeat and Renewal* (Simon & Schuster, 1980) for its realistic treatment of this issue. "It's probably the best book I've read on the subject, because Nixon talks about the fact that, okay, you can come back, but the former defeat is still there. Nixon went to his grave as a maligned figure; he never quite left the legacy he wanted to. The same is true for me. I can have the best life I can possibly have, but I'm still a blind person." Though blindness, he insists, is the single best thing that ever happened to him (because it opened new doors and pointed him in new directions), it's still an inconvenience and source of occasional frustration. "There are days when the life I lead, at its best, still is not as good as being able to see. It's not like I ever get over that. There are days when I'd love to be back in that safe little room. A lot of them."

- *To begin a comeback, first change your mind.* The reason he's *not* back in his little room is that the Stovall of today is a different person—a person who won't allow himself to go there. "When you change your mind about who you are, everything becomes possible. The difficulties are still there; the obstacles still exist. I don't *see* any better today than I did when I walked out of that TV room. But my whole world has changed, because I changed my mind about who I am and what I do. My difficulties are no more than yours or anybody's who will read this book. We're only as big as the smallest thing it takes to divert us from our goal." What sets the new Stovall apart from the old is attitude: He made a conscious decision to be brave, to get up out of his chair and venture forth, even if the cost was that every now and then he'd step on a rake. He pushed himself. He sums up the difference between his old and new selves this way: "Failure feels fear and retreats. Success feels the same fear and moves forward anyway."

- *Pursue your passion.* "I have never met anyone I felt was lazy or stupid," Stovall says. "I have, though, met people who are pursuing the wrong course. We all know people who can barely drag themselves through a substandard performance each workweek, but who will jump out of bed at 4 A.M. on Saturday to go fishing, skiing, etc. Find the right game, and everyone is a winner." He says he's read, on tape, the biographies of some 1,500 "great men and women" who achieved their personal and professional goals. "I can find very few things that these people had in common except a sense of their own destiny, their own place in history. They believed they were put on this earth to perform a certain task, and that this task would not be accomplished without their best efforts. This kind of personal accountability will lead to greatness in any area of life."

- *Liberate "Someday Isle."*   This is Stovall's whimsical name for the place to which adults consign the "unrealistic" ambitions of their youth. "It's a picture-postcard kind of place where the weather is always perfect and everything is always wonderful, except that nothing ever happens. Every time we think of our long-forgotten dreams and goals, we say to ourselves, 'Someday I'll do this' or 'Someday I'll do that.' But someday never comes." That's a tragedy, he thinks, because people brave or imaginative or just plain persistent enough often find ways of making the "unrealistic" entirely practicable. If a dream still has the power to power to motivate you, liberate it. "I defy you," says Stovall, "to find a statue or a monument erected to anyone because they were realistic."

- *Don't quit!*   It's true, Stovall says, that success breeds success. "But failure also breeds failure. Once you've had a setback and embraced it, it's easier to opt for failure a second time." So don't embrace it. Keep swinging. In his most recent book, *The Way I See The World,* Stovall writes: "Failure is not defeat. It is merely a stepping stone to your destiny. As a totally blind person, I believe I could hit a baseball thrown by the best pitcher in the major league if you would allow me to keep swinging until I got a hit. Sooner or later, I would hit one, as long as I kept trying. So, in the final analysis, the only true failure is to stop trying."[1]

Kevin Maxwell

◆━┄ ≡◊≡ ┄━◆

# Kevin Maxwell

*Founder of Telemonde and Former CEO
of Maxwell Communications*

*"One could have—should have—abandoned ship."*

KEVIN MAXWELL'S KIDS took pride in their pop, the big record set-ter. None of the other kids' dads, they could be certain, had gotten himself into the *Guinness Book of World Records* alongside the world's strongest man, tallest building, deepest diver, biggest burrito, or other spectacular superlatives. The nuance, though, that Kevin's children failed to grasp was that their dad had not been singled out for a positive achievement—quite the opposite. Here's what Guinness had to say:

> On September 3, 1992, newspaper heir Kevin Maxwell became the world's biggest bankrupt following the death of his father, Robert Maxwell, with debts of pounds 406.8 million ($813.6 million).[1]

Look up "Bankruptcy" in the index, and Guinness takes you straight to Maxwell.

Pandora Maxwell, Kevin's wife, told the BBC she'd had a devil of a time quelling her children's initial enthusiasm:

> It's something that is quite difficult to explain to them—[that] it isn't actually that good a thing. I mean, it's all right if you're the highest high jumper or the fastest runner of all time. To be in the Guinness book of records the biggest bankrupt of all time is no great honor. That's some-thing that they don't understand. They don't really understand the ins and outs of it. Because if they did, I'd ask them to explain it to *me*.

By the "ins and outs," she was referring to Maxwell's half-decade legal and financial ordeal following the mysterious death of his father, British newspaper publisher Robert Maxwell—an ordeal so vast, so costly, and so politically charged that it has become the stuff of several books and at least one television documentary. In one of the knottiest criminal proceedings ever in English legal history, Maxwell found himself accused of having robbed and defrauded 32,000 innocent pensioners of their old-age savings. He was looking at a potential 12 years in prison. The trial consumed five full years of his life, made him easily one of the most hated men in England, and yanked out from under him the thick carpet of corporate perks and privileges on which he previously had trod. At his financial nadir, the cocky young man who once had jetted around the world aboard the Concorde found himself waiting in line with other indigents to apply for public welfare.

The onset of all Maxwell's troubles began in the predawn of an early November morning in 1991, when his father—the bullying, charismatic, and luxuriantly eyebrowed media tycoon Robert Maxwell—jumped, fell, or was pushed to his death from his yacht, while cruising off the Canary Islands. One might truly say that Maxwell's troubles began the moment that his father's ended.

## Heir to Robert Maxwell's Scandal and $4.4 Billion in Debt

Found floating face-up and naked in the North Atlantic, Robert Maxwell caused the same notoriety in death that he had in life. "It is a measure of Maxwell's fame, his zest for self-publicity and extraordinary personality combining to make him Britain's best-known businessman, that for weeks afterward people would, as in the Kennedy assassination of 1963, talk of where they were and what they were doing the moment they heard he had vanished," Maxwell newspaper editor and biographer Roy Greenslade wrote, following the potentate's death.[2]

Preliminary evidence pointed toward a heart attack, not drowning, though conclusive evidence never materialized. Was it an accident? Maxwell afterward put forth the claim that his father fell to his doom while groggily relieving himself off the side of the boat in the early hours of the morning. Or was it murder? Some suggested that Maxwell's torn muscles indicated there might have been a struggle. A long list of possible conspiracy-theory suspects—ranging from the KGB to the New York Mafia and the Israelis—spoke to the heterogeneous array of heavy hitters that Robert Maxwell had managed to antagonize during his 68 years.

In the end, the most popular theory accepted by the public was that Robert Maxwell had simply committed suicide. His family insists this is impossible—that if you knew the man, you'd know he'd never kill himself. But his death, accidental or not, neatly coincided with a crisis in his business life. During the months leading up to Robert's death, his media empire, built largely on debt, was wobbling, on the verge of collapse, no longer able to support the weight of its titanic borrowings. Had Robert lived, he would have had to face the consequences himself. Now all eyes turned to Kevin.

In fact, Maxwell's claim to being a comeback champ rests far less on his having built some great, new, gleaming business edifice than on his having crawled out of the stygian pit of failure and disgrace dug for him by his father. Guinness was right to honor him for negative achievement, but his extraordinary accomplishment isn't that he holds the title of biggest bankrupt. It's that, having suffered the consequences of that distinction, he isn't now divorced, dispirited, dead, or languishing in jail.

Robert Maxwell—the digger of Maxwell's pit—had been so mighty that no one seemed able to say no to him—bankers, especially. Six feet tall, 290 pounds, with Groucho Marx eyebrows and jet-black hair (dyed twice a month), he was famous for traumatizing his subordinates, firing senior managers (including his two sons), and then hiring them back later, after his rage had cooled.

His troubles were largely of his own making: He'd expanded aggressively, incurring new debts as he acquired new media properties, including the *New York Daily News* and the Macmillan publishing house. In the last months of his life, he saw revenues from his publicly held Maxwell Communications Corporation and Mirror Group Newspapers (not to mention his many privately held companies) shrivel from recession and debt. As business conditions deteriorated and bankers demanded payment, he faced a financial crisis greater than any he had faced before. How would he respond?

"When the recession came, and the interest rates doubled in practically one year, my father made the catastrophic decision to brazen it out and to borrow more money, basically to ride out the recession," Maxwell recalled in *The Trial of Kevin Maxwell,* a 1996 BBC documentary about Maxwell's legal and financial troubles. "Nobody in the business, not myself or any of my father's fellow directors, had the strength to stop him, once he'd made his mind up."

Maybe a sensible program of asset sales would have reduced Robert's exposure, but the brazen buccaneer didn't take that safe and unexciting route. Instead, he began juggling assets, trying to use securities owned by his public companies to prop up the value of his private holdings, upon which much of his empire depended. Then, suddenly, Robert turned up dead.

When Robert Maxwell's body was positively identified, Kevin Maxwell cried—a rare display of emotion for the self-contained young man. Then he dried his tears and assumed the chairmanship of MCC, with his brother Ian taking the helm of the Mirror Group. Side by side, united, they faced the television cameras. Both sons made a public vow to carry on, managing all the while to maintain a surprising degree of cool. It was the first manifestation, post–Robert Maxwell, of what many would refer to as Kevin Maxwell's remarkable sangfroid. No less an authority than Maxwell's wife proclaimed him "a master of the art of hiding how he actually feels."

In scarcely more than a month, despite Maxwell's efforts, the Maxwell empire collapsed under the weight of $4.4 billion in debt, and evidence emerged that among the assets Robert Maxwell had juggled in his frenzy to save his private empire had been his employees' pension funds. To most observers, it looked as if Maxwell *père* knowingly had robbed more than 30,000 pensioners of their old-age monies in a cynical attempt to save his own ample skin.

Shareholders were stripped of their shirts, pensioners feared for their pensions, and Ian and especially Kevin now had every reason to fear the law. Who would not naturally suppose that they—being senior stewards of the Maxwell empire—had also played a conscious part in their father's apparent villainy?

As events exploded around him, Kevin scarcely had time to mourn. "The collapse of my father's business happened so quickly after his death," he explained. "There wasn't any time to grieve or have anything like a normal reaction, because we were thrown into the deep end of the deepest hole imaginable."

In June 1992, both brothers were arrested, accused of fraud. On top of that, the courts pronounced Kevin liable for the $813 million missing from the Maxwell pension funds. With a stroke of the magistrate's pen, Maxwell instantly became a record setter—the world's biggest bankrupt.

Robert Maxwell had said, many times during his life, "I do not plan to leave my children an inheritance." In this, he proved better than his word.

## The Rise of Robert Maxwell and the Creation of His Empire

Robert Maxwell did not start out life big or strong or rich—or even with the surname Maxwell. He was born Jan Ludwig Hoch in 1923 to a pair of unemployed Jewish farm workers in the village of Slatinske Doly, then part of Czechoslovakia. "We lived like pigs; really like pigs," he told Nick Davies, one of his newspaper editors and biographers. "We ate anything we could get our hands on, and I mean anything. I can never remember eating meat as a child, except sometimes chicken. I can remember eating soup all winter, but there was never anything in it. It was gruel, slops. Sometimes it was potatoes or beans or maize, but it was never enough."[3] In the mornings, he would scavenge for bread.

Having quit school after only three years of formal education, teenaged Jan was selling trinkets on the streets when the Nazis stormed western Czechoslovakia in 1939. Although he escaped to France and volunteered along with other Czechs for the French Foreign Legion in 1940, his parents, four siblings, and grandparents all died in the Holocaust. Subsequently, though hardly religious, Maxwell was a great supporter of Israel, and he is buried on the Mount of Olives.

One way or another, he eventually made his way to England and signed on as a volunteer with the British Army, where he worked in military intelligence. His capacity for languages was phenomenal (at the end of his life he'd be adept in nine). By one account, he learned English in six weeks. In 1945—the same year he won a Military Cross for heroism—he married a French Huguenot named Elisabeth Meynard, whom he met in Paris just after its 1944 liberation. At the age of 21, Hoch laid out his ambitions to his sweetheart: "I want to make my fortune, and then I want to go into Parliament." Elisabeth was impressed by the man who'd ultimately decided—after a couple of false starts—to call himself Ian Robert Maxwell, and was even more so by 1964, when he was a multimillionaire and member of Parliament.

Pergamon Press made Maxwell rich. Stationed in Berlin with the British Foreign Office after the war, Maxwell realized that there was money to be had in the publishing of scientific textbooks and materials, and so he purchased an existing publisher and renamed it Pergamon. He found he could charge high prices. "It's no use trying to compete with me, because I publish the authoritative journal in each field," he told *Forbes* in 1987, showing off his tough-guy braggadocio. "I'm dealing in high-penalty information. If you're building a chemical plant and you don't know about the latest development in that area, the mistake could cost you pounds 10 million, so people will pay pounds 1,000."[4] He was right. Pergamon Press minted money. By 1964 he'd managed to establish a business reputation that facilitated his run for the House of Commons.

Things weren't so rosy by 1971. That year the British Department of Trade and Industry filed a report that proved devastating for Maxwell. "Notwithstanding Mr. Maxwell's acknowledged abilities and energy," it read, "he is not in our opinion a person who can be relied on to exercise proper stewardship of a publicly quoted company." The indictment stemmed from what the *New York Times* called "London's most garish corporate melodrama in years."[5] In 1969, Maxwell tried to sell a controlling interest in Pergamon to the New York financier Saul Steinberg, but Steinberg later backed out of the deal, maintaining that Maxwell had misrepresented the company's worth. When it was revealed that Maxwell had violated a takeover code, he was booted off the board of Pergamon by the principal shareholders. In 1970, Maxwell lost his seat in Parliament, at least in part because of the messiness of the whole affair. He'd been ousted. Never crazy about the unruly Czech Jew in its midst, the City of London establishment had essentially seized on his hubris and chucked him out by the ears. For the rest of his life, Maxwell would soothe the burn of his outsider status by turning it into a point of pride.

At school, not yet a teenager, Kevin Maxwell had a job delivering newspapers, so he read with some consternation the headlines that detailed his father's troubles from 1969 to 1971. By then, after the death of a son in a car crash and of a daughter with acute leukemia, the Maxwell children numbered seven, and Kevin, the second-youngest, was the most deeply affected by his father's woes. The other kids at school mocked him. Yet Kevin seemed rarely inclined—then or now—to make a nasty comment about his father, which at the time was all the more remarkable given the beatings he took from Maxwell at home.

Poverty and war had been Robert Maxwell's teachers; he was determined to be no less a formidable instructor for his own children. "I want you to push them," Maxwell urged young Kevin and Ian's teachers at school. "Show them no mercy." Having definite ideas about how kids should be raised, he showed little mercy himself. In exchange for privilege—his three sons would all receive scholarships to Balliol College in Oxford—he expected excellence. If Kevin brought home a school report that complimented him on general excellence but suggested one area in which a little more effort might be needed, Robert's eyebrows would shoot up at the "little more effort," and Kevin would be whipped. The number of lashes depended on "the degree of his dissatisfaction," Kevin told the *Daily Telegraph*.[6] The beatings went on until Kevin was in his midteens, and they were severe enough to attract the attention of his headmaster at school.

School wasn't the only testing ground; the dinner table was, too. At home in Oxford, mealtimes were trials. Robert picked his kids' brains to make sure they were keeping abreast of their lessons, and Sundays were the worst, because he'd usually bring home Pergamon authors or business acquaintances and put the children to the test in front of the crowd. Ghislaine, the youngest and also his favorite, once burst out crying because she couldn't define the world *theocracy* fast enough for him in front of guests. He repeatedly advocated the three Cs—*concentration, consideration,* and *conciseness.* He also liked to lecture on good manners, even though his own were horrible. Tom Bower, Maxwell's biographer and critic, has written:

> Maxwell, one can assume, unconsciously disliked some aspects of his personality and reacted violently if he perceived it in others. In his children, he wanted to forestall the development of his own characteristics. Since by all accounts his children are in some respects the antithesis of their father, he was clearly successful.[7]

By 1974, Robert Maxwell had reacquired Pergamon by going into debt. Though the company had fared badly under its old ownership, Maxwell made it profitable again. His zestiest decade as a businessman kicked off smashingly in 1980. Maxwell Communications Corporation (MCC) was born when he acquired the United Kingdom's largest printer and turned its failing fortunes into $28 million in pretax earnings by 1983. (His hacking of 6,000 of the 13,000 employees off the payroll helped.) Then, in 1984, he fulfilled his dream of owning a newspaper when he acquired the six newspapers of the Mirror Group. Immediately he launched a rivalry with Rupert Murdoch's *Sun.* He aimed, he later said, to create one of the world's 10 largest communications empires by 1990, projecting annual revenues of up to $8 billion.

## The Next Generation of the Maxwell Empire

Kevin's assignment, meanwhile, was simple: Conquer America. After Kevin graduated from Oxford, Robert dispatched him to the United States. The young man's orders were to establish a military and defense publishing business for his father. And Kevin complied. Despite the beatings, despite his father's unhuggable personality, Kevin still felt called to work for Robert, who'd nurtured in him and in his older brother Ian a deep-seated ambition to join the family enterprise.

Kevin's project was humming along nicely—until Robert, in one swift stroke, fired him.

Their tiff had arisen over a woman, Pandora Warnford-Davis. Kevin had met her at Oxford, and the two wanted to marry. Robert, however, would not allow this—he thought them too young, and he simply didn't like the woman. Pandora, for her part, didn't much care for Robert. Worse, she said so. She quickly earned the distinction of being one of the few people in the world to stand up to him, giving him as good as he gave, and enthusiastically flouting his wishes. When Robert forbade her from going to America to join Kevin in 1983, she went anyway. Next, Robert demanded that Kevin put her on the first plane back to Britain. Pandora again refused.

Robert's response was to fire Kevin—not in person, but by fax. Even for Kevin, who by now was quite the connoisseur of abuse, this was an extraordinary moment. He says, "The most difficult thing that ever happened to me was being fired by my father because I wanted to marry my wife." Kevin lived with Pandora in America, where he got a job with CBS Publishing. In 1984, they returned to England to get married on a chilly but bright day in May. (They had decided to move the date up, in light of the fact that Pandora was pregnant with their first child.) Robert not only insisted he would boycott the wedding, but further threatened to fire Ian—the best man—if he went.

In the end, after his bluff was called, Robert showed up at the last minute, spoke a few well-wishing words at the reception, and then departed early so that he could catch a football match.

Then the newlyweds, still maintaining their independence, returned to the United States, where they lived for another year. But after this protracted interlude, Maxwell told Pandora he wanted to rejoin the family, that he was determined not to be cast out permanently. What factors drew him back? As Maxwell explains, "Duty, number one. It was a very strong sense of duty. And secondly, the excitement of working with someone who was in a very public and recognized and exciting area. It's very hard to find, even today, an area that is more interesting than media." Speaking to the *Times* of London in 1996, Pandora added another: "He felt that his father wanted and needed him, and he had always wanted to work for the family business."[8] So, eventually, a truce was reached. Father and son made up, and Maxwell and Pandora returned to England. That was the good part. The bad was that forever after this, Maxwell would be the subject of a tug of war between his wife and father. Robert would demand he spend more time at the office, Pandora that he spend more time at home. As Pandora told the *Daily Mail:* "Kevin was always pulled by his heart. But it's very difficult when you have to say: 'Who comes first? My wife and children, or my father and the business?' He was constantly tugged in two directions and it was very, very difficult for him."[9]

As his family grew, Maxwell deeply dove into the family business, with Robert taking full advantage, often belittling and demeaning him. "Can't you be a real man?" the elder Maxwell yelled at the younger on at least one occasion when Kevin failed to perform up to Robert's standards. During meetings, he'd bark at Kevin to shut up, and he'd pretend to confuse him with Ian during introductions. The licks were brutal, but the father's grooming quickly turned the heir into a killer businessman. The foundations for what Maxwell himself would later term a "bloody arrogance" were soon established.

Robert spent a lot of time cultivating his reputation as an international figure, wining and dining and meeting and greeting players from all over the world, particularly Russia and Eastern Europe. That left Kevin, the burgeoning young executive, with more and more responsibility. As the Maxwell conglomeration continued to add to its myriad of private holdings, the younger Maxwell found himself at the center of business deals worth billions of dollars, all before he was 30 years old.

Physically, he looked like a young shark—sleek, lean and wiry, with thick black hair and chiseled cheekbones—a cross between John F. Kennedy, Jr., and a James Bond movie villain. He was unflappable, inscrutable, debonair, and accustomed to moving frictionlessly among aristocrats and power brokers. Thanks to his father's megalomania, he had access to costly and exotic toys. Mere mortals might get from A to B by cab or limo. But Maxwell, when commencing an international trip, thought nothing of departing via helicopter from Maxwell corporate headquarters in central London. He would arrive at Heathrow, where special passport officials would expedite his passage, waving him swiftly through. On at least one occasion, the Concorde was held waiting for him.

Maxwell and his father were running 350 companies; they employed some 16,000 people. It couldn't help but go to his head. "I ended up being given positions of responsibility at a very young age, in my twenties, so that by the age of 28 or 29 I was running Macmillan, one of largest imprints, and wasn't ready for it," he says. "It's nepotism—you get put into positions ahead of the curve. I had ability, but that's not the same thing as necessarily being the right person to be the number-two guy for a company like Macmillan, not at the age I was."

As Kevin's authority expanded, Robert's appetites—both private and corporate—seemed to go into overdrive. The elder Maxwell seemed bent on consuming everyone and everything. By the end of the 1980s, his already ample bulk had swelled on a diet of hamburgers and buttermilk, scrambled eggs and baked beans, cheese and grilled chicken, smoked salmon and peanuts. Eschewing petite champagne flutes, he drank his bubbly in half-liter glasses. He'd stuff a handful of beluga caviar into his mouth while the other hand was busy scooping up more.

Though he remained capable of generosity and good deeds (most notably, he paid for the airlifting of children from Chernobyl following the nuclear accident there in 1986), his social behavior degenerated: He'd fail to show up at dinners where he was the guest of honor; he'd crash events to which he hadn't been invited. At Malcolm Forbes' seventieth birthday party (an extravaganza in Tangiers to which Maxwell *had* been invited), Maxwell dressed up in a gold-embroidered djellaba, complete with pasha's turban and Turkish slippers. Later, the corpulent conglomerateur attempted (according to one account) to gain admittance to Forbes's residence by scaling its railings.

Maxwell's behavior in his own offices ranged from the preemptory to the deliberately rude. He'd keep a banker waiting on the phone for an hour while he lectured a *Daily Mirror* underling on how to do his job. When he did get to work, he was a one-man show, conducting big deals on the phone and shredding important faxes without telling anybody else on staff. His rages were titanic, and he seemed to take delight in pulling rank and yelling "You don't know what you're talking about" at Kevin in front of other people. At the end of the 1980s, Maxwell kicked Kevin out of his sight and sent him and his family back to the United States. Kevin and Pandora found a house in Connecticut and a nanny for their kids. Four weeks later, Kevin came to her and said they were returning—Robert had changed his mind and wanted them back in England. Pandora was livid.

On his return, the younger Maxwell asked his staff if they could install a weight sensor in the hallway floor between his office and his father's, so that he might have a few seconds' warning when Big Bob was en route. The staff declined. "He'd kill us," they said. In the end, that's figuratively what Big Bob did—he killed everybody off. He made bad decisions that doomed his empire and snuffed out the jobs and pensions of his employees.

## The Maxwell Empire Begins to Totter

Eager to hit annual sales of £3 billion, the elder Maxwell embarked on a debt-backed feeding frenzy, gobbling up a wide variety of companies, including newspapers, television stations, computer makers, and pharmaceutical companies. He was especially proud of his acquisition of U.S. publisher Macmillan in 1989. But none of this new glory came cheap. MCC's debt burden swelled to better than $2.3 billion. By 1990 to 1991, fighting tough economic times, Maxwell found himself owning some 800 companies whose sales totaled £997 million—far short of his vaunted £3 billion. Some of his ventures, such as *The European* (a weekly Europewide color newspaper he launched in 1990), were hemorrhaging money. And still he bought! In 1991 he put still another property on his plate: New York's tabloid newspaper, the *Daily News*.

Struggling to boost liquidity, Maxwell sold off Pergamon Press—his original golden goose. But the sale was too little, too late. Hobbled by the $2.3-billion debt that the Macmillan acquisition brought, as well as enormous private debt, the whole empire had begun to totter, and Maxwell now began to play what would become his endgame: shuffling assets in a last-ditch effort to prop up the share price of stock in MCC, his public company. Keeping it high was crucial, because MCC stock was the collateral he'd used in order to get loans for his ailing privately owned companies, the Robert Maxwell Group (RMG). If the share price fell, Maxwell would have to offer more shares as collateral, thus leaving him with even less borrowing power. Meanwhile, more and more of his private debt was coming due. His banks were calling in their chits, and Maxwell was hard pressed to pay.

Enter the pension funds.

More than $1.4 billion in securities belonging to the pension funds and treasuries of Maxwell's private companies were transferred to the privately held RMG companies, to help hold up the empire. The magnitude of the existing debt guaranteed, however, that should the private companies go bust, there'd be no way to get the securities back. The pensioners would just be out of luck. And that's what happened: When Robert died, everything in his tattered kingdom collapsed, including his employees' chances of ever receiving a Maxwell company pension.

No one, of course, will ever know for sure what Maxwell was thinking when he made these transfers, and much hinges on his death: If it was accidental, or if Maxwell was murdered, then it's possible to imagine that he might have been hoping to ride out the recession by maintaining his secret juggling act, eventually putting the assets back where they should have stayed all along. This is what Kevin Maxwell contends—that his father stood a good chance of clearing things up and saving his empire had he lived. But if the elder Maxwell committed suicide, then the evidence seems completely damning: In order to keep up corporate appearances a little longer—and, not incidentally, to keep enjoying his yacht, his jet, and other perks—he knowingly consigned his workers to an old age of poverty.

When the depletion of the pension fund was revealed, public anger in England went white-hot, with many fingers pointing straight at Kevin Maxwell: He'd been his father's second in command, after all. How could he not have known? Surely, he must have been in on the scheme.

Nothing in the younger Maxwell's life had prepared him for this moment. Up to then, he'd considered being fired by his father to have been the worst trial he'd ever have to face. But this? No comparison. "Being fired from a job is one thing," he says. "Having a business collapse around you and being charged with fraud—that's a different order of magnitude." Just how different was something he and his family were soon to discover.

## The Legal Problems Begin: Kevin Maxwell Is Arrested

"Piss off! We don't get up for an hour!" In the wee hours of a June morning in 1992, Pandora Maxwell, awakened by a loud knocking on her home's front door, irately slammed open her second-story bedroom window to see what all the commotion was about. The people milling around down below looked like reporters, so she gave them a blast of the same vitriol that had made her Robert Maxwell's most famous antagonist this side of Rupert Murdoch. When the men didn't go away, she lifted up the window higher and tried again. "I am about to call the police," she announced, her words like spitballs.

"We are the police," the gentlemen replied.

The arrest of Kevin and Ian Maxwell, though shocking to the Maxwell family, didn't come exactly as a surprise. Public antipathy against the brothers had been building steadily, even before the discovery of the missing funds. After their father's mysterious death, Kevin and Ian had been brought before a House of Commons Select Committee investigating the Maxwell scandal. The session—covered by television cameras—didn't go well for either of them. The brothers chose to invoke their right to remain silent and to let counsel answer for them. On television, that didn't look good—Kevin declining question after question. What was he hiding? After all, this was the person who only recently had stood before the cameras and declared that the Maxwell companies were on solid footing, when he must have known that they were not. This latest appearance made it look as if Kevin and Ian didn't care what anyone thought and couldn't (or wouldn't) explain their actions. It seemed to matter to no one that the brothers previously had offered to cooperate fully with the committee, providing the session could be held in private, without reporters present.

The media, for its part, had a field day with the Maxwells. Here was a rich irony indeed: the sons of the press lord, hounded by the press. Of many possible Maxwell photo opportunities, none proved more tantalizing to the London tabloids than the brothers' arrest. Initially, Kevin had been tipped off by the case controller responsible for implementing his arrest that the police intended to go about their business in a way that would allow him to maintain some dignity—picking him up quietly, without any media present.

It didn't happen that way. Rather, it later seemed to Maxwell that the police had tried to milk his arrest for maximum coverage. Video cameras were there to film the police knocking on his door. Photographers were waiting downtown, to snap his picture at the jail house. More pictures showed him being transported from there in handcuffs to the Old Bailey—in a police van big enough for all the Dallas Cowboys. As a bitter Pandora later noted, the police usually didn't handcuff even rapists.

"It was staged for maximum effect," Maxwell later said to the *Financial Mail on Sunday*. "The policeman said he didn't want me to shave, so I would look as scruffy as possible. I told him to sod off and went upstairs to shave. The whole object was to maximize the indignity."[10] He maintains that the investigators, England's Serious Fraud Office, needed a conviction, and so they wanted to stage an arrest that was sure to make him look "guilty, guilty, guilty." The newspapers the next day were splattered with "gotcha" headlines.

The ordinary Briton didn't much care for Kevin Maxwell. He'd walk down the street, and passersby would yell "Crook!" at him. One day when his order was ready at a popular restaurant, his waitress slammed down his plate and shouted, "I hope you choke yourself on it!" He received hate mail and death threats. At one point, Maxwell's legal defense team commissioned an opinion poll to determine the public's perceptions of their client. Persons polled used such words as *fraudster, crook, selfish pig, leech, bastard, scheming,* and *slimy.*

Equally rough, Maxwell says, was his case's slow slog through the courts. He later remembered asking his lawyers in 1992 when they thought the trial would be over. They told him mid-1994 at the latest. His trial didn't start until May 1995, nearly three years after his arrest, and after 190 days of pretrial and jury-trial hearings in 1994.

"You'd go to court and the judge would say, 'This hearing's postponed for three months or four months or five months," Maxwell says. "[That's] when you realize you've got the machinery of the state and there's nothing you can do about that. It's like the *Exxon Valdez* headed for the rocks; there's nobody on the bridge, you can't do anything about it. There are days when you get incredibly depressed by the sheer weight of the whole oppressive side of the government that's out to get you. We had everything from wiretapping, to mail being opened, to being followed. And then you add a layer of media interest; there was enormous sustained media coverage of the affair. That becomes a physical oppression, and it does get you down." He adds: "You feel threatened."

While the legal war raged, Maxwell found himself having to fight smaller skirmishes as well: He sought and won an injunction against a planned London musical called *Maxwell: The Musical Review,* which lambasted his father to the tunes of Gilbert and Sullivan. (One retooled song was called "I Am the Very Model of a Modern Megalomaniac.") He and his lawyers claimed—successfully—that it would prejudice the jury pool.

Despite it all—the major and the minor strife—Kevin and Pandora managed, for the most part, to maintain a normal family life—no small accomplishment, under the circumstances. Maxwell spent as much time as he could spare with his five kids, well aware that Tilly, Teddy, Eloise, Chloe, and Madeleine (by the end of the trial, a sixth, Thomas, was on the way) might not have a chance to get acquainted with their dad later on, if he was sent to prison. (Rather wryly, he'd also play preemptive disciplinarian by explaining that just because Dad might go to jail, that's no excuse for misbehavior.) He learned to cook, helped with Sunday lunches, and kicked soccer balls in the backyard. The Maxwells tried to give the kids a regular life, with its full share of the quotidian, be it making ornaments at Christmas time, or playing an instrument for the school band.

There were bumps. Kids at school teased the eldest child, Tilly, just as Maxwell had been ridiculed at school over his father's Pergamon scandal. But Maxwell had consciously sought to build a big family with Pandora, and he now says that his family is really what sustained him through litigation and the prospect of prison:

> I was pretty fortunate to have a pretty indomitable wife, a great bunch of kids, and a large and supportive wider family and friends. I think it's something that a lot of people in any kind of difficulties would recognize. At the end of the day, if you're respected and loved by anybody when the rest of humanity is throwing shit at you, it tends to be reassuring. It's a comfort and it's a great source of solace. Essentially, you have a center in your life where you're going to be supported, as opposed to crapped on.

The family had been forced to move by the bankruptcy into a former old people's home near Pangbourne, and even that was being paid for not by Maxwell but by Pandora's father. Later, they were able to relocate to a modest house (paid for by Pandora's parents) in the village of Moulsford, 18 miles from Oxford. Although her parents and his mother were helping him out, Maxwell was still legally bankrupt until 1995, so he and his brother Ian were eligible for government legal aid to pay for their defense costs. That they took it made people mad, too.

## The Key to Kevin's Defense

Finally, the trial lurched into the dock. Kevin, Ian, and two other Maxwell financial advisers were the defendants. Tom Bower, author of *Maxwell: The Final Verdict*, summarizes the charges thusly:

> In essence, the defendants were accused of using shares belonging to the pension funds to repay the Maxwells' private debts while aware that, because of [Robert Maxwell Groups]'s insolvency, there was no chance of reimbursing the pension funds. That risk, the prosecution alleged, was dishonest and known to be dishonest when the defendants conspired to use the pension fund shares.[11]

Of the defendants, only Kevin Maxwell faced two charges. The first alleged that Maxwell had conspired with his father to defraud the pension funds by using $160 million worth of pension fund stock in an Israeli computer imaging firm, Scitex, to raise bank credit, well aware that the empire wouldn't be able to pay it back. The second, against Kevin, Ian, and two others, alleged that they had misused $35 million worth of stock in Teva Pharmaceuticals Industries Ltd. in an attempt to attain more credit from National Westminster Bank for a loan to private Maxwell companies.

Compared to the O.J. Simpson trial, which was wrapping up the same summer that Maxwell's was getting started, the Maxwell trial lacked sex appeal. It depended on no bloody glove, no knife, no incriminating footwear. Instead, a parade of prosecution lawyers, accountants, and bankers—69 witnesses in all—stepped up to help make sense of a baffling paper trail of memos, faxes, letters, and bank statements. The jury leaned in closer in an effort to understand the intricacies of call deposits, stock lending, and foreign-exchange transactions. Though crowds of spectators clogged the court on the opening day in May 1995, public interest in the case waned as summer wore on.

Despite the four months of prosecution evidence, the crux of the case was fairly simple: Did Kevin Maxwell know that the shares they put at risk were owned by the pension management company, and was their risk dishonest? In October, audiences reappeared as Maxwell finally took the stand for a marathon 21 days to claim his innocence. The key to his defense: Robert Maxwell.

On July 5, 1991, Kevin Maxwell had been beckoned to his father's office. According to Maxwell, his father showed him an amended contract that transferred the beneficial ownership of Scitex shares from BIM, the pension management company, to the Robert Maxwell Group. One sentence, stipulating that BIM's shares would pass to RMG only after receipt of payment, was crossed out and dismissed as "nonsense" by the elder Maxwell. From then, based on his father's word, Maxwell believed that BIM had transferred the share ownership to RMG, regardless of payment, on July 5. To his extreme vexation, Maxwell was unable to find the amended contract during trial preparations. The prosecutor, Alan Suckling, hoping to trip him up, denied that the meeting had ever taken place.

"Mr. Suckling, you have to say that," Maxwell countered, meeting him head on. "My defense has not changed for years. I saw the amended agreement. I believe it was valid." Explaining to Suckling why he put stock in his father's word, Maxwell said, "I had implicit faith in my father and I trusted him. I had years of experience working with him, of his methods, that included transactions involving pension fund assets. It was the ordinary course of business for him and I accepted it."

Later on, he added: "Did I, for a second, consider we were jeopardizing the ability to pay pensions? Absolutely not."

Fireworks were popping between Maxwell and prosecutor Suckling. During another heavy pressing, Maxwell, denying the prosecutor's claims that he was dishonest, shot back with: "You are a prosecutor who wants to send me to jail and you want me to say something different." He huffed, "I am not going to help you."

Maxwell presented the same story for the Teva shares. Over drinks on October 30, 1991—the last time they met face-to-face—his father transferred ownership of $35 million worth of Teva shares from BIM to RMG. Afterward, Maxwell testified, he thought the shares belonged to

RMG. Again, he swallowed it because of "years of working with my father." His father didn't show him the paperwork, but he still believed him. "I relied on what he said to me," Maxwell said.

Furthermore, Maxwell testified that numerous staff members, bankers, auditors, and lawyers knew of his father's relaxed habit of moving assets around in "one big group," with paperwork "following later." Also, he denied that he dishonestly risked the Scitex and Teva shares because he thought that they could eventually be repaid through a group of perfectly acceptable "intercompany accounts." Finally, he confessed to being "bloody arrogant" in his thinking that the group could survive to repay the pension funds. "I was probably one of the most arrogant people you will ever meet," he said. "I could not imagine failure."

Maxwell admitted, now, to lies and mistakes stemming from that arrogance. Yes, he'd lied to banks. Yes, he'd shared "a significant responsibility" for the collapse, mainly because he wasn't his father: "I didn't have the stature, I didn't have the reputation. I didn't have 40 years of business experience." One of his main contentions was that if his father had not died what was most likely an accidental death while relieving himself over the side of the boat, he would have come roaring back to try and save his empire. For anyone other than his father to attempt it, Maxwell said, was an impossibility.

Kevin Maxwell was an energetic, persistent, and sympathetic presence on the stand, and he quelled some of that famed inscrutability to give his all to illuminating his father. Maxwell had to explain what it was about his father that could make a son not only stick around so faithfully, but trust him so blindly. He had to make it clearer how he'd tied himself to the man who played such a large part in getting him into this mess, a man who, Maxwell admitted, would "stretch the law as far as he could."

"He was motivated by power, the ability to influence events, the ability to make a difference, to change things," Maxwell testified. "He was an exceedingly generous individual." At the same time, "He was capable of being a bully. . . . He was a big man, he had enormous charisma and a commanding presence. Given his weight and bulk, he could dominate and did dominate every meeting that he attended."

Bearing bad news to Bob Maxwell? Maxwell reported that the unlucky messenger "would have a strip torn off him in front of everyone else." As punishment, senior employees were often given grunt work, such as opening the mail. Nor did Robert Maxwell bear criticism very well. "It was possible to change his mind," admitted Maxwell, "but it would be very rare, and it would be extremely and physically grueling to achieve. The arguments were frequent, and he was as abusive to me as to others."

Kevin Maxwell's own story starts with a plate of French beans. In the mid-1960s, after Maxwell *père* had already established a fortune in publishing, the family would take month-long cruise holidays to Italy, typically calling at Elba, Corsica, Sardinia, Naples, Capri, and the Aeolians before hitting a few Greek islands and what Elisabeth Maxwell, Robert's wife since 1945, calls "their picturesque little harbors." Robert was the domineering father of nine, a strict disciplinarian and corporal punisher, but during the holidays he'd usually ease up on the children. Then one night somebody put a plate of French beans in front of 7-year-old Kevin.

Kevin simply wouldn't eat them. He hated French beans. Eat them, Robert said. No, said Kevin, even after his father threatened to lock him up in his cabin. Kevin didn't give in for two days. Only under the threat of a rope lashing did he finally relent. In her memoir *A Mind of My Own* (HarperCollins, 1994), Elisabeth Maxwell reports that Kevin, in between "convulsive sobs," stood up to his father and said, "I give in, but only because you are bigger and stronger than me, and for no other reason."[12] It was hardly the last time that Robert would exert his authority, or that Kevin would submit.

Eventually the question was put: Why hadn't Kevin Maxwell, at some point, just opted out?

"What sane person would want to be in the Central Criminal Court, on trial charged with conspiracy to defraud pensioners?" Maxwell asked. "So the sane reaction is that, of course, there must have been a moment when one could and should have abandoned the ship.

"But if I was being honest with myself I don't think I had the ability to leave him. We had an extremely complicated relationship. It was not only chief executive–chairman, it was father–son."

The jury stayed out longer than any in English history—deliberating for almost 50 hours over 11 days. During its deliberations, Maxwell was on edge, leaving home each morning not sure if he'd be able to return for the night, jumping at the ringing of beckoning phones. He'd already packed a bag for Brixton prison; he had a radio, a change of clothes, *Don Quixote*, and some unread Dickens ready. He'd also been getting a little insight on the prison mafia from a friend, because these things are good to know.

As a verdict becomes more and more imminent, a defendant's focus grows narrower and narrower, Maxwell says, "till you get to the point when the jury's out and considering their verdict. Then you can't really focus on anything. At the start of the process you have quite a broad horizon. By the end you're focusing on a single point, because it's one of those moments in life there is no gray. It's black or it's white. You're convicted or you're acquitted. And your life will be so completely different depending on the outcome."

Now here he was, back in court, pacing in circles, awaiting the decree with his brother Ian. His fingers were so tightly intertwined behind his back that his knuckles were white.

On the 131st day of the trial, the seven women and five men of the jury were ready to announce their verdict: not guilty, all around.

While Ian shed happy tears and kissed his wife all over her face, Kevin was noticeably more self-restrained. He smiled and pumped the jury's hands. An hour and a half later, the brothers left the building, arms around each other's shoulders. Maxwell later said he didn't want to make that big a show because he knew he might face the prospect of further charges.

## Fighting Further Accusations

Only one week after the brothers' acquittal, the Serious Fraud Office announced that it wanted to put Kevin Maxwell up on another trial on new fraud charges involving roughly $300 million. If the first trial had tried to show that pension fund assets were dishonestly used to prop up the ailing private side of the empire, the new allegations asserted that other assets from the public MCC and Mirror Group Newspapers (MGN) holdings had been used for the same nefarious end. Maxwell vowed to "fight this new challenge with vigor and determination and with absolute confidence that I will be proven innocent."

It wasn't necessary. In September 1996, the court ruled that a second prosecution by the Serious Fraud Office would represent an unfair and abusive use of power—that Maxwell, in effect, could not be tried twice for the same alleged crime. Maxwell's legal trials were over—for the time being, at least—but not his troubles.

The public did not exactly welcome Robert Maxwell's sons back into its bosom. Britons bristled at the fact that the brothers, being bankrupts, had been defended at public expense. The cost of prosecuting *and* defending the Maxwells came to more than £20 million (roughly $40 million), which made it the most expensive case in British legal history. Many Britons still think the Maxwells got off easy: that the prosecution was too lax, the evidence too dry and complex, and the brothers' explanations too implausible and too at odds with the testimony of prosecution witnesses.

But on the other hand, Robert Maxwell's sons had not exactly gotten off scot-free. The years in court, the worry, the sleepless nights—it all had left its mark on Kevin Maxwell. He was not the same brash young prince he'd been before the crackup. As he says, you can't help but meditate upon your existence when things go topsy-turvy:

> [Say] you're put in front of a jury, and you have five years of negative reporting which says that the decisions you made were crap. Unless you're Toad in "The Wind and the Willows," and you bounce back from everything completely oblivious of everything and become madder as you go, you do learn. You learn, and you are humbled. You are definitely much more [aware] of all the bits and pieces that go together to make a successful business, or even a successful person. I mean, you're not the same person after the event of the magnitude that I went through.

Or, as Maxwell said to the *Financial Mail on Sunday* the week after his acquittal:

> I was very angry about it in 1992—with what I saw then as the unfairness of the system, facing multiple investigations. . . . But that anger has gone completely, and I think what has replaced it is a degree of understanding to accept the process, that with all the unfairness and the problems, the fact was that there was a case to answer.[13]

Maxwell had beaten the machinery of the state; he'd shouldered the sins of the father he both loved and feared; perhaps he'd even gained hard-won wisdom and a measure of humility. But he could not afford— literally—to sit and contemplate his past. Instead, working side by side with Ian, he was ready to begin rebuilding his business life. In fact, amazingly enough, he had already started while the trial was in progress, working on new business ventures, going to his office at 5 A.M. to "get in a full day" before court began. He says he thought it was essential that he not let the trial become his entire life. He and his brother, he says, "made the absolutely conscious decision that the trial and the litigation and all of that came second. The first priority was to work, and we did." Now, acquitted and committed, he looked forward to getting back to business full time, unimpeded.

## Starting Over: Looking for His First Job

Maxwell had gotten 300 job offers back in 1992, when his trial was just beginning, by resorting to what some called a cheap publicity stunt— applying for public assistance. He had hied himself down to his local Job Center—the English equivalent of the welfare office—and put himself on the dole. The event made for quite a picture in the newspapers: The former billionaire's son in an unemployment line, waiting for a handout. Whether this really was a stunt or, as he claimed, a move born of legal necessity (so he could qualify for public defense), the resultant publicity netted him a cache of job offers. Many turned out to be bogus, but others weren't. Suddenly, he had his choice of doing everything from selling pyramids to reading meters.

Up to then, he and Pandora had been paying their domestic bills with money given them by his family and her parents. Maxwell knew this arrangement could go on only so long—that someday, and the sooner the better, he'd need to find work. But work promised something more than money: It gave him an outlet—something else to think about—during the long years of courtroom maneuverings. There was a third benefit as well: He got to know his brother. Robert Maxwell had always striven to keep the two apart, playing a strategy of divide and conquer even within his own family. With him gone, the brothers now discovered they made a good team—in business and in court. And Maxwell took no little comfort in the fact that he had a blood companion to see him through his troubles. "My brother and I went through this thing together," he says. "A burden shared is actually easier."

Sifting through his 300 offers, Maxwell's interest was piqued by one in particular from a headhunter, one Elliott Price. When he went for his interview, however, Maxwell discovered—somewhat to his surprise—that Price was Asian. Maxwell asked the man about the seeming disparity between his name and his ethnicity. Price replied that if he'd made a point of always announcing his ethnicity, he'd never have been given the time of day by "white bastards like you." Maxwell liked the guy immediately, and vice versa. Price, knowing of the Maxwell family's high-level business connections in the Soviet Union and the Eastern Bloc, offered to pay Kevin and Ian to make one "introduction" a month between these acquaintances and Price's clients. As a bonus, the brothers got office space in the Price's West End headquarters.

The Maxwell name still went far in Russia, because Robert had dropped millions there when he was building up his publishing empire. Kevin Maxwell had been to Russia nearly 50 times with his father, and now, during the trial, he hopped to Moscow roughly once a month for business. The brothers did well for their new employer, and eventually expanded their consulting practice to include work for Westbourne Communications, a company established by Robert Maxwell's former personal secretary. Though Maxwell found the travel and the consulting work itself demanding, he was grateful for the income. "On the clients that we had, and the business side of life, we put the highest priority," he says. "And if that meant we had to get up at four o'clock, if that's what it meant in order to be able to do [business], five hours before the court day started," then that's what they did. When the court day was over, they'd return to the office. Adds Maxwell, "Self-motivation has never been a problem."

By the time Kevin Maxwell's bankruptcy ended automatically in 1995, and the bulk of his and Ian's court woes ended in 1996, the Maxwell brothers had dabbled in a little bit of everything. Although an attempt to establish a satellite television business in Russia had not panned out, they'd succeeded in, among other things, starting a new company called Maximov Publications, which published *Who's Who*–type guides to Russian government. In September 1996, with the specter of imprisonment finally removed by the British court's decision not to proceed with a second Serious Fraud Office trial, Kevin was free to roll up his sleeves and pursue ideas—including a new one he had in the field of telecommunications.

Through his consulting work for Westbourne, Maxwell had met and counseled several telecommunications clients, and from his work with them he began to appreciate opportunities within the field. "Once I understood the basic nuts and bolts" of it, he says, "I got very interested in the industry, the size and the scale of it, and the fact that it was international and pretty closely aligned with my previous background." He'd already acted as a matchmaker between businesses. Now he was proposing to do matchmaking of a different kind, linking up whole regions of the globe by selling them *connectivity*—fiber-optic cable capacity, for example, or Internet and voice service. A small, fast, aggressive communications provider, he believed, could compete effectively with larger, slower firms in hooking up Europe and the United States with less-developed regions (for example, the Middle East and Southern Africa).

## Creating a New Company in the Telecommunications Business

In 1997, Maxwell established a media-related investment company, describing it as "a modest corporate beginning." Then, in March 1998, he achieved a minor coup, acquiring some fiber-optic phone lines at a bargain price. What he bought in bulk, he leased at retail, recouping his investment in just six months. All the while, under much secrecy, he was setting up what would later become Telemonde, Inc., a company specializing in selling fiber-optic bandwidth. To get the company started, he borrowed money from friends and private individuals. For collateral, Maxwell had to put up his family's home in Moulsford and his mother's French chateau.

Late 1998 threw him another legal curve. In October he was issued a writ by the Department of Trade and Industry (DTI), the same government group that had issued the damning 1971 report against his father, for his "continued non-cooperation" in the investigation of Robert Maxwell. He had sought assurances that the DTI wouldn't ask him about matters for which he'd already been tried or investigated. "I have absolutely nothing to hide, but if you have been though a criminal trial like I have you just don't want to go through another one, you just don't," he told reporters, adding, "It's like something out of Kafka."[14]

Maxwell again went to court, this time to defend his right to refuse to answer. Rather than pay for expensive lawyers, he chose to represent himself. Against him, the DTI fielded a team of 20 legal experts. In the end, the lone wolf won. In March 1999, a High Court judge ruled that Maxwell's fears of unfair treatment were reasonable, and that the DTI could interrogate him only under the strictest conditions. Said the judge: "The potential burden that the questioning may place on Mr. Maxwell does seem to me at risk of going beyond that which an unrepresented individual can reasonably be required to accept." After the ruling, Maxwell declared it "a victory for common sense."

Two months later, Maxwell's ship finally started coming in. In May 1999, he succeeded in getting Telemonde listed on NASDAQ's tertiary over-the-counter market. By August, the new public company had a $350 million market value, making Kevin and Pandora Maxwell's stake worth almost $30 million. Maxwell announced that Telemonde meant to make still more millions by helping to hook up developing countries, such as Oman and Bangladesh, to the information superhighway, using cheap and efficient telecom links. Later, he made another announcement: He personally would help to compensate the still-suffering pension victims, who had been bailed out only partly by the English government. He could not make restitution yet, he said, noting that his new wealth wasn't yet cash but only paper. But his professed intentions put the pensioners in a new and unaccustomed position: rooting for Kevin Maxwell's success.

After almost eight years of fighting legal and financial battles, after suffering the shame of being heir to the "Crook of the Century"— Maxwell appeared to have finally trumped his enemies and critics. If living well is the best revenge, then he was starting to enjoy his. A reporter for the *Sunday Times* of London, sitting down with the revitalized tycoon in August, wrote that Maxwell "exuded the confidence of a man winning back his dignity."[15] And why not? Compared to Kevin Maxwell's comeback, Robert Maxwell's own (winning back control of Pergamon in 1974) looked puny.

Nor was Kevin the only Maxwell who was prospering. His twin sisters Christine and Isabel had become (on paper, at least) even more successful in the business world than he—millionaires in their own right. In 1982, Christine, working for her father, helped him acquire Information On Demand, an early online information broker. Later, after their father's death, the daughters joined forces, moved to Silicon Valley, and, in the mid-1990s, started an Internet business (the McKinley Group) that developed a search engine called Magellan. In 1996, they sold out to Excite, netting some $18 million. Christine, now dubbed by the trade press "one of the two most powerful women on the Internet," has gone on to start an Internet publishing business, while Isabel started 1999 with a $6.5-million stake in CommTouch, an email operation financed largely by Paul Allen. Like Kevin, the twins give every indication of having normal family lives. The English magazine *Tatler,* describing the resurgence of the whole Maxwell clan, concluded a recent article by saying: "Around the world there are plenty of investors who have confidence that Robert's children understand the electronic businesses of the new age, and how to make money from them. The Maxwells are back. Like it or not."[16]

Surely, Robert Maxwell would have been pleased to know he had left his children more than just a lot of heavy baggage—he evidently had left them the elements necessary for their own survival. Whether by nature or nurture, he had programmed his children to be strong and resourceful. Says Maxwell "If you're born with a silver spoon, you can choose to enjoy the fruits of that and the social life that goes with it, [or] you can try to make something of it. In my own case and my brother's and two of my sisters', we're trying to actually use what we've learned, and build on that."

But for Maxwell, *trying* has turned out to be the operative verb. As this book was heading off to press, his company, Telemonde, was heading into troubled waters. Though it had gotten off to a flying start, in November 1999 it filed a document with the SEC saying it might not be able to remain in business if it could not raise additional debt and equity. What had happened?

Put simply, one of Maxwell's principal competitive advantages had disappeared: He'd acquired cheap capacity on fiber-optic cables, buying it in bulk from such giants as MCI WorldCom and Global Crossing. His business plan was to resell it to third-world clients. In 1999, the telecom market saw a rapid price decline in the transatlantic bandwidth capacity industry. This meant that what Maxwell had contracted to sell no longer struck his customers as such an attractive buy. His customers defected. And Maxwell was left unable to honor his contracts to sell the capacity he'd acquired from such big players as MCI WorldCom and Global Crossing. Kevin now stood in technical default on purchase agreements totaling some $88 million.

The first half of 2000 brought at best mixed developments. On the plus side, Telemonde reported it had signed a number of new contracts, including one worth $16 million with Spanish telecommunications carrier Jazztel to provide capacity on Telemonde's fiber optic link between Madrid and London. On the negative side, in February the National Association of Securities Dealers (NASD) placed a so-called scarlet letter on the company's ticker symbol (changing it from TLMD to TLMDE). This warned investors that the company stood in danger of being delisted, should it to fail successfully to answer questions posed by the SEC concerning its registration document. Telemonde's president, Adam Bishop, professed confidence that these questions would be answered to the Commission's full satisfaction.

They weren't. The SEC did not judge its questions to have been fully addressed. Telemonde had to submit an amended registration statement, and, while waiting for it to clear SEC scrutiny, was booted off NASDAQ altogether and relegated to trading in the "pink sheets"—the lowest rung on U.S. securities markets. On the night the company acknowledged its delisting, its shares were selling for $0.94, down from $8.50 in 1999.

"Reports of my death are greatly exaggerated," a jaunty Maxwell quipped in mid-March, borrowing Mark Twain's famous line. He was eager to allay any misgivings the world might have about his and his company's prospects. Telemonde, he pointed out, was still a start-up, and was saddled with a start-up's growing pains. Difficulties were to be expected. "Why should it be *easy* to create a $100- or $200-million vehicle from scratch?" he asked rhetorically. "This is a business adventure, and we're doing our very best. Yes, we've had some checks and turbulence, but we're entirely confident of our ability to get the ship back into reasonable shape."

What about the delisting? "The temporary listing of Telemonde on the pink sheets is just that," he insisted, "temporary." The company fully anticipates being relisted in April or early May, just as soon as its amended registration form earns SEC approval. "We have been compliant with the SEC's requirements since November 1999—that is, we are a fully reporting public company. We have, however, fallen foul of the listing requirements of the NASD, which require the company's filing to have received a 'no comment' from the SEC," he explained.

Maxwell further noted that Telemonde's descent into the pink sheets had not precipitated a further fall-off in its share price (there not being a world of room between 94 cents and zero) and that the daily trading volume was holding up respectably. He noted, as well, that Telemonde had retained all its key staff during its pink period, and that it was continuing to add customers to its client roster. Telemonde's relisting, he insisted, would be "simply a matter of working through the comments of the SEC." Concluding on an upbeat note, he said: "Watch this space!"

Okay, we will. But right now, for the sake of argument, let's assume Maxwell is, as the English like to say, "full of it." Let's assume that by the time you read this, all that's left of Telemonde is a grease spot on the information superhighway—that the company will have gone bust. This would seem to be what a number of Maxwell's fellow Britons are hoping it will do.

Adam Jones, a writer covering Telemonde's descent into the pink sheets for the *Times* of London, said in tones that might easily be mistaken for glee that Kevin's company had now achieved "plankton status in the Wall Street food chain." He then went on to note that "Telemonde has not been completely ignored by the U.S. business aristocracy, though. The Forbes publishing empire is preparing a book on business comebacks that will devote a chapter to Maxwell's return. It may turn out to be a very short chapter."[17]

We disagree. We think a person who's been to hell and back isn't likely to succumb to a 90-degree day. We think he'll prevail—if not with his current company, then with some future one. As noted at the outset, of this chapter, Maxwell's claim to fame (or at least to his being a comeback champ) rests less on his having made a great success of Telemonde—which, to be fair to him, he still might do—than on his having extricated himself manfully from the smoking wreckage left him by his father. He shouldered his father's sins. He paid his father's price. And then, having done so, he hitched up his trousers and went on to live another business day. Against daunting odds, Maxwell's optimism, his health, his marriage and the integrity of his and Pandora's large and boisterous brood have emerged intact. He survived his enemies. What's more, he's only 41—his mature business life still awaits him. As the media of his homeland have lately been forced to admit, Kevin and the whole Maxwell clan are back—like it or not.

# NOTES

## Chapter 1

1. John Wiehman, "From Ashes to Fleece: In the Wake of a Tragedy, a Shining Example of Compassion Emerges," *Backpacker,* March 1996, 5 [editorial].
2. Peter Michelmore, "One Boss in a Million," *Reader's Digest,* October 1996, 94.
3. Richard Jerome, "Holding the Line: After Fire Wrecked His Mill, Aaron Feuerstein Didn't Let His Workers Down," *People,* 5 February 1996, 122.
4. Louis Uchitelle, "The Risks of Keeping a Promise," *New York Times,* 4 July 1996, p. D-1.
5. John W. McCurry, "TW's 1997 Leader of the Year: Aaron Feuerstein," *Textile World,* October 1997, 34.

## Chapter 2

1. Tom Monaghan with Robert Anderson, *Pizza Tiger* (New York: Random House, 1986), 3.
2. Monaghan and Anderson, 3.
3. Monaghan and Anderson, 7.
4. Monaghan and Anderson, 61.
5. Monaghan and Anderson, 81.
6. Monaghan and Anderson, 149.
7. Monaghan and Anderson, 150.
8. Monaghan and Anderson, 149.
9. Monaghan and Anderson, 154.
10. Monaghan and Anderson, 154.
11. Monaghan and Anderson, 163.
12. Monaghan and Anderson, 167.
13. Monaghan and Anderson, 168.

14. Monaghan and Anderson, 179.
15. Monaghan and Anderson, 190.
16. Monaghan and Anderson, 232.

## Chapter 3

1. Mike Wilson, *The Difference Between God and Larry Ellison: Inside Oracle Corporation* (New York: William Morrow, 1997), 237–238.
2. Rich Karlgaard, "Larry Ellison," *Forbes ASAP,* 7 June 1993, 71.
3. Wilson, 262.
4. "From Rags to Riches," *Which Computer?,* January 1992, 43.
5. "Company Profile: Oracle Goes Out to the Woodshed," *Tech Street Journal,* January 1991, 8.
6. Karlgaard, 71.
7. Wilson, 21.
8. Wilson, 18.
9. Wilson, 5.
10. Wilson, 42.
11. Wilson, 160.
12. Joshua Greenbaum, "No More Genghis Khan," *Management Review,* May 1992, 29.
13. John Soat, "Our Adolescence is Over," *Information Week,* 15 June 1992, 40.
14. Edward J. Bride, "Note: Maturity," *Software Magazine,* May 1991, 6.
15. Wilson, 180.
16. Richard Brandt, "The Selling Frenzy That Nearly Undid Oracle," *Business Week,* 3 December 1990, 156.
17. Peter Nulty, "Oracle Systems," *Fortune,* 6 September 1993, 76.
18. Julia Pitta, "The Arrogance Was Unnecessary," *Forbes,* 2 September 1991, 138.
19. Wilson, 11–12.
20. Janice Maloney, "Larry Ellison is Captain Ahab and Bill Gates is Moby Dick," *Fortune,* 28 October 1996, 119.
21. "From Rags to Riches," 43.
22. Danica Kirka, "Oracle Conquers Woes, Returns to Profitability," *Los Angeles Times,* 27 April 1993, sec. D2, p. 29.
23. Soat, 40.
24. Don Clark, "Change of Heart at Oracle Corp.," *San Francisco Chronicle,* 15 July 1992, p. B1.
25. Clark, p. B1.

26. *Red Herring,* June 2000.
27. *Red Herring,* June 2000.
28. *Business Week,* 8 May 2000.
29. Soat, 40.
30. Wilson, front cover.

## Chapter 4

1. Ruth Handler with Jacqueline Shannon, *Dream Doll: The Ruth Handler Story* (Stamford, CT: Longmeadow Press, 1994), 225.
2. Handler and Shannon, 161.
3. Handler and Shannon, 155.
4. Lisa Petrillo, "All-Business Barbie," *San Diego Union Tribune,* 29 December 1994, p. E-1.
5. Handler and Shannon, 47.
6. Handler and Shannon, 3.
7. Handler and Shannon, 12.
8. Handler and Shannon, 145.
9. Handler and Shannon,
10. Handler and Shannon, 178.
11. Handler and Shannon, 185.
12. Lisa Miller Medag, "From Barbie Dolls to Real Life," *Time,* 8 September 1980, 88.
13. Barbara Vancheri, "Barbie to Breast Cancer," *Pittsburgh Post-Gazette,* 11 October 1994, p. D-1.
14. Handler and Shannon, 202.
15. Petrillo, p. E-3.
16. David Groves, "A Doll's Life," *Los Angeles Times,* 10 November 1994, p. E-5.
17. Joanne Davidson, "Handler Overcame Nightmares," *Denver Post,* 5 February 1996, p. 4.

## Chapter 5

1. Ron Popeil with Jefferson Graham, *The Salesman of the Century* (New York: Delacorte Press, 1995), 9.
2. Popeil and Graham, 10–11.
3. Popeil and Graham, 11.
4. Popeil and Graham, 14.

## Chapter 7

1. Donald Trump. *Trump: The Art of the Comeback* (New York: Random House, 1997), 197.

2. Pete Hamill, "T. Without Sympathy," *Esquire,* December 1989, 59.

3. Donald Trump, "America Needs a President Like Me," *Wall Street Journal,* 30 September 1999, p. A26.

4. Maureen Dowd, "Living La Vida Trumpa," *New York Times,* 17 November 1999, p. A25.

5. Adam Nagourney, "Trump Proposes Clearing Nation's Debt at Expense of the Rich," *New York Times,* 10 November 1999, p. A19.

6. Larry Reibstein, "Trump: The Fall," *Newsweek,* 18 June 1990, 38.

7. Milo Geyelin and Neil Barsky, "Single, 10-Letter Word Pressured All to Set Trump's Bailout: Bankruptcy," *Wall Street Journal,* 27 June 1990, p. A2.

8. Trump (1997), 223–224.

9. *Current Biography Yearbook, 1984,* 401.

10. *Newsmakers: 1989 Cumulation,* "Donald Trump," 482.

11. *Newsmakers,* 482.

12. Trump (1997), 46.

13. Trump (1997), 46–47.

14. Trump (1997), 51–52.

15. Monci Jo Williams, "Trump's Troubles," *Fortune,* 18 December 1989, 157.

16. Reibstein, 41.

17. Stratford Sherman, "Donald Trump Just Won't Die," *Fortune,* 13 August 1990, 75.

18. Trump (1997), 6.

19. Richard Stern and Tatiana Pouschine, "Can Donald Pay His Hotel Bill?," *Forbes,* 8 July 1991, 43.

20. Larry Light and Joseph Weber, "The Donald's Trump Card," *Business Week,* 23 March 1992, 74.

21. Shawn Tully, "An Ex-Loser is Back in the Money," *Fortune,* 22 July 1996, 86.

22. Mark Bowden, "The Art of the Donald," *Playboy,* May 1997, 88.

23. Sherman, 75.

24. Mitchell Pacelle, "Trump, Bankers Are Shaping a Deal to Use Casino Empire to Retire Debt," *Wall Street Journal,* 12 November 1993, p. A2.

25. Trump (1997), xii.

26. Trump (1997), xii–xiii.

27. Trump (1997), 51.

28. Trump (1997), 151.

29. Craig Horowitz, "Trump Gets Lucky," *New York,* 15 August 1994, 26.

30. Bowden, 88.

31. Jesse Angelo, "Trump Nixes Sales of His Ailing Casinos," *New York Post*, 3 February 2000, p. 42.

## Chapter 8

1. Lawrence Linderman, *Playboy*, May 1980, 55.
2. Linderman, 53.
3. Michael Katz, *Sport*, July 1982.
4. Linderman, 62.
5. Linderman, 62.
6. *TV Guide*, 30 June 1975.
7. Jack Newfield, *Only in America: The Life and Crimes of Don King* (New York: William Morrow, 1995), 32.
8. Newfield, 34.
9. Linderman, 64.
10. Newfield, 48.
11. Newfield, 53.
12. Newfield, 71.
13. Norman Mailer, *The Fight* (New York: Little, Brown, 1997), 115.
14. Mailer, 116.
15. Amy Walman, "Promoter's Praises Sung on His Day," *New York Times*, 14 June 1979.

## Chapter 9

1. David Mildenberg, "Risk at Every Turn," *Charlotte Observer*, 1 October 1995, p. A-1.
2. Mildenberg.
3. John Wildman, "Smith Rode Love of Cars to the Top," *Charlotte Observer*, 28 November 1990, p. A-10.
4. Mildenberg.
5. Suzanne Oliver, "A Fan-Friendly Sport," *Forbes*, 3 July 1995, 73.
6. Ed Hinton, "Big Wheel," *Sports Illustrated* Special Issue, 1999.
7. Ed Hinton, "Crash But No Smash," *Sports Illustrated*, 14 April 1997, 92.

## Chapter 10

1. John Burgess, "Can U.S. Get Things Right Anymore? Hubble Telescope, Space Shuttle Problems Raise Questions About American Technology," *Washington Post*, 7 March 1990, p. C-1.

## Chapter 11

1. Jim Stovall, *The Way I See the World* (Tulsa, OK: GSN, 1999), 99.

## Chapter 12

1. *Guiness Book of World Records*, 1998, 126.
2. Roy Greenslade, *Maxwell: The Rise and Fall of Robert Maxwell and His Empire* (Secaucus, NJ: Carol, 1992), 302.
3. Nicholas Davies, *Death of a Tycoon: An Insider's Account of the Fall of Robert Maxwell* (New York: St. Martin's Press, 1993), 16.
4. *Current Biography* (New York: H. W. Wilson, 1988).
5. Craig R. Whitney, "Robert Maxwell, 68: From Refugee to the Ruthless Builder of a Publishing Empire," *New York Times*, 6 November 1991, p. D-23 [obituary].
6. Eric Bailey, "Can he Ever Forgive His Father?" *Daily Telegraph*, 13 May 1996, p. 13.
7. Tom Bower, *Maxwell: The Outsider* (London: Viking, 1988), 93.
8. Ginny Dougary, "Gilt-Edged Bonds," *Times* (London), 16 November 1996, Features.
9. Linda Lee-Potter, "Bob Wouldn't Come to the Wedding . . . and When He Did, He Left Early for a Football Match: Continuing Pandora Maxwell's Story of the Shame and Disgrace of Her Family in the Wake of the Maxwell Scandal," *Daily Mail*, 27 October 1992, p. 22–23.
10. William Kay, "Kevin Maxwell: 'When the Jury Go Out, You Don't Know If You're Going to Brixton or Coming Home,' " *Financial Mail on Sunday*, 28 January 1996, p. 8.
11. Bower, 384.
12. Elisabeth Maxwell, *A Mind of My Own: My Life with Robert Maxwell* (New York: HarperCollins, 1994), 349.
13. Kay, p. 8.
14. Johnathan Prynn, "Maxwell Faces Court Action," *Evening Standard*, 9 October 1999.
15. John Waples, "The Fall and Rise of Kevin Maxwell," *Sunday Times* (London), 8 August 1999, Business.
16. Tim Willis, "Return of the Maxwells," *Tatler*, April 2000, 211.
17. Adam Jones, "Bayou Dave Keeps Faith with Maxwell," *Times* (London), 8 March 2000, 33.

# ACKNOWLEDGMENTS

I WAS FORTUNATE to have the help of many people during the creation of this book, and it is both my privilege and my pleasure to be able to thank a few of them by name.

In 15 years of writing for business publications I never have met a more thorough, professional, indefatigable, good-natured, or resourceful researcher than Joan Fitzsimons of the *Forbes* library. It was she who supplied most of the background material for the profiles. *Forbes* institutionally was generous in giving me many hours of her time. But Joan personally was generous in the way she invested herself unstintingly in the success of this project. I owe her a tremendous debt of thanks.

My editor at *Forbes*, Jim Michaels, helped shape this book from its inception, thoughtfully (and trenchantly) parsing our original list of some 60 candidates down to the 12 you find here. It is no exaggeration to say that Jim was busy putting his own stamp on the manuscript right up until the moment of publication.

Barbara Strauch (at Forbes) and Ruth Mills (at John Wiley & Sons) urged the writing of the book along, providing a helpful kick whenever I needed one.

Given the exceptionally tight deadlines under which this book was produced, the following chapters might never have seen daylight, but for the timely, welcome, and highly professional help provided me by three editorial colleagues: Allyn Freeman (Don King, Ruth Handler, and Tom Monaghan), Andy Erdman (Donald Trump and Larry Ellison), and Gregory Kirschling (Kevin Maxwell).

I wish also to thank Henning Gutmann, formerly of John Wiley & Sons, who picked me for this job, and Larry Alexander, now with Wiley, who subsequently took over management of the project. Of the personnel at many institutions and business organizations who contributed suggestions for potential candidates, I am especially indebted to Alisa Picerno of MassMutual. Every year, in cooperation with the U.S. Chamber of Commerce, MassMutual singles out heroic and deserving businesspeople for its Blue Chip Enterprise Awards.

To my wife, I can only say: Honey, you were right. I should have heeded your instinct about this project sooner. And to my legal advisor and friend of almost 30 years Jon Davis: Ditto, Jon (all except the "honey" part).

Finally, I want to thank the 12 "comeback champs" themselves, without whose guts, ingenuity, self-confidence, and indomitable will we'd have no story at all to tell.

# INDEX

---